Islamophobia and Radicalization

John L. Esposito · Derya Iner
Editors

Islamophobia and Radicalization

Breeding Intolerance and Violence

Editors
John L. Esposito
The Bridge Initiative
Georgetown University
Washington, DC, USA

Derya Iner
Charles Sturt University
Sydney, NSW, Australia

ISBN 978-3-319-95236-9   ISBN 978-3-319-95237-6   (eBook)
https://doi.org/10.1007/978-3-319-95237-6

Library of Congress Control Number: 2018948173

© The Editor(s) (if applicable) and The Author(s) 2019
This work is subject to copyright. All rights are solely and exclusively licensed by the Publisher, whether the whole or part of the material is concerned, specifically the rights of translation, reprinting, reuse of illustrations, recitation, broadcasting, reproduction on microfilms or in any other physical way, and transmission or information storage and retrieval, electronic adaptation, computer software, or by similar or dissimilar methodology now known or hereafter developed.
The use of general descriptive names, registered names, trademarks, service marks, etc. in this publication does not imply, even in the absence of a specific statement, that such names are exempt from the relevant protective laws and regulations and therefore free for general use.
The publisher, the authors and the editors are safe to assume that the advice and information in this book are believed to be true and accurate at the date of publication. Neither the publisher nor the authors or the editors give a warranty, express or implied, with respect to the material contained herein or for any errors or omissions that may have been made. The publisher remains neutral with regard to jurisdictional claims in published maps and institutional affiliations.

Cover image: © Gokmen Karci
Cover design by Fatima Jamadar

This Palgrave Macmillan imprint is published by the registered company Springer Nature Switzerland AG
The registered company address is: Gewerbestrasse 11, 6330 Cham, Switzerland

Contents

1 Introduction: Relationships Between Islamophobia and Radicalization ... 1
Derya Iner

Part I Co-existence

2 Islamophobia and Radicalization: Roots, Impact and Implications ... 15
John L. Esposito

3 Reacting to Islam: Islamophobia as a Form of Extremism ... 35
G. Douglas Pratt

4 Marocanization of Dutch Islamophobia and Radicalization of Dutch Moroccans ... 55
Sam Cherribi

Part II Crosspollination

5   Interweaving Islamophobia with Radicalism: Feeding
    the Radicals with the Anti-Halal Debate   73
    Derya Iner

6   Can Islamophobia in the Media Serve Islamic State
    Propaganda? The Australian Case, 2014–2015   97
    Nahid Afrose Kabir

7   Muslim Civil Society Under Attack: The European
    Foundation for Democracy's Role in Defaming and
    Delegitimizing Muslim Civil Society   117
    Farid Hafez

8   Islamophobia in Al-Qa'ida's and IS' English-Language
    Magazines   139
    Julian Droogan and Shane Peattie

Part III Countering Terrorism & Islamophobia

9   Deepening Divides? Implementing Britain's Prevent
    Counterterrorism Program   161
    Paul Thomas

10 How Counterterrorism Radicalizes: Exploring the
    Nexus Between Counterterrorism and Radicalization   179
    Haroro J. Ingram

11 When the 'Right Thing to Do' Feels So Wrong:
    Australian Muslim Perspectives on 'Intimates'
    Reporting to Authorities About Violent Extremism   203
    Michele Grossman

Part IV Responses

12 Men on a mission: Engaging with Islamophobia
and Radicalization in Australia 1863–1957   225
Katy Nebhan

13 Islamophobia and Stigmatising Discourses:
A Driving Force for Muslim Active Citizenship?   245
Mario Peucker

14 Tackling the Twin Threats of Islamophobia and
Puritanical Islamist Extremism: Case Study of the
Hizmet Movement   265
Ozcan Keles, Ismail Mesut Sezgin and Ihsan Yilmaz

Index   285

NOTES ON CONTRIBUTORS

Sam Cherribi is Senior Lecturer at Emory University in the Department of (MESA & Economics). Prior to moving to Emory in 2003, Dr. Cherribi served as a Member of Parliament in The Netherlands for two consecutive four-year terms (1994–2002). Cherribi's most recent book is *Fridays of Rage: Aljazeera and the Arab Spring*, published by Oxford University Press in 2017 and Les Imams Marocains Face au Libéralisme. Bouregreg, 2017. His first book, *In the House of War: Dutch Islam Observed* was published in paperback in 2013, and hardback in 2010 by Oxford University Press.

Julian Droogan is Senior Lecturer in the Department of Security Studies and Criminology, Macquarie University. He leads a number of funded research projects on surveying violent extremist audiences, promoting social resilience and cohesion, and evaluating preventing violent extremism programs. His research interests include extremist narratives, terrorism and political violence in the Indo-Pacific, and the history of terrorism. Julian is Editor-in-Chief of the *Journal of Policing, Intelligence and Counter Terrorism* (Routledge).

John L. Esposito is University Professor and Professor of Religion & International Affairs and Founding Director of the Alwaleed Center for Muslim-Christian Understanding and The Bridge Initiative: Protecting Pluralism—Ending Islamophobia at Georgetown University. Past President of the American Academy of Religion and Middle East Studies Association, his more than 60 books include: *Shariah Law: What*

Everyone Needs to Know, *Who Speaks for Islam?: What a Billion Muslims Really Think*, *Unholy War: Terror in the Name of Islam*, *The Islamic Threat: Myth or Reality?*, *Islam and Democracy after the Arab Spring*, *Islamophobia and the Challenge of Pluralism in the twenty-first century*.

Michele Grossman is Professor and Research Chair in Diversity and Community Resilience at the Alfred Deakin Institute for Citizenship and Globalisation, Deakin University in Melbourne, Australia, where she is also convenor of the AVERT (Addressing Violent Extremism and Radicalisation to Terrorism) Research Network. Her Australian research on community reporting thresholds has been replicated and extended in the UK through an Economic and Social Research Council grant (ESRC-CREST) in 2016–2017. Her publications appear in journals including *Terrorism and Political Violence*, *Critical Studies on Terrorism*, *Behavioural Sciences of Terrorism and Political Aggression* and *Journal of Ethnic and Migration Studies*.

Farid Hafez (Political Science, University of Vienna) is currently lecturer and researcher at the University of Salzburg, Department of Political Science and Sociology. He is also Senior Research Scholar at Georgetown University's 'The Bridge Initiative'. In 2017, he was Fulbright visiting professor at University of California, Berkeley and in 2014, he was visiting scholar at Columbia University, New York. Since 2010, Hafez is the editor of the *Islamophobia Studies Yearbook*, and since 2015 co-editor of the annual *European Islamophobia Report*. Hafez is an award-winning author and has published more than 70 books and articles, including high ranking academic journals.

Derya Iner is Senior Lecturer and research coordinator at the Centre for Islamic Studies, Charles Sturt University, teaching and researching subjects on contemporary issues related to Islam, Islamic cultures and Muslims. She completed her Ph.D. in Cultural Studies and Gender Studies in Wisconsin-Madison (USA). Iner's research focus on Islamophobia, especially women and children's experience with Islamophobia, Western Muslim Youth and Religious identity, and early twentieth century Ottoman intellectual history. Iner is the chief investigator and editor of the *Islamophobia in Australia 2014–2016 Report*, whose second issue is in progress.

Dr. Haroro J. Ingram is a visiting fellow with the Department of International Relations, Australian National University.

Nahid Afrose Kabir is an Associate Professor in the Department of English and Humanities at BRAC University, Dhaka, Bangladesh. Nahid Kabir worked as a Senior Research Fellow at the University of South Australia, Adelaide (2011–2016), and Research Fellow at the Edith Cowan University, Perth, Australia (2005–2010). Currently, Nahid Kabir holds Adjunct Professor positions at Georgetown University, Washington DC, USA, and Edith Cowan University, Perth, Australia. She is also an Adjunct Senior Research Fellow at the University of South Australia. During 2009–2011, Kabir was a Visiting Fellow at the Center for Middle Eastern Studies at Harvard University, USA.

Ozcan Keles is a non-practicing Barrister, a Ph.D. candidate in Islam and human rights at the University of Sussex, the executive editor of the *Journal of Dialogue Studies* and the chairperson of the London-based Dialogue Society. His research interests include the sociology of human rights and Islam, social movement practice, Islamic activism, British Islam, the Hizmet movement, violent extremism claiming an Islamic justification and dialogue studies.

Katy Nebhan is a historian with a particular interest in Australian masculinities and the development of minority communities within a distinctive Australian culture. She has worked on heritage preservation in New South Wales and has written on the Afghan cameleers, Australian Muslim history and popular culture. She is currently working on a research project at Centre for Islamic Studies and Civilisation, Charles Sturt University.

Shane Peattie was formerly a research assistant in the Department of Security Studies and Criminology, Macquarie University. Has a Master of Policing, Intelligence and Counter Terrorism with a Master of International Security Studies from Macquarie University. His research has examined Salafi-jihadist narratives and their use in violent extremist propaganda.

Mario Peucker is as postdoctoral research fellow at Victoria University's Institute for Sustainable Industries and Liveable Cities. He has conducted research and published on active citizenship of ethno-religious minorities, inclusion-exclusion dynamics and far-right political movements since 2003, both in Europe and Australia. He has authored books *Muslim Active Citizenship in the West* (2014, Routledge, co-authored with Shahram Akbarzadeh) and *Muslim Citizenship in Liberal Democracies. Civic and Political Participation in the West* (2016, Palgrave) and published numerous book chapters, refereed articles in prestigious academic journals (e.g., *Ethnic and Racial Studies*; *Politics and Religion*) and many research reports.

Prof. G. Douglas Pratt taught religious studies at the University of Waikato, New Zealand, for 30 years. Now retired, he is an Adjunct Professor at the University of Bern, Switzerland, an Honorary Professor at the University of Auckland, New Zealand, and a Team Leader on an international research project, *Christian-Muslim Relations: A bibliographical History*, University of Birmingham, England. His research interests encompass Christian-Muslim relations, interreligious dialogue, and contemporary religious issues. He has recently published *Christian Engagement with Islam: Ecumenical Journeys Since 1910* (Brill, 2017) and *Religion and Extremism: Rejecting Diversity* (Bloomsbury, 2018).

Ismail Mesut Sezgin is an honorary fellow at The Centre for Governance, Leadership and Global Responsibility, Leeds Business School. He gained his Doctorate from the Institute for Spirituality, Religion and Public Life at Leeds Beckett University and is the Executive Director of the Centre for Hizmet Studies. His thesis was titled Moral Responsibility in Contemporary Islam. His research interests include ethics, Islam, Political Islam, Sufism and Turkish Politics.

Paul Thomas is Professor of Youth and Policy at the University of Huddersfield, UK. Paul's research focusses on how policies such as community cohesion and the Prevent strategy have been enacted by ground-level practitioners. It has led to the books *Youth, Multiculturalism and Community Cohesion* (Palgrave, 2011) and *Responding to the Threat of Violent Extremism—Failing to Prevent* (Bloomsbury, 2012), as well as articles in many leading journals. His recent research has focussed on implementation of the 'Prevent duty' in English schools and colleges and on barriers to community members reporting concerns about an 'intimate' becoming involved in violent extremism.

Ihsan Yilmaz is Research Professor and Chair of Islamic Studies and Intercultural Dialogue at the Alfred Deakin Institute for Citizenship and Globalisation, Deakin University, Melbourne, Australia. His research is focused on Turkish politics, especially the issue of religion and the secular state, along with research into political participation and legal pluralism in Muslim minority communities, particularly in the United Kingdom and Australia.

List of Figures

Fig. 8.1　A thematic network generated from *Inspire*'s first fourteen issues　146
Fig. 8.2　A thematic network generated from the first thirteen issues of *Dabiq*　150
Fig. 10.1　Iatrogenic drivers of radicalization　184

LIST OF TABLES

Table 6.1　Media representation of Islamic/Muslim topics,
　　　　　　August 2014–January 2015　　　　　　　　　　102
Table 6.2　Australian Newspaper Readership, 12 months,
　　　　　　March 2014–March 2015　　　　　　　　　　　103

CHAPTER 1

Introduction: Relationships Between Islamophobia and Radicalization

Derya Iner

Tackling the relationship between Islamophobia and Radicalization from different perspectives, this book reflects on different types of interactions between Islamophobia and Radicalization. The first part of the book explores the co-existence between Islamophobia and Radicalism that is assumed to be neither coincidental nor independent from one another. This push and pull factor is also referred to "reactionary radicalism". The second part of the book reflects on the recycling relationship causing mismatches, overgeneralizations and sometimes dismiss of Islamophobia and Radicalism when engrained in one another. In the third part, the relationship between Islamophobia and Radicalization is likened to a medicine causing another sickness while intending to cure it. This relationship is medically termed as *iatrogenic* relationship, which is most applicable to the CVE programs today. The last part of the book focuses on a deviating relationship that breaks the vicious cycle of the fringes feeding each other. This is achieved by the mainstream Muslims who develop positive perception and response individually, perform civic citizenship as a community and adopt spiritual and social

D. Iner (✉)
Charles Sturt University, Sydney, NSW, Australia
e-mail: diner@csu.edu.au

© The Author(s) 2019
J. L. Esposito and D. Iner (eds.), *Islamophobia and Radicalization*,
https://doi.org/10.1007/978-3-319-95237-6_1

motivation as a religious philosophy (or mindset) to generate positive attitude and action.

Although radicalization is a generic category defining the process of adopting extreme political, social and religious ideals, it is interchangeably used for Islamist Radicalization. According to the British government's definition, extremism is slightly different than radicalization as a vocal and active opposition to fundamental values like democracy, rule of law and individual liberty[1] Violent extremism promotes or engages in violence as a means of furthering one's radical political, ideological or religious views.[2] Violent extremism and terrorism are also used interchangeably.

Islamophobia is defined as anti-Muslim racism by the recent Runnymede Trust report, which addressed the word Islamophobia first time in 1997,[3] whose level can range from an ideology to violent extremism/terrorism. In this collection, radicalism is used interchangeably when referring to Islamist radicalism or generically to denote levels of extremity.

Islamophobia and Islamist Radicalism are exclusivist ideologies which survive and thrive by blaming, defaming and despising the other and such exclusivist ideologies do not occur in a vacuum. Reflecting on the socio-political context, John Esposito in Chapter 2 provides us with the historical roots of Islamophobia and Radicalism. Islamophobia like other discriminatory ideologies (i.e., racism, anti-Semitisms and xenophobia) has deep-seated roots, and its resurgence dates back to the Iranian Revolution of 1979, hijackings, hostage taking, the September 11 attacks and more recently ISIS. In addition to these significant acts of terrorism, far-right groups, politics and media are addressed as the auxiliary forces reinforcing and normalizing Islamophobia in the West.

Esposito points out that like Islamophobia, Islamic radicalization has deep roots in bias and discrimination, xenophobia and racism. Political and socioeconomic causes should also be considered prior to discussing ideological indoctrination. Religion is identified in this regard, not as a reason but as a tool for legitimizing narratives of marginalization while recruiting and mobilizing followers in the Muslim world and from the West.

While Western societies are increasingly multicultural and multi-religious, Esposito suggests Western governments adopt a more robust policy of inclusion and for Muslim communities to continue with organically blending their religious and cultural identities with Western dynamics including citizenship and healthy nationalism. Esposito suggests that the ISIS brand influencing the marginalized Muslims youth in the West can be debunked if the internal cracks are sealed.

Socio-political ideologies and groups cannot function independently from their surrounding environments. The first section of the book focuses on the co-existence of Radicalisation and Islamophobia. Among the examples of this co-existence in the last few decades are: Al Qaida's use of the term "War on Islam" in responding to Al Qaida, ISIS and the "War on Terror" rhetoric popularized by the Bush administration and more recently by the Trump administration, the spike of Islamophobic attacks following the Islamist terrorist attacks,[4] the increasing far-right groups in tandem with the increasing visibility of ISIS in the West and as captured as a case study in this book, the effective ISIS recruitment among the Moroccan youth of the Netherlands, where Moroccanized Islamophobia is in force under the leadership of the Islamophobe Geert Wilders.

Although existence of the radicalization is not an excuse for the presence of Islamophobia (or vice versa), the relationship between the two needs to be investigated further. Yet, the correlation of such multifaceted social realities is beyond statistical calculations. Douglas Pratt in Chapter 3, theorizes this relationship through an analysis of the co-reactive radicalization concept. Pratt provides a conceptual framework for understanding and analyzing extremism, particularly religious extremism, and defines religious it as the extremity (margins) or centering (intensifying) of an existing religion. Addressing pluralism as the hallmark of post-modernity, the author addresses the role of exclusivism in paving way to extremism. Pratt introduces reactive co-radicalization, which can develop into parallel and reactionary extremisms. Islamophobia can be counted as one of them. The author focuses on two examples to unpack Islamophobia as a form of reactive co-radicalization: the 2009 Swiss ban on the building of minarets and the 2011 Norwegian massacre carried out by Anders Behring Breivik.

Sam Cherribi coins Pratt's term as 'reactive radicalization' focusing on the Morrocanized Islamophobia in the Netherlands in Chapter 4. Cherribiconfronts the pressing question of why more Dutch-Moroccan youth have joined ISIS than any other ethnic group in the Netherlands by examining rising anti-Moroccan rhetoric within the Islamophobic discourse. Cherribi proposes that religion "functions as a race boundary" and argues that this racialization process has made it extremely difficult for Moroccan youth to access Dutchness. He critiques the news media for circulating this Islamophobia, particularly in the over-reporting of Wilder's 'fewer Moroccans' promise. Geert Wilder built, through his Party for Freedom, a unique brand intended for Dutch internal consumption by targeting Moroccans, and in the process launched a successful party-model for other far-right political parties in the West. The consequence of this Islamophobia is articulated as a 'reactionary extremism', which the author suggests is contributing to radicalization within both the dominant and dominated groups, such as mass killers like Anders Breivik and joining ISIS.

While co-existing reactionary radicalism is in force for the fringe groups, the relationship between Islamophobia and Radicalism is not limited to reactionary radicalization. Presenting an ironic relationship between Islamophobia and Radicalism, Derya Iner in Chapter 5 argues that there is Islamophobia in Radicalism discourse and likewise, there is Radicalism in Islamophobia practice, using the anti-halal debate in Australia as a case study. She argues that Islamophobia is tacitly embedded in the Radicalism discourse by reducing all Muslims to terrorist suspects through the deliberately blurring of the lines between terrorists and ordinary Muslims in political, media and academic discourses. Iner discusses that this approach helps in strengthening the Islamophobic arguments equating all Muslims to terrorists even in seemingly unrelated matters like the halal debate. Likewise, the Radicalism embedded in Islamophobia but neglected by the public allows for the denial of Islamophobic extremism by assuming the convict is not ideologically motivated but mentally sick, and not part of an organization but a lone wolf. Similarly, branding Islamophobes under different group names and dismissing varying levels of extremism among them, portrays them as harmless local groups. After discussing the diametrically opposite attitude towards their Muslim counterparts, Iner concludes that such disparity towards similar types of cases causes overestimation of Islamist terrorism and underestimation of Islamophobic terrorism while leading to an unnecessary social panic on the one hand and absolute denial in the other based on the convict's religious and ideological background.

As the most influential players in society, politicians, media and academia have a significant impact on shaping public perception. Focusing on the media component, Nahid Afrose Kabir in Chapter 6 documents these Islamophobic tendencies through the content analysis of two selected Australian media outlets, *The Australian* and *The Advertiser*, within a six-month period (from August 2014 to January 2015). Based on her previous studies, which outlined the frustrations of Muslims in response to their negative portrayal in the media, Kabir explores the ways in which media representations of Muslims can marginalize vulnerable Muslim youth and steer them towards radicalization. Kabir's content analysis and comparison of the two media outlets concludes that the selective representation of news and images by *The Australian* (as compared to *The Advertiser*) can be considered Islamophobic and reinforces Islamic State propaganda in furthering division between Muslims and non-Muslims.

While the lack of a clear distinction between ordinary Muslims and terrorists in the public discourse inadvertently makes ordinary Muslims pay the bill for Islamist terrorism, certain Islamophobic institutions deliberately do this in order to defame, exclude and paralyze the integrated, successful, contributing, civic and vocal Muslims of Islamic communities. Farid Hafez in Chapter 7 analyzes how the erudite and institutional stream of Islamophobia, i.e. the Islamophobic think tanks in Europe, defame active and organized Muslims by systematic production of biased knowledge. Hafez focuses on the Brussels-based 'European Foundation for Democracy' (EFD) and argues that by outing "Muslim Brotherhood," as a dangerous Islamist group and associating active and vocal Muslims of the community with the Brotherhood, the EFD discards the vocal and active actors of the Muslim civil society. Hafez likens the allegations about the Brotherhood to the conspiracy theories of Jewish world domination. Such allegations "allow for the widening of the Muslim threat, including not only violent extremists, but putting potentially every Muslim civil society organization under suspicion". A systematic effort to portray ordinary Muslims as terrorist suspects is a reoccurring concept (also addressed by Iner) and Hafez's thought-provoking chapter sets the ground for future research to explore the impact of powerful Islamophobic think tanks in shaping public and politic opinions about the mainstream and high achieving civic Western Muslims.

Following the reactionary extremism debates offered by Pratt, Cherribi and Kabir, the vilification of ordinary Muslims due to the inadvertently blurred lines as argued by Kabir and Iner and the systematically driven connections between ordinary Muslims and terrorists discussed by Iner and Hafez, in Chapter 8, Julian Droogan and Shane Peattie address the repercussions in the violent extremist discourse, providing critical empirical data by focusing on the thematic analysis of Al Qaida's and ISIS's e-magazines *Inspire* and *Dabiq*. Droogan and Peattie find that Islamophobia/anti-Muslim discrimination as a concept was rarely addressed in both magazines. However, Islamophobia in the broader sense as a form of structural and systemic violence and discrimination targeted at Muslims in non-Western and Muslim majority appears more frequently than the narrower form of Islamophobia. Both *Inspire* and *Dabiq* frequently address 'Western malevolence', 'occupation of Muslim lands', "West at war with Islam," "blasphemy" and "humiliation," all of which generally relate to perceived Western impressions of aggression, violence, and oppression within the Muslim world. The meta global theme 'Islam is at War'—and the implicit clash of civilizations thesis that it rests upon—is also another recurring theme of the e-magazines.

There is a relative absence of the 'Islamophobia and Discrimination' theme and a strong presence of the much broader 'Western Malevolence' and "Islam is at War" themes in both magazines. Both focus predominantly on Middle Eastern politics written by the non-Western editors, who would be less informed about the Western Muslims' experience with Islamophobia in the West. Yet, from the vulnerable Western Muslim youth's point of view, the narrower and broader forms of Islamophobia can be seamlessly connected through their own experience with Islamophobia in the West.

The debates on counterterrorism in this collection draw attention to another dimension of Islamophobia that appears both in "soft" and "hard" counterterrorism measures but not independently from the political landscape and media. Within this context, the authors argue that counterterrorism measures are counterproductive by focusing on British and Australian examples and considering the issue from Muslim communities' point of view.

Paul Thomas in Chapter 9 examines Britain's Prevent counterterrorism program to argue that counter-radicalization measures reinforce and reflect Islamophobia through their overt focus on British Muslims in implementation and discourse, as they suggest that extremism is a widespread problem for Muslim communities. Thomas draws on his previous empirical data on the implementation of 'community cohesion' policies to argue that, while alternative non-stigmatizing policies could offer a constructive vehicle for anti-extremism and counterterrorism work, they are sidelined, with Prevent favored as a "strategy overtly focused on British Muslims". In providing an overview of the development of Prevent and literature to develop a theoretical contextualization of recent developments in British multiculturalism, the article argues that "the available grounded evidence shows Britain's Prevent program to be a tainted brand that needs to end." The study suggests that the Prevent program initially operated to stigmatize Muslims and deepen problematic community divides, and that these divisions have not only been cemented, but also securitized through the implementation of Prevent 2. Thomas illustrates the way in which specific political events related to Muslims provided the opportunity for "the ideological drive towards large-scale surveillance and suspicion of Muslims per se to be accelerated." He critiques the way in which the impact of the surveillance and monitoring of Muslims through Prevent 2 is most obvious in schools and colleges. Thomas also provides examples from research and news reports to support his warning in regard to the exacerbating impact of counterterrorism strategies on the deepening divides between Muslims and the broader community.

Haroro Ingraham in Chapter 10 argues that counterterrorism measures are counterproductive in terms of harming the Muslim community and helping the radicals' causes. Ingraham discusses that both 'hard' (e.g. anti-terrorism raids) and 'soft' (e.g. counter violent extremism) measures may drive radicalization towards Islamist extremism while fueling far-right groups. Ingraham maintains that the relationship between CVE and radicalization as an illness caused by medical treatment (i.e. iatrogenic radicalization) and analyzes three ways in which counterterrorism strategies may inadvertently drive radicalization. The first one is the myopic and disproportionate focus of counterterrorism efforts on Muslim communities (supported by the example of unprecedented counterterrorism laws and heavily policed anti-terror raids), which helps in deepening the divide. The second is "soft" countering measures that align with the government-approved version of Islam and Muslim leaders. This is also counterproductive as it reinforces the militant Islamists' "sold-out Muslims" allegation. The third relates to how counterterrorism strategic communications may inadvertently reinforce (rather than counter) violent extremist propaganda by showing the terrorist groups as more than what they are. If the dynamics leading to *potential* harm and further radicalization is understood, both "hard" and "soft" counterterrorism measures can be utilized more effectively.

The broken relationship between the government stakeholders and the Muslim community during the CVE processes are captured in Chapter 11. Michele Grossman argues that ineffective and loaded countering measures under the prevalent Islamophobic climate cause cutting off the main and most effective sources of preventing radicalization. Grossman begins with the premise that states 'intimates', especially close friends and family, are critical to early intervention in radicalization cases, yet community reporting can be difficult when experienced as a 'harm'. Interviewing based on interviews with community members, community leaders, and government stakeholders, the study provides an insightful view of what the reporting means for the community, unpack the disparity between the reporting campaigns and the Muslim community perspective and its implications from a countering point of view. The study states that intimates perceive reporting to authorities as a last resort. Grossman empathetically comments on the loneliness of the reporting experience as articulated by community participants, and the loss of power and control they experience through the reporting process. The findings require a revisit of reporting campaigns to shift the dialogue and improve trust between government and communities.

The previous chapters discussed the factors leading vulnerable Muslim youth to radicalization and mainstream Muslims to being targets of Islamophobia and being labeled as terrorist suspects. As mainstream Muslims are heavily impacted both by Islamophobia and Radicalization, it is important to investigate Muslims' responses in different platforms. This section unpacks the Muslim responses at the individual, community and movement levels.

Reflecting on the historical roots of contextualized and institutionalized Islamophobia, Katy Nebhan examines the responses to racism and Islamophobia by Australia's Muslim pioneers in Chapter 12. She reflects on how these early Muslim immigrants responded to Islamophobia as a marginalized, often disadvantaged and minority group within a largely White Australia.

Nebhan analyzes the narratives of some of the most vocal of these early Muslim settlers, referred as the Afghan cameleers, to highlight the ways they positioned themselves within a hostile and Islamophobic nation that actively promoted institutionalized racism through the White Australia Policy. The Orientalized and eroticized cameleers who were perceived as 'imperial possessions' at best, were for a long-term written out of history and "references to them as Afghan cameleers conveniently places them in this sphere of existence namely for their 'use' rather than for themselves". The chapter traces the levels of racism that the cameleers were subjected to, from not being allowed to bring their families over to Australia and being treated as social outcasts, to experiencing discrimination and violence which was deemed acceptable due to the emergence of the White Australia Policy. Nebhan argues that the voices and cultures of the cameleers were written out of the national historical narrative in an attempt to dilute their foreignness and assimilate their presence into a white Australian imagination. Nebhan examines the writings of both Musakhan and Allum to highlight the distinct ways in which they represented themselves and their place within Australia. Despite blatant racism and resistance by ardent unionists, Musakhan actively pursued opportunities to belong by representing himself as a British subject and a loyal citizen, while Allum who believed in the quintessential Australian idea of egalitarianism, modeled himself on the evolving and masculinist 'types' of the Australian character. The chapter documents the 'reluctant Muslim' type who stood against reacting to White Australia through radicalization in an effort to belong in their new home. What is evident is that their idealism appears to have remained despite active resistance to [their] presence.

Early Muslims' navigation through racism and Islamophobia is an empowering example for Muslims today faced with Islamophobia in the West. In Chapter 13, Mario Peucker focuses on contemporary Muslims' responses in the West, particularly in Australia. Peucker argues that the substantive equal citizenship of Muslims in Australia has been inhibited by socioeconomic disadvantage, as well as discrimination, vilification, stigmatization and experiences of exclusion, characterized as Muslims' contested citizenship status. The author examines how Muslims in Australia "claim, enact and negotiate their citizenship" and the findings suggest that most Australian Muslims explained that their civic or political engagement has been driven by a desire to transform society by dispelling misconceptions about Muslims. Some Muslims found that Islamophobia became a motivating factor for their activism, while suggesting that this may not be the case, as Islamophobia is also paralyzing for other members of the community. The article offers insight into the civic and religious identity of active Muslims who emphasized optimism and strength as characteristics which allow them to invest in political and civic work. The participants also provided commentary on why some Muslims withdraw or remain passive in the face of Islamophobia. Breaking the vicious cycle between Islamophobia Radicalization, this chapter demonstrates how Muslims can develop their own constructive responses by performing positive citizenship.

In addition to historical and community responses, it is essential to understand the ways in which transnational Islamic movements cope with the global spread radical and violent extremist ideologies while striving to survive and thrive in the West regardless of the Islamophobic climate. Keles, Sezgin and Yilmaz examine the *Hizmet* (Service) movement as a transnational movement present in the Western scenery since 2000s. Keles et al. argue that Islamophobia and Islamist extremism feed each other. The association of Islam with extremism and terrorism leads to Islamophobia and anti-Muslim crime, which supports the perception that the war on terror is 'truly' a war on Islam. Keles et al. suggest that in a post-modern and post-truth world, traditional and moderate Islamic scholars have struggled to meet the demand to develop Islamic social, cultural and political discourses and paradigms that address contemporary challenges that can be conceptualized as 'theological deprivation'. After highlighting the need for addressing "the lack of knowledge of Islamic studies and lack of intercultural understanding", Keles et al. focus more specifically on the Hizmet movement to analyze its approach to the "twin threats" that are Islamophobia and Radicalization. The authors argue that Hizmet's direct refutations of violent extremism through its teachings and values can act as a positive counter-narrative to the teachings of Islamist extremists. They also examine Hizmet's indirect approach to deradicalization by comparing it with 'reactive' government policies which the authors critique for creating 'suspect communities'. Hizmet's "deradicalization by default" approach is presented as an alternative, where the teachings of the movement are internalized and reinforced through practice, thus rooting out extremist and Islamophobic representations of Islam. The movement practices these values through education, relief work, media and dialogue, which are analyzed in the chapter to present its impact on challenging extremism. The authors also consider the limitations that the Hizmet movement faces in acting as an alternative to attractive Islamist extremist ideology to vulnerable Muslims who are drawn to its forceful Islamist representations. The case study provides an important, alternative perspective to deradicalization from within Muslim majority communities and societies.

Notes

1. Akimi Scarcella, Ruairi Page, and Vivek Furtado, "Terrorism, Radicalisation, Extremism, Authoritarianism and Fundamentalism: A Systematic Review of the Quality and Psychometric Properties of Assessments," *PLoS One* 11, no. 12 (2016): 1.
2. Failsal J. Abbas, "Is It Called 'Terrorism' or 'Violent Extremism'?," *Huffington Post*, March 6, 2015, https://www.huffingtonpost.com/faisal-abbas/is-it-called-terrorism-or_b_7499384.html.
3. Runnymede Trust, *Islamophobia—20 Years on, Still a Challenge for Us All* (London: Runnymede Trust, 2018).
4. Derya Iner, et al., "Islamophobia in Australia 2014–2016," in *Islamophobia Report*, ed. Derya Iner (Sydney, NSW: Charles Sturt University, 2016); Paul McGeough, "Make America Hate Again: How Donald Trump's Election Has Emboldened Bigotry," *Sydney Morning Herald*, November 19, 2016, http://www.smh.com.au/world/us-election/hate-crimes-surge-in-donald-trumps-america-20161117-gsrjpx; and TellMAMA, "The Geography of Anti-Muslim Hatred: Tell Mama Annual Report 2015," *Faith Matters*, London. Retrieved on September 5, 2016.

PART I

Co-existence

CHAPTER 2

Islamophobia and Radicalization: Roots, Impact and Implications

John L. Esposito

Like anti-Semitism, xenophobia and racism, Islamophobia has long and deep historical roots. Its resurgence was triggered by the Iranian revolution, hijackings, and hostage-taking, as well as the 9/11 attacks and subsequent terrorist attacks in Europe by Al Qaeda and more recently ISIS. The global response to terrorism has included an emphasis on countering radicalization and combatting violent extremism (CVE). At the same time, Islamophobia, fear of Islam and Muslims has grown exponentially and become normalized in popular culture in America and in Europe. What is the relationship of Islamophobia to radicalization and militant movements like Al Qaeda and ISIS? Where do we go from here? What is the way forward?

Iran's Islamic Revolution: A Powerful Lens

The Iranian revolution or Iran's Islamic revolution 1978–1979 stunned religious and political leaders, academic experts and the media alike. The toppling of a powerful Shah, who had the second largest modern military in the Middle East and an ambitious modernization program and

---

J. L. Esposito (✉)
Georgetown University, Washington, DC, USA
e-mail: jle2@georgetown.edu

© The Author(s) 2019
J. L. Esposito and D. Iner (eds.), *Islamophobia and Radicalization*, https://doi.org/10.1007/978-3-319-95237-6_2

Western allies (US, Great Britain and other European countries), by the aged Ayatollah Ruhollah Khomeini and a broad-based opposition was totally unexpected. The subsequent call by Khomeini for the export of Iran's "Islamic revolution" and the invasion of the American embassy and taking of hostages became the "Lens" through which many in the West encountered Islam and Muslims. Fear of Iran's export of "radical Islamic fundamentalism" was reinforced by Shiah uprisings in Saudi Arabia, Bahrain and Kuwait, the assassination of Anwar Sadat, Egypt's president by Egyptian Islamic Jihad militants in 1981.

By the 1990s and the Fall of the Soviet Union, fear of "the Green Menace" (Islamic fundamentalism) had replaced the Red Menace as a major international threat. Fears of radical Islam, its threat to the Middle East and to the West, loomed large: Saddam Hussein's call for the world's Muslims to rise up and wage holy war against Western Crusaders during the Gulf War of 1990–1991 was a chilling reminder of Ayatollah Khomeini's threat to export Iran's Islamic Revolution. It confirmed fears of a militant, confrontational Islamic threat or war against the West. The support that Saddam enjoyed from leaders of Islamic movements in Algeria, Tunisia, the Sudan, and Pakistan reinforced the arguments of those who view Islam and the Muslim world as on a collision path with Western priorities and interests. Critics also warned that fundamentalist terrorism had been exported to new battlegrounds, America and Europe. US Vice President, Daniel Quayle in an address at the US Naval Academy, warned that "radical Islamic fundamentalism" was a major threat to the United States—comparable to those posed by communism or Nazism in the twentieth century.

The bombing of New York's World Trade Center in March 1993 reinforced fears that a global "fundamentalist" holy war had been exported to America. Islam was portrayed as a triple threat to the West: political, civilizational and demographic. Samuel Huntington's "The Clash of Civilizations" in 1993 warned of the dangers of an impending clash of civilizations between Western and Islamic civilization and blurred the distinction between Islam and mainstream Muslims using phrases like, "Islam has bloody borders."[1] The article and subsequent book became an international best seller and became part of the political vocabulary of many policymakers, political commentators, and media.

Belief in an impending clash between the Muslim world and the West was also reflected by media headlines and television programs in America and Europe with provocative headlines and titles: "A Holy War Heads

Our Way,"[2] "Jihad in America,"[3] "Focus: Islamic Terror: Global Suicide Squad," "Algerians in London Fund Islamic Terrorism,"[4] and "I Believe in Islamophobia."

Fear of militant Muslim terrorist attacks obscured the extent to which Islam and the vast majority of mainstream Muslims had been brush-stroked by the horrific actions of religious extremists and terrorists. November 1997 proved a watershed moment. Britain's Runnymede Trust report identified and named the elephant in the room, the existence of bias and discrimination towards Muslims. *Islamophobia: A Challenge for Us All*, named and defined anti-Islam and anti-Muslim bias, Islamophobia, as "the dread, hatred and hostility towards Islam and Muslims perpetrated by a series of closed views that imply and attribute negative and derogatory stereotypes and beliefs to Muslims."[5] It results, the report noted, in exclusion (from economic, social, and public life), discrimination, and the perception that the religion of Islam has no values in common with and is inferior to the West and that it is a violent political ideology rather than a source of faith and spirituality like the other Abrahamic religions, Judaism and Christianity.

TERRORISM AND POPULAR CULTURE

The 9/11 attacks in the US, subsequent terrorist attacks in Europe and beyond were used to legitimate fear not only of the terrorists but also of Islam and of Muslims.

> We should invade their countries, kill their leaders, and convert them to Christianity. We weren't punctilious about locating and punishing only Hitler and his top officers. We carpet-bombed German cities; we killed civilians. That's war. And this is war.[6] (Ann Coulter, *National Review*)

> Islam is something we can't afford any more in the Netherlands. I want the fascist Qur'an banned. We need to stop the Islamisation of the Netherlands. That means no more mosques, no more Islamic schools, no more imams.[7] (Geert Wilders, Dutch politician and leader of the Party of Freedom)

> Western European societies are unprepared for the massive immigration of brown-skinned peoples cooking strange foods and maintaining different standards of hygiene.... All immigrants bring exotic customs and attitudes, but Muslim customs are more troublesome than most.[8] (Daniel Pipes, Columnist and Political Commentator)

In the aftermath of 9/11 and the attacks in Europe, the relevance and viability of multiculturalism as a policy in the United States and Great Britain were challenged by France and others who charged that it contributed to domestic terrorism: retarding Muslim assimilation and civic engagement, perpetuating foreign loyalties, and providing a space for militant radicals. The process of integration, in which immigrant citizens and residents could retain their religious and ethnic differences, was rejected by many, in particular the Far Right in Europe, which demanded total assimilation.

In 2002, the European Monitoring Center on Racism and Xenophobia (EUMC) published *The Summary Report on Islamophobia in the EU After 11 September 2001*, which documented increased and widespread acts of discrimination and racism against Muslims in fifteen EU member countries and warned that Islamophobia and anti-Semitism were becoming acceptable in European society.[9]

In 2004, the Runnymede Trust, in a follow to its earlier report, concluded that Islamophobia was a pervasive feature of British society and characterized media reporting on Muslims and Islam as biased and unfair.[10] It noted that far-right anti-immigrant political parties and political commentators in Europe demonized Islam and Muslims, and the net result was a virulent form of cultural racism.[11]

Underscoring recognition of the international dimension of Islamophobia, Kofi Annan, then Secretary General of the United Nations, in 2004 convened an international conference at the UN. "Confronting Islamophobia: Education for Tolerance and Understanding."

> [When] the world is compelled to coin a new term to take account of
>
> increasingly widespread bigotry—that is a sad and troubling development. Such is the case with "Islamophobia." ... Since the September 11 attacks on the United States, many Muslims, particularly in the West, have found themselves the objects of suspicion, harassment, and discrimination.... Too many people see Islam as a monolith and as intrinsically opposed to the West.[12]

In the US, a 2006 USA Today–Gallup Poll found that substantial minorities of Americans admitted to having negative feelings about or prejudices against people of the Muslim faith and favor using heightened security measures with Muslims to help prevent terrorism.[13] Fewer than half of the respondents believed US Muslims are loyal to the United States. Nearly one-quarter of Americans, 22%, said they would not like to have a Muslim as a neighbor; 31% said they would feel nervous if they noticed a Muslim man on their flight, and 18% said they would feel nervous if they noticed a Muslim woman on the flight. About four in ten Americans favored more rigorous security measures for Muslims than those used for other US citizens: requiring Muslims who are US citizens to carry a special ID and undergo more intensive security checks before boarding airplanes in the United States.

Despite this data in contrast to Britain's Runnymede, the extent of bias and discrimination in America towards Islam and Muslims was under-reported and remained unidentified and unnamed. It was not until August 2010 and the debate and mobilization against the building of the so-called mosque at ground zero that for the first time a major news outlet used the term Islamophobic, Time Magazine's cover story asked "Is America Islamophobic?"[14]

The Normalization of Islamophobia

Park 51, a plan to build a $100 million 15-story Muslim Community Cultural Center and luxury condos at 49–51 Park Place in Manhattan two blocks from the site of the World Trade Center revealed the depth of anti-Islam and anti-Muslim sentiment, attracting national and international attention. Although approved by local government and community officials, it suddenly became a national focal point for protest and demonstrations led by outside anti-Islam activists, Robert Spencer and Pamela Geller, founders of Stop Islamization of America, who called it the "Ground Zero Mosque" even though it was not at Ground Zero.

Time magazine cover story "Is America Islamophobic?" reported a poll finding that twenty-eight percent of voters did not believe that Muslims should be eligible to sit on the US Supreme Court and nearly one-third believed that Muslims should be barred from running for President.[15]

In the subsequent fallout, efforts to erect or expand existing mosques across America met with fierce and at times violent backlash and were often labeled "command centers for terrorism." In many US states, a movement to prevent anti-Sharia legislation was introduced despite the fact that there has been no significant attempt to introduce Sharia in America and that it is impossible to do so under the US Constitution.

By 2015–2016 Islamophobia had grown exponentially and negative media coverage of Islam and Muslims hit an all-time high. Domestic and international terrorist attacks (AQ, ISIS), mass and social media coverage and American and European national politics and elections were major catalysts in the growth of Islamophobia. Fear of Islam and Muslims (not just militant extremists and terrorist) became normalized in popular culture. According to Public Religion Research Institute, "no religious, social, or racial and ethnic group [was] perceived as facing greater discrimination in the U.S. than Muslims."[16] One could say the same thing for conditions in many European countries.

The exponential growth and normalization of Islamophobia in turn has had a significant impact on domestic policies that threatened Muslim civil liberties, influenced the radicalization of Muslim and non-Muslim militant extremists, and informed and legitimated Western foreign policies: from US and EU responses to the Arab Spring and Arab Winter and US and EU acceptance of a military coup, July 3, 2013, led by General Abdel Fattah El Sisi which overthrew the democratically elected government of Mohamed Morsi and subsequent support for authoritarian allies in the Middle East in the name of a securitization to assure the stability of governments and Western interests in combating violent extremism.

American and European Elections

American political elections became a major driver or trigger in the 2008 and 2012 Obama presidential elections and 2016–2017 American and European elections. In primary battles for the 2016 US presidential election, Republican candidates like Donald Trump, Ben Carson, Ted Cruz, Rick Santorum, and Newt.

Gingrich raised questions that underscored an Islamic or Muslim threat or incompatibility.

Donald Trump advocated a temporary freeze on all foreign Muslim immigration, as well as the monitoring or even the forced closure of American mosques. When CNN's Anderson Cooper asked Trump if "Islam is at war with the West." He responded **"Islam hates us**.... There's tremendous hatred there… We have to get to the bottom of it. There is an unbelievable hatred of us…"[17] Trump then continued, "And we have to be very vigilant. We have to be very careful, and we cannot allow people coming into this country who have this hatred of the United States and of people that are not Muslim."

In a Republican debate hosted by CNN the following day, Jake Tapper asked Donald Trump if he meant "all 1.6 billion Muslims." He responded, "I mean a lot of them."[18]

Ben Carson declared that a Muslim would have to reject the tenets of Islam to become president of the United States.[19] Republican presidential candidates and some thirty-one, more than half, governors called for a freeze on accepting Syrian refugees fleeing the civil war.

The Trump administration reflected the anti-Islam beliefs of Trump and his appointees. Members of the Trump cabinet and administration, like Steve Bannon, White House Chief Strategist, Rex Tillerson, Secretary of State and James Mattis, Defense as well as Jeff Sessions, the Attorney General and Mike Pomeo, Director of the CIA and later replacement for Rex Tillerson as Secretary of State, all had one thing in common: a track records of saying Islam is not a religion but a dangerous political ideology.

In Europe, anti-Muslim prejudice was closely linked to the "War on Terror" with an anti-immigrant and anti-Muslim drumbeat about the impending demise of Europe's religious (Christian) identity and cultural heritage. Soon, critics warned the continent will be transformed into "Eurabia," or in Great Britain, "Londonistan."

The institutionalization of anti-Muslim prejudice was illustrated by anti-hijab and/or burqa and burkini (Muslim women's swimsuit) bans in France, Germany, Belgium and Austria, a ban on building mosques in Switzerland. Surveys in France reported that 68% of French citizens believed Muslims were "not well integrated into society," 55% said the "visibility of Islam is too large," and 60% were concerned about Muslim's refusal to integrate into French society. In a survey in Germany 79% of those surveyed said that Islam was "the most violent religion."[20]

Far-right political parties, like the British National Party led by Nick Grifin, the Netherland's Party for Freedom of Geert Wilders, Marine Le Pen's National Front and other right-wing nationalist and populist parties espoused anti-immigrant and in particular anti-Muslim policies and fanned the flames of Islamophobia with unbalanced and inaccurate narratives about Muslims and Islam. The BNP warned that Islam "presents one of the most deadly threats yet to the survival of our nation"[21] and Wilders maintained "The Koran is an evil book that calls for violence, murder, terrorism, war and submission.... We need to stop the Islamisation of the Netherlands. That means no more mosques, no more Islamic schools, no more imams."[22]

The net result of xenophobic, anti-Muslim and racist far-right extremism in Europe and America could be seen in the rhetoric and attacks on Muslims and mosques and significant election performance of far-right political parties in Europe and election of Donald Trump in America, and their common opposition to Muslim immigration, specifically to the tens of thousands (part of the 4.7 million of Syrian refugees) of immigrant victims of Syria's brutal civil war.

Media's Powerful Role

Media (mass and social media) have played a critical role in the exponential growth of Islamophobia, providing a platform for anti-Islam and anti-Muslim statements, accusations and condemnations by political leaders, media commentators, and a host of "preachers of hate" as well as hate speech and hate crimes.

Mass media with its penchant for explosive, headline events, rooted in the common maxim, "If it bleeds, it leads." Far right political, media and religious commentators spoke out publicly and often indiscriminately not only against militant Muslims but also brush-stroked Islam and the vast majority of mainstream Muslims, asserting with impunity what would never appear in mainstream broadcast or print media regarding American Jews, Christians and established ethnic groups. Huntington himself retained in his book a controversial statement he made in his article that "Islam has bloody borders."

A comparison of media coverage in 2001 vs. 2011 demonstrated the shocking disparity of coverage. A study by Media Tenor, "A New Era for Arab-Western Relations,"[23] found that out of nearly 975,000 news stories from US and European media outlets, networks significantly reduced coverage on events in MENA to actions of Muslim militants.

In 2001, 2% of all news stories in Western media presented images of Muslim militants, while just over 0.1% presented stories of ordinary Muslims. In 2011, 25% of the stories presented militant image, while 0.1% presented images of ordinary Muslims, their faith, beliefs, attitudes and behaviors.[24]

The net result was an astonishing imbalance of coverage: a significant increase in coverage of militants but no increase at all over the 10 year period in the coverage of ordinary Muslims. By 2015–2016 Islamophobia had gotten worse, became normalized: for example—80% of American, British and German coverage was negative.[25]

At the same time, social media became a major source for news and information and with it an exponential growth in anti-Islam and anti-Muslim websites and diatribe with international and domestic consequences. An Organized Islamophobia Network (OIN) , with major funding and engineered Islamophobic campaigns and messages, anti-Muslim and anti-immigrant emerged. A cottage industry of pundits, bloggers, authors, documentaries, and elected officials were cultivated by ideological, agenda-driven anti-Muslim polemicists, and their funders.

An August 2011 Center Report, Fear, Inc., documented that $42.6 million flowed from seven foundations over 10 years to support Islamophobic authors and websites.[26]

A CAIR Report in 2013, "Legislating Fear: Islamophobia and its Impact in the United States,"[27] reported that the inner core of the US-based Islamophobia network enjoyed access to at least $119,662,719 in total revenue between 2008 and 2011.

The Complex Sources of Radicalization

The causes of radicalization and violent extremism are more complex than ideological indoctrination, they include: bias and discrimination, xenophobia and racism as well as political and socioeconomic causes. Studies of Islamophobia and of terrorist groups and individuals have confirmed that authoritarian regimes in Muslim countries and US and European foreign policy towards Muslim-majority countries, not religion, are the primary causes or grievances of most militant groups and of homegrown terrorists.

A 2011 study, "Homegrown Islamist Terrorism: Assessing the Threat,"[28] assessing the motives of homegrown terrorist attacks in the US from 2001 to 2011 concluded that the number of attacks were greatly exaggerated and that the main motive was US foreign policy, reported that "Most Homegrown Islamist Terrorists Believe that the United States is at War with Islam."

While there is no definitive generic "homegrown jihadist terrorist" profile, similarities do exist. Links to Foreign Terrorist Organizations were not directly involved with the vast majority of "homegrown jihadist terrorist" plots. A study of the four attacks by American Muslim terrorists in the Army identified that they were all loners. Two of them had mental illnesses, but most importantly, after analyzing their statements during interrogations, Marc Sageman concluded that:

The wars against Muslims had transformed their dual American-Muslim loyalty into a divided loyalty, American versus Muslim. Imminent negative change in status, such as impending discharge, detention, or unwanted deployment abroad, catalyzed their anger into action.[29]

Their actions were driven by identity, a feeling of a lack of belonging, and personal anger at being unjustly treated. Other American violent extremists believed that they were defending their community, the global Muslim community (*ummah*). "Many attribute this change to specific events, such as watching the mass murder of Muslims, invasion of a Muslim land, unfair prison time, or learning about egregious injustice against comrades."[30]

A study of more than 140 terrorist plots in Europe found that although Islamist terrorist attacks in Europe in 2015 made major headlines, there had been a long history of jihadist terrorism in Europe, dating back in 1980s, mostly influenced by the increasing involvement of Europe in conflict zones in the Middle East.[31] This involvement, usually supporting one group against another, led to more organized transnational sense of identity and networks of jihadists in Europe.

Today diverse terrorist groups are connected through loose networks, often part of a transnational, evolving, and expanding network. The cells are usually self-financed and rally around charismatic local leaders. Because the network is complex, intelligence communities often have difficulty keeping track. The primary catalysts that brought Al Qaeda and ISIS to life were political, economic and social grievances, rather than religion. Islam was used to buttress and legitimate militant extremist ideologies and acts of terrorism.

"Online recruiters and organizers of terrorist organizations have sought people who have problems, and often do not know much about religion. A typical candidate for recruitment is often someone who is isolated, who does not have a healthy family life and finds solace in cyberspace. Young girls, for example, who did not interact well with parents, were abused at home, didn't have good friends, or were bullied at school were drawn to ISIS by the promise of marriage, a good life and are therefore predisposed to religiously indoctrinated by ISIS."[32]

Sources of Alienation and Radicalization

While the majority of American and European Muslims are mainstream and moderate, a small minority have been alienated by their country's domestic and foreign policies. A minority, in most countries a very small minority, are radicalized.

In contrast to most American Muslims, who despite difficulties, can and have pursued the American dream, the experience of many European Muslims has been different. Whereas Muslim migration to America often consisted of well-educated immigrants seeking a better life, leaving authoritarian regimes, or Muslims pursuing better educations and professional careers, many of Europe's Muslim immigrants have been laborers or refugees with minimal educations and language skills welcomed by "host countries" to fill lower paid jobs. Many came with the intention of eventually returning to their homeland and their host countries were not anticipating the majority would stay and become permanent citizens.

American and European Muslims have struggled with a crisis of identity (Where do I belong in this society?), a double identity: national and religious. Often younger generations find themselves alienated both from their American or European identity and from the traditional national and religious identities of their parents. Media's disproportionate coverage of Muslim terrorists and their acts of terrorism, Islamophobic writings and statements by anti-immigrant and anti-Muslim far-right political parties, political leaders, media commentators and the exponential growth of Islamophobic websites as well as ill-conceived anti-terrorism legislation, bias discrimination, hate speech and hate crimes have reinforced among Muslims in the West that their multiple identities were and are incompatible and that they will never be accepted as full and equal citizens in their societies.

The role and results of Islamophobia in fostering radicalization helps explain the susceptibility and desire of potential recruits for an alternative or more "authentic" identity. It is a reaction by some against living in a culture where young second and third generation Muslims feel like misfits, alienated both from their immigrant parents' or grandparents' cultures and from that of their adopted homelands where anti-Muslim and anti-Islam bias and discrimination marginalizes and alienates them.

Homegrown extremist Muslim militants often feel marginalized, demonized for something they can't control (i.e. their Muslim identity and background). Militant Islam is presented as an escape into a new and more authentic identity. It promises and offers a weapon to "fight" back against the hate they feel from society—the more Islamophobic the environment, the more pressure there is to radicalize out of self-preservation.

What most people watch in the media is completely different from what many potential young recruits watch. They watch online platforms such as on YouTube. They are attracted to conspiracy videos, which are so professionally produced and use the Islamophobic discourse of the western leaders, and the acts against Muslims, to catch the attention of the youngsters.

Leaders of militant Muslim organizations and YouTube sheikhs provide a basic Manichean good-evil dichotomous worldview and sense of community. They show and exploit the abuses at Abu Gharib and Guantanamo and use these facts to foster radicalization, violence and terrorism. They condemn Western societies' Muslims who live as minorities, often victims of the Islamophobic rhetoric and policies of Western governments leaders and political parties, of white nationalist violent rhetoric and actions, of bias and discrimination and hate crimes. They offer an imagined religio-political community without borders, one with a regional or global vision, mission and goal. New followers are drawn to this militant global ideology with the zeal and vigor of new converts to an ultra-patriotic transnational ideology and a commitment to violent militancy.

While European countries have provided a land of socioeconomic opportunity for some Muslims, many have struggled in low paying jobs, living in depressed ghetto areas, lacked access to a good education and had limited job skills and/or were unemployed with little hope for a better life. These conditions feed and reinforce a sense of social exclusion, marginalization and alienation second-class citizenship, contributing also to problems with crime and drugs. A minority have then become vulnerable to recruitment by jihadist groups and their militant interpretations of Islam. The Molenbeek community in Brussels, Belgium, a community that many Muslim jihadists have come from including one of the 9/11 plotters, is a prime example. The similarities among many young jihadists there is striking. Their parents were and are traditional, rural Muslims, who immigrated to Belgium, usually living in Brussel's ghettos, earning just enough to make ends meet. Many were and are non-practicing Muslims and some turned to a life of crime and dealing with drugs.[33]

Muslim youth from stable economic and social backgrounds, well educated, and employed are not exempt from becoming radicalized, especially when they see a double standard not only in their economic status, civil liberties and future but also in the foreign policies of their country and/or other Western governments such as a reluctance or selective espousal of democracy and human rights and support for authoritarian regimes in the Muslim world.

Is Religion the Primary Catalyst for Radicalization, Political Violence and Terrorism?

Major polls by Gallup, PEW and others have consistently reported that Islam is a significant component of religious and cultural identity in Muslim countries and communities globally. Gallup World Polls of Muslims (2001–2008) in some 35 Muslim countries reported the most frequent response by those polled as to what they admired most about themselves and associated with Arab/Muslim nations was "attachment to their spiritual and moral values is critical to their progress."[34]

Pew polls and others have continued to confirm these findings. Thus the use of Islam by violent extremists as an instrument for legitimation and mobilization is not surprising. However, the most frequently cited reason for joining violent extremist groups has not been religion but authoritarian, unrepresentative and repressive governments. A power vacuum in Syria and Iraq enabled separatist movements, particularly the self-named Islamic State or ISIS, to garner supporters, and take hold and govern large swathes of territory. This was exacerbated by Sunni-Shia sectarian conflict and exploitation by Iran and some Gulf countries like Saudi Arabia in proxy wars.

For groups like the Islamic State, religion has been a tool to legitimate narratives of marginalization, anguish and discontent, and to recruit and mobilize followers in the Muslim world and from the West. ISIS execution videos, initially released (October 2006–April 2013 Al-Furqan Media Foundation) underscored the importance of political and socioeconomic grievances as motivations to join: Western military invasion, occupation and support for authoritarian regimes, the Iraqi and Syrian governments' killing of tens of thousands of civilians and "crimes" committed by individuals/groups (Iraqi soldiers, police, and government workers), Islamophobia and its impact on the lives and civil liberties of Muslims.

An imprisoned Iraqi jihadist in Europe explained his motive to join ISIS as "The Americans came... they took away Saddam, but they also took away our security. I didn't like Saddam, we were starving then, but at least we didn't have war. When you came here, the civil war started."[35] Many Iraqi Sunnis' joining ISIS had very little, if at all, to do with religion, or a caliphate. They blamed the coalition (America and the UK) for the invasion and for handing over Iraq to the Shia, the loss of their positions, livelihood and the secure life of their community.[36]

Many returnees from Syria and Iraq have stated that the first impetus to join ISIS was not due to religious belief or indoctrination or blind hatred of the West, but because of media materials, in particular social media, the coverage of the carnage, in particular of the slain Muslim children and women in Syria at the hands of the Assad regime. Moral outrage at these atrocities enhanced sympathy and sense of solidarity and identification with an "imagined community."[37]

While the main recruitment venue of ISIS in Europe has been cyberspace, the venues for recruitment process have included prisons, mosques, and sports facilities.[38] For some, the main motive was political, for others social discontent, social networks, or militant religious preachers. Political grievances include foreign involvement in the Middle East and broader Muslim World, Western support for authoritative leaders and repressive governments. Some, when faced at home with the bias, discrimination, hate speech and hate crimes of Islamophobia have become radicalized and turned to violence and terrorism.

A distinctive difference between Al Qaeda and ISIS has been their use of Islam. Al Qaeda leadership and propaganda machines have used Islamic discourse. Whereas ISIS leadership and propagandists have relied heavily on pop-culture and the promise of "a better life." Recruiters do not speak about the religion of Islam when they initially recruit for ISIS. They speak about how Western governments Islamophobia, their hatred and discrimination against Muslims, their inequality and marginalization in society; issues of poverty, education, and employment. ISIS recruiters strongly emphasize the caliphate as a utopian government that sees and treats everyone equal and is a just community and society.

Emphasis religion or religious extremism as the primary cause for militant Muslim movements like Al Qaeda and ISIS ignores the real causes: political and socioeconomic conditions and grievances, reinforces Western foreign policies that strengthen and prop up authoritarian Arab and Muslim governments like Egypt, Saudi Arabia and the United Arab Emirates regarding them as sources of stability and security.

ISIS recruiters do not recruit Muslims who have considerable knowledge of Islam, practicing Muslims with no family or law enforcement issues. ISIS targets have been youngsters who have a troubled past and lack a strong self-identify as Muslims. Polls have shown that generally the two groups that don't become victims of recruitment are: practicing Muslims who are literate in Islamic teaching and secular Muslims who have good friends, good community, and functioning families. Whereas the vulnerable recruits are those who do not have good friends, have had problems with law enforcement, were bullied when they were little, alienated, have family problems, and do not have good knowledge or practice of Islam.[39]

CONCLUSION

The exponential growth of Islamophobia and anti-immigrant policies in recent years and its impact on American and European politics and societies enhances the political influence of anti-Muslim politicians, activists and organizations, It enables the passing of legislation and security measures that threaten the safety, security and civil liberties of mainstream Muslim citizens and immigrants in general. It also increases a sense of marginalization, alienation and outrage and thus the danger of radicalization among a distinct minority.

Rampant unchecked Islamophobia in American and European societies and the political rhetoric and actions of some Western governments predictably make Muslim minorities feel that they have no place, no level playing field, and are second-class citizens who are demonized and too often seen as guilty until proven innocent. Despite this reality and the barbaric acts in Europe and America as well as in Muslim countries by terrorists and organizations like Al Qaeda and ISIS, the numbers of their followers have remained small relative to the 1.6 billion Muslims in the world. Moreover, major polls in the Muslim world and the West have consistently shown that despite the efforts and propaganda of militant groups like Al Qaeda and ISIS, majorities of Muslims have rejected the violence and terror and are loyal citizens who like their non-Muslim counterparts become and wish to be part of the mosaic in their countries.

A Pew Research Center report (November 2015) found overwhelmingly negative views of ISIS across Muslim majority countries including Indonesia, Senegal, Turkey, Nigeria, Burkina Faso and Malaysia.[40]

The Doha Institute's 2015 Arab Opinion Index (December 2015) reported that approximately 89% of the Arab public—spanning from Saudi Arabia to Mauritania to Jordan to Kuwait to Palestine to Egypt—viewed ISIS negatively.[41] Its few supporters' grievances were rooted in the region's politics and conflicts. The strategies cited by respondents to combat ISIS included: (1) support for a democratic transition in the Arab World (28%); (2) resolving the Palestinian cause was the second most common response (18%).

According to a Zogby poll (2016) in eight Muslim majority countries, "Muslim Millennial Attitudes on Religion and Religious Leadership,"— three-quarters of those polled believe groups like ISIS and Al Qaeda are a complete perversion of Islam.[42] This included 9 in 10 respondents in the UAE and Morocco as well as 83% of those in Egypt, 65% in Bahrain, 61% in Jordan, 58% in Palestine, and 57% in Saudi Arabia.

Like it or not, Western countries have become and will continue to become more and more multicultural and multi-religious. Diversity must be seen and fostered as a potential strength not an inevitable threat. A true and inclusive multiculturalism must be embraced, one that has a place for people of all ethnic backgrounds and faiths. America and Europe must pursue **a more robust policy of inclusion** of its Muslim citizens, their equality and civil liberties, and eschew Islamophobia as they do anti-Semitism and racism. Islam and the vast majority of Muslims are not the problem.

Muslims must be recognized and treated as equal citizens and neighbors not regarded as tolerated guests or foreigners in host countries. The exponential growth of Islamophobia and the media's disproportionate coverage of violence and extremism and failure to adequately cover the broader contexts of mainstream Muslim lives and beliefs reinforce a sense of second-rate citizenship and marginalization as well as fuel the growth of xenophobia, white supremacy and racism. These conditions not religion can lead to radicalization.

Muslim religious leaders and communities through their schools, mosques, community centers, non-government organizations must continue to reformulate and reassert their faith in Western societies, incorporate those attitudes and values that enable them to blend their religious and cultural identity and values with a healthy sense of nationalism and citizenship. Where needed, they must continue to be active representatives and witnesses of their faiths to non-Muslim fellow citizens and partner with national and local religious and civic organizations.

Finally, America and Europe need to break the ISIS brand. ISIS established a brand, they had marketing and propaganda strategies, including very well-made productions, and they keep building on it, mostly citing Islamophobic discourse and using the problems that Muslims are facing in the West. Richard Stengel, Under Secretary for Public Diplomacy and Public Affairs at the State Department during Obama Presidency, said that according to their research 80% of ISIS fighters don't know much about Islam and ideology or religion are not their driving force. Rather, 80% of ISIS messages were about positive things, about how beautiful life in the "caliphate" and how the Muslims should "migrate" there. Their videos are of ISIS members playing with kids, giving food and fruits to children, nice infrastructure etc. Unlike Al Qaeda, ISIS called for doctors, engineers, architects, plumbers, and others, to migrate there to help build a state. They are not only calling for fighters and martyrs. They aim to make Muslims think that life is better in the "caliphate" so they should migrate there instead of being discriminated and marginalized in America or Europe.[43]

Basically, America, Europe, and Muslims in the West need to find ways and methods to appeal to the millennial Muslims, breaking what ISIS tried to build, but also building their own brand of justice, anti-discrimination, pluralism and inclusion to counter Islamophobia and radicalization.

NOTES

1. Samuel Huntington, "The Clash of Civilizations?," *Foreign Affairs*, https://www.foreignaffairs.com/articles/united-states/1993-06-01/clash-civilizations (1993).
2. Fergus M. Bordewich, "A Holy War Heads Our Way," *Readers Digest* (January 1995).
3. "Jihad in America: The Grand Deception," http://www.granddeception.com/#sthash.j34WVkq2.dpbs (2013).
4. "Algerians in London Fund Islamic Terrorism," *Sunday Times* (January 1, 1995).
5. *Islamophobia: A Challenge for Us All*, https://www.runnymedetrust.org/companies/17/74/Islamophobia-A-Challenge-for-Us-All.htm (London: Runnymede Trust, 1997).
6. Ann Coulter, "This is War," *The National Review* (September 14, 2001).
7. Geert Wilders, "Profile: Geert Wilders," *The Guardian*, https://www.theguardian.com/world/2009/feb/12/profile-geert-wilders (October 16, 2009).
8. Daniel Pipes, "The Muslims Are Coming! The Muslims Are Coming!," *National Review* (November 19, 1990).
9. "Summary Report on Islamophobia in the EU After 11 September 2001," European Monitoring Centre on Racism and Xenophobia, https://www.theguardian.com/world/2009/feb/12/profile-geert-wilders (May 2002).

10. "Islamophobia, Issues, Challenges and Action," Runnymede Trust (London: 2004).
11. Ibid.
12. Kofi Annan, "Secretary-General, Addressing Headquarters Seminar on Confronting Islamophobia, Stresses Importance of Leadership, Two-Way Integration, Dialogue," United Nations, http://www.un.org/press/en/2004/sgsm9637.doc.htm (2004).
13. Lydia Saad, "Anti-Muslim Sentiments Fairly Commonplace," Gallup, http://news.gallup.com/poll/24073/antimuslim-sentiments-fairly-commonplace.aspx (August 2006).
14. "Is America Islamophobic?," *Time Magazine* (August 30, 2010).
15. Ibid.
16. "Anxiety, Nostalgia, and Mistrust: Findings from the 2015 American Values Survey," *Public Policy Research Institute*, https://www.prri.org/wp-content/uploads/2015/11/PRRI-AVS-2015.pdf (Washington, DC, 2015).
17. Theodore Schleifer, "Donald Trump: I Think Islam Hates Us", *CNN*, https://www.cnn.com/2016/03/09/politics/donald-trump-islam-hates-us/index.html (March 10, 2016).
18. "Transcript of Republican Debate in Miami, Full Text," *CNN*, https://www.cnn.com/2016/03/10/politics/republican-debate-transcript-full-text/index.html (March 15, 2016).
19. Martin Pengelly, "Ben Carson Says Muslim President Would Have to 'Subjugate' Beliefs," *CNN*, https://www.theguardian.com/us-news/2015/sep/27/ben-carson-muslim-president-subjugate-beliefs (September 27, 2015).
20. "L'image de l'Islam en France," IFOP pour Le Figaro, http://www.lefigaro.fr/assets/pdf/sondage-ipsos-islam-france.pdf (October 2012).
21. "BNP Calls for an End to Immigration from Muslim Countries," *BBC News*, http://news.bbc.co.uk/2/hi/uk_news/politics/election_2010/8639097.stm (August 23, 2010).
22. Ian Traynor, "'I Don't Hate Muslims. I Hate Islam,' Says Holland's Rising Political Star," *The Guardian*, https://www.theguardian.com/world/2008/feb/17/netherlands.islam (February 16, 2008).
23. "Reviewing Tone and Coverage of Islam: 2005–2016," Media Tenor, https://www.mediatenor.cz/wp-content/uploads/2015/02/ADR_2015_LR_WEB_PREVIEW.pdf (2016).
24. Ibid.
25. Ibid.
26. "Fear Inc.," Center for American Progress, http://www.americanprogress.org/issues/religion/report/2011/08/26/10165/fear-inc/ (2011).
27. "Legislating Fear: Islamophobia and Its Impact in the United States," CAIR, http://www.cair.com/images/islamophobia/Legislating-Fear.pdf (2013).

28. "Homegrown Islamist Terrorism: Assessing the Threat," *Journal of Public and International Affairs*, https://jpia.princeton.edu/sites/jpia/files/jpia2011-2.pdf#page=109.
29. Marc Sageman, "Misunderstanding Terrorism" (University of Pennsylvania Press, 2017), p. 144.
30. Ibid.
31. "Homegrown Islamist Terrorism: Assessing the Threat," p. 109.
32. Lesaca, Javier, "On Social Media, ISIS Uses Modern Cultural Images to Spread Anti-Modern Values," The Brookings Institution, https://www.brookings.edu/blog/techtank/2015/09/24/on-social-media-isis-uses-modern-cultural-images-to-spread-anti-modern-values/ (September 24, 2015).
33. Johan Leman, "At the Intersections Migration, Religion and Extremism: Pluralism in Today's EU," Rumi Forum Luncheon, http://rumiforum.org/migration-religion-extremism/ (May 3, 2016).
34. John L. Esposito and Dalia Mogahed, *Who Speaks for Islam: What a Billion Muslims Really Think* (New York: Gallup Press, 2008), p. 86.
35. Lydia Wilson, "What I Discovered From Interviewing Imprisoned ISIS Fighters." *The Nation*, https://www.thenation.com/article/what-i-discovered-from-interviewing-isis-prisoners/ (2015).
36. Ibid.
37. Sageman, "Misunderstanding Terrorism."
38. Peter Nesser, "Islamist Terrorism in Europe: A History." The New America Foundation, https://www.newamerica.org/international-security/islamist-terrorism-in-europe/ (May 9, 2016).
39. Leman, "At the Intersections Migration, Religion and Extremism: Pluralism in Today's EU."
40. Jacob Poushter, "In Nations with Significant Muslim Populations, Much Disdain for ISIS," Pew Research Center, http://www.pewresearch.org/fact-tank/2015/11/17/in-nations-with-significant-muslim-populations-much-disdain-for-isis/ (November 2015).
41. "The 2015 Arab Opinion Index," Arab Center for Research & Policy Studies, https://www.dohainstitute.org/en/News/Pages/The_2015_Arab_Opinion_Index_Results_in_Brief.aspx (December 2015).
42. "Muslim Millennial Attitudes on Religion and Religious Leadership," Tabah Foundation, http://mmasurvey.tabahfoundation.org/downloads/mmgsurvey_full_En_web.pdf (Abu Dhabi 2016).
43. "Schieffer Series: Breaking ISIL's Brand," Center for Strategic & International Studies, https://www.csis.org/events/schieffer-series-breaking-isils-brand (May 2016).

CHAPTER 3

Reacting to Islam: Islamophobia as a Form of Extremism

G. Douglas Pratt

INTRODUCTION

Foremost among the problems confronting the world today is the troublesome manifestation of extreme forms of Islam. Islamic extremism may be regarded as the 'sharp end' of what is popularly referred to as 'Islamism'. Sometimes these terms are used synonymously when in fact they are not. 'Islamism' refers to a wider concept and phenomena of intentional and intensifying Islamic identity and polity that can manifest in many quite peaceful but also clearly assertive ways. Islamic extremism, which is what concerns us here, is quite fissiparous. There are many different and sometimes competing groups, such as Islamic State (ISIS), Al-Qaida, Boko Haram, Al Shabab, and many others. They are often bound together in some form of coalition, or they may engage in intergroup rivalries.

A second problem is the reactionary response to Islamic extremism that generalizes to a fear of, or anxiety about, Muslims as such. At times it is

G. D. Pratt (✉)
University of Auckland, Auckland, New Zealand
e-mail: d.pratt@auckland.ac.nz

G. D. Pratt
University of Bern, Bern, Switzerland

© The Author(s) 2019
J. L. Esposito and D. Iner (eds.), *Islamophobia and Radicalization*,
https://doi.org/10.1007/978-3-319-95237-6_3

accompanied by an almost visceral rejection of anything to do with Islam. The internal diversity of the Muslim *Ummah* (notional single and global community) is ignored, discounted, or simply not known; and rivalrous distinctions within even the field of Islamic extremism are likewise glossed. Muslim rhetoric of the unity of Islamic identity and community is taken at face value, so reinforcing a (mis)-perception of Islam as a domineering monolith. And with the seemingly incessant headlines of violent Islamist extremism there comes the inevitable result that much media commentary, and too many people, tend to equate 'extreme' with 'mainstream', thereby tarring all Muslims with the same brush. So an oversimplified perception ensues: Muslims are 'the same', and Muslims are 'extreme'.

Yet it is Muslims, rather than non-Muslims, who more often the victims of Islamic extremists. And at the same time many Muslims may find themselves victimized by non-Muslims who have succumbed to Islamophobic anxieties and allied prejudices. Muslims with no link to Islamic extremists become the targets of hostile reaction, very often from persons who are not even connected to the sites and contexts of Islamic extremism. Such peaceful ordinary Muslims are themselves subject to an increasing reactionary extremism emanating from many non-Muslim quarters. These reactions are aimed, disturbingly, at any—indeed all—Muslims virtually everywhere. This fearful reaction to all things Islamic is the reactionary problem of Islamophobia.[1] It is itself a form of extremism. And where Islamophobia is supported by religious perspective and argument, it is arguably a form of religious extremism—Jewish, Christian, Hindu and Buddhist varieties of Islamophobia abound along with political-oriented, or simply secular, right-wing Islamophobia.[2] One does not have to look too far or hard at contemporary print, video and social internet media to see examples of this.

For instance, in Thailand there is evidence of reactionary Buddhist extremism in response to a perception of the danger posed by Islam and Muslims. A Buddhist culture, confronted with the specter of so-called jihadi terrorism, responds with forms of violent behavior that, on the face of it, runs counter to predominant religious teachings and sensibilities.[3] This has been seen even more graphically and violently with the recent purge of Muslim Rohingyas from Buddhist Burma (Myanmar).[4] And today individuals and organizations in the West, especially in Germany and the UK, have a declared mission to 'confront and demolish the foundations of Islam' in a polemical war of words.[5] And there is a deep 'othering' of Muslims presently emanating from right-wing and fundamentalist Christian quarters in the United States, Australia, and parts of Northern Europe, especially. This is seen very clearly in the many media reports of Islamophobic statements and actions that appear virtually daily. The reactionary extremism that is Islamophobia is a truly globalized phenomenon.[6]

Among a number of cases that could be considered I wish to focus on two dramatic instances—the 2009 Swiss ban on the building of minarets and the 2011 Norwegian massacre carried out by Anders Behring Breivik. These are examples of what I have come to think of as the extremism of mutually reactive co-radicalization.[7] The Swiss case issued in a message of *implicit exclusion*; the Norwegian affair enacted a *displaced elimination*. One expressed blanket rejection; the other dealt in death. Yet each gives evidence of a process of radicalizing values, beliefs, attitudes etc. that, relatively speaking, resulted in some form of extreme outcome. Further, my contention is that what emerged as Islamophobia in these cases arose out of the radicalization of sets of guiding ideas (theology, ideology) that varyingly impact persons, whether individually (as with Norway's Breivik) or collectively (as with those Swiss who banned the building of minarets). Following a scene-setting description of these two cases, I shall briefly discuss some hermeneutical and conceptual tools for understanding and analyzing these sorts of extreme acts. I will return to the two cases before concluding with a discussion of reactive co-radicalization and its applicability to Islamophobia, especially in the context of political changes now registering within many other parts of the world.

FEAR OF MUSLIMS: TWO CASES OF EXTREME REACTION

In 2009 a citizen's referendum in Switzerland voted to ban the erection of minarets. At the time there were some 200 mosques in the country, but only four with a minaret. However, two mosques had sought planning permission to erect a minaret each, and it was their applications which sparked a right-wing reaction aimed at, and eventually achieving the addition of a single sentence to article 72 of the federal constitution forbidding the building of any more minarets in the country. This occurred despite the advice of the Federal Council, all the main other political parties, the Churches and others to not go down this path. Now, so long as this addition remains, there will be no more minarets built in Switzerland. On the one hand it would seem a case of political overkill: building code restrictions and allied requirements at the local level had precluded, without rancor, the building of minarets in many locations, just as they preclude new church towers or steeples. Switzerland wasn't exactly at risk of being transformed overnight into a minaret-dominated landscape. Other European countries have their flash-point issues with Islam—often centered on female attire—however, as Mayer noted 'The symbolic nature of the minaret … acquired a central place in the political debate in Switzerland … but larger anxieties and issues hide behind the minaret question'.[8]

On July 22, 2011, Norway witnessed a horrific assault from within. A young Norwegian man, Anders Behring Breivik, then only 32, detonated a bomb in the capital of Oslo, destroying a government building in which several people died and many more were injured. Shortly thereafter, in a surreal attempt to precipitate an uprising against Islam, he set about executing 69 individuals, mostly young people, who were attending a political (Labor) youth camp on the island of Utoya. Breivik's Facebook profile at the time stated his political views were 'conservative' and that his religion was 'Christian'. His self-published manifesto (he used the Anglicized form of his name, 'Andrew Berwick', as the author) gives clues and statements concerning his ideology and rationale. It states 'the fear of Islamization is all but irrational'.[9] Breivik goes on to claim there 'is no Resistance Movement if individuals like us refuse to contribute'[10] and that his manifesto 'presents the solutions and explains exactly what is required of each and every one of us'.[11] He rather chillingly asserts, in the context of Islam in Europe, that: 'It is not only our right but also our duty to contribute to preserve our identity, our culture and our national sovereignty by preventing the ongoing Islamization'.[12] So, what are we to make of Breivik's actions and motives? How might his motives and actions be assessed?[13]

Tools for Analysis and Understanding

Each of these cases, in their own way, demonstrates Islamophobia in action. But in order to understand the deeper significance and meaning of them we need to identify some conceptual tools. Accordingly, I begin by asking: what do we mean by 'extremism' as such? The term most obviously evokes a sense of being at the margins, of existing on the boundary, or of functioning at the edge; in other words, extremism suggests, naturally enough, 'extremities'. Any organization or group that is in this sense extreme will tend to manifest a tenuous link to whatever is the relative 'center', or else give evidence of a loose connection to the normative tradition to which it sees itself as belonging. Arguably, this is the case with extreme groups such as Boko Haram in Nigeria, or al-Qaeda in Saudi Arabia: normative religio-political cultures in each case outlaws these groups as extreme. And most Muslims around the globe eschew such movements as even properly Islamic. In other cases, such groups may not be outlawed, but they are generally regarded as being on the margins of society, as is the case with some extreme right-wing groups and political parties in Europe, for example. In such situations as these, extremism expresses a relative 'heterodoxy' contrasting with the prevailing orthodoxy, whether in terms of religion or politics.

However, extremism can refer to something else altogether, even, indeed, the opposite of being 'at the margins', namely, being at—or claiming to be—the center. So al-Shabab in Somalia, perhaps; and certainly ISIS, or the so-called Islamic State, at the height of its power across great swathes of Syria and Iraq. And there are signs of assertive political Islamism, and with it the prospect of Islamic extremism being manifest, gaining ground in places like Turkey, Malaysia and Indonesia, as well as elsewhere.[14] Within many Western societies the political ground-shift to the right is very evident, and not always to do with the present triumph of neo-conservative economics. Religious and cultural shifts are also very evident. Thus in some cases we see such heretofore marginal—as in 'extreme'—groups, whether political or religious, gravitating toward the center. This is not because they now are less extreme, but rather because the 'center' or 'normative' tradition has shifted *its* orientation in the direction of the extremist position. An extremist ideology or group will likely claim the relevant central position exclusively for itself. In so doing, it will proclaim its interpretation and application of the relevant normative tradition intensely and very particularly. In these cases 'extremism' connotes degrees of intensity or sharpness of focus: it suggests 'fanaticism', and this can apply as much to a broad, even centrist, constituency as to an otherwise marginalized one. Extremism in this context takes its own wider group identity—its religion or tradition—to an 'extreme', not by a move away from the center but rather by intensifying self-understanding and self-proclamation as representing, or being, the center. In this mode extremism expresses an *ultra-orthodox* outlook in contrast to a prevailing orthodoxy.

It is important to note that, either way, religious extremism belongs necessarily to a religion or religious tradition. For religious extremism, by definition, has to do with the extremity (margins) or centering (intensifying) of an existing religion with which the extremist is identified. Despite inclinations of what can be loosely referred to as the 'moderate majority,' often reacting to an extremist's claim to religious legitimacy by denying that said extremists are in fact bona fide members of the religion, in reality such extremists do belong, and so do constitute a problem for the religion they claim to represent. For instance, many Muslims abjure the self-profession of an Islamic extremist group as genuinely Muslim, and Christians will often deny far-right extremists' claim to a Christian identity. But extremists *of* those religions *come from* their religion: this is what makes them religious extremists in distinction from other forms of extremism—political, or environmental, or anti-vivisectionist, for example—which may happen to have a particular religious identity but for which the cause evoking the extreme positions does not require or involve religion as such.

However, religious extremists supposedly gain, by virtue of their particular interpretation of religious texts and their application of religious values, divine or otherwise transcendent sanction for their policy and actions. The religious extremist requires a specific religious identity as the primary reference for self-legitimization. And for the most part, I suggest, the nub of the problem of religious extremism vis-à-vis the relevant tradition is the degree to which that tradition is able to accommodate and address internal, let alone external, diversity. For religions appear to have an inherent tendency to exclusivity and uniformity, despite inherent values such as compassion, tolerance, and inclusion that are also often evident. This seeming paradox is perhaps seen in the distinction between 'conservative' and 'liberal' strands within most religions. It brings me to the underlying issue of diversity and the problematic response of exclusion.

Plurality, or diversity, names much of the context of contemporary life. Religious and cultural—not to mention ethnic, racial, and gender—diversity is a facet of our time in a way that is, arguably, qualitatively different from almost anything hitherto. Indeed, it has been said an affirmation of plurality is a hallmark of so-called post-modernity, which itself is a cipher for the present widespread experience, if not also affirmation, of diversity per se; 'Being consciously multifaith is part of being a post-modern society'.[15] But, of course, religious extremists eschew diversity and resist multifaith tolerance, let alone acceptance. Nevertheless, today, in just about all quarters of the globe, the religious dimension of any given community is pluriform. But if the capacity to cope with diversity is a hallmark of the understanding of a modern secular society, it is anathema to a religious extremism, including Islamism or other hardline versions of Islam, whether Sunni or Shi'a. Extremism, of any sort, is inherently intolerant of whatever it perceives as intrinsically oppositional or problematically 'other' to it.

Broadly speaking, the fact of diversity may be, and is, responded to in a range of ways, although most would fall under one of the following: exclusivism, inclusivism, and pluralism.[16] These provide the contextual paradigms for responding to diversity; they may be regarded as providing options for accommodating, or resisting, religious plurality. Certainly, they denote various means of dealing, both cognitively and behaviorally, with the sheer fact of religious diversity.[17] It is exclusivism, however, which is of particular concern. For it is clearly the case that a distinctive and rigid form of exclusivism is particularly obvious in certain forms of religious fundamentalism.[18] Exclusivism is indeed an element of all fundamentalist ideologies, whether religious or otherwise. A fundamentalist perspective, for example, is inherently absolutist: all other relevant phenomena are simply explained on its terms, or viewed in a relativizing, even nugatory, way with reference to it. As a mind-set, it expresses the modern quest for universality and coherence: only one truth; one authority; one authentic narrative that accounts for all; one right way to be. Religious exclusivism involves the identification of a particular religion (or form of that religion) as being, in fact, the essence and substance of true and universal religion *as such*, thereby excluding all other possibilities. From this viewpoint the exclusivist's religion is the 'Only One Right One' because, for the exclusivist, it is axiomatic that there can *only be* one way that is right or true. The exclusivist position holds that this universality is materially identified with one religion, namely that of the exclusivist. All 'others', indeed anything or anyone who opposes or contradicts the exclusivist, is necessarily denied and so devalued, even to the point of elimination.

Exclusivism, comes in at least three variants, however: open, closed, and extreme or 'hardline rejectionist'. An *open exclusivism*, while maintaining cognitive and salvific superiority may at least be amenably disposed toward the other, if only to allow for—even encourage—the capitulation (by way of conversion, for example) of the other. By contrast, *closed exclusivism* simply dismisses the 'other' out of hand. Relationship to the 'other', especially the religious 'other', is effectively ruled out. The 'other' may be acknowledged as having its rightful place, but that place is inherently inferior to that of the closed exclusivist who, by definition, prefers to remain wholly apart from the other. By contrast, *extreme exclusivism* gives expression to hardline rejectionist exclusivity, the viewpoint that asserts an exclusive identity to the extent that the fact and presence of an 'other' is actively resisted, even to the point of taking steps to eliminate the other. This marks a distinct shift from the closed form of exclusivism, understood more simply as the exercise of a right to withdraw into itself, in some sectarian fashion. This is where what might be otherwise denoted as 'fundamentalism' reveals itself to be a distinctly different kind of phenomenon.

The distinguishing feature denoting extreme exclusivism is the negative valorizing of the 'other'—howsoever defined—with concomitant harsh sanctions and limitations imposed upon the other. It is this level of exclusive religion which, in its hostility to variety or 'otherness', inherently invalidates alterity; it intentionally opposes and denies the 'other' as having any validity. This is the path to the dehumanization of fellow human beings. It is this level or version of religious exclusivism which lies at the heart of so much religious strife, not to mention terrorism and insurgency, and thus poses an acute challenge to those who would advocate religious freedoms, toleration, and peaceful co-existence. Here, exclusivism denotes active *exclusion*.

The exclusivism inherent in extreme religious fundamentalism or, in the case of Islam, forms of Islamic extremism, thus involves the negation of otherness (alterity) as determined by the specific ideology. The negation of otherness is perhaps critical, for it involves a devaluing and dismissal of the 'other', whether in terms of rival community or competing alterities, be they ideological or some other form of 'competitor'. In the process of negating the other, the self is asserted as inherently superior. The religious 'other' on this view is often cast as 'satanic', or at least seriously and significantly labeled as a hostile opponent, and so hostilely regarded. However expressed or referenced, it will be clear enough that the exclusivist is applying a key value-set of negativity to otherness per se, and concomitantly asserting self-superiority. A consequent sanctioned imposition of an exclusivist program may lead to the legitimizing of extremist actions: articulated negative judgements and values may lead to extreme and violent behaviors. For once there is in place a sense of transcendent sanction for programmatic action, the way to viewing extreme behaviors as legitimate in achieving desired outcomes is eased.

Sanctioned imposition and legitimated extremism are the two sides of the one coin in the currency of contemporary terrorism. Submission to the dictates of the extreme exclusivist is a matter of necessary imposition—as Afghani women found to their cost, for example, at the hands of one form of extremist Islam, and young Nigerian girls at the hands of another. And the alternative to even an involuntary submission is outright destruction: hence, from the Taliban's fundamentalist perspective, the great cliff-carved Buddha 'idols' had to be destroyed. How else does the fundamentalist extremist ensure that the imposition that has been sanctioned can actually be effected? In a nutshell, at the extremity of exclusive religion lies an inherent, and inevitably enacted, invalidation of otherness and variety as the necessary corollary of an unyielding religious exclusivism.

There is, however, a rather sharp question to be posed; a paradox of sorts to be discussed at this juncture. Is there a proper way of speaking of exclusive religion, or of religion in terms of exclusive identity, without necessarily falling into the pit of exclusivist extremism? On the one hand a measure of exclusivity—as in, being unique—is logically required for clarity of identity, and a necessary prerequisite for dialogical engagement, for example; yet, on the other, when taken to an extreme, exclusivity of identity militates against any sort of dialogical rapport by becoming exclusionary—and that is a hallmark of extreme religion.

The distinction between exclusivity and exclusivism is the interpretive lens which needs to be factored into a critical understanding of Islamophobia. Not all Muslims are exclusionary exclusivists; that is the province of extremist ideologically driven religious—in this case, Muslim—identity. However, particularity of Islamic belief denotes exclusive identity in the sense of uniqueness. And that can, and does, find expression in many forms and variants, for uniqueness also implies particularity as opposed to some generic and abstract universality.

Having now reviewed some analytical tools that can be applied to the question of religious extremism as a phenomenon, I return to our two European cases of reaction to the presence of Islam and the question of reactive co-radicalization. The world today is faced not only with the problem of Muslim extremists but also with religious radicalization expressed by different religions as, in effect, a parallel and reactionary extremism. Islamophobia, in some cases at least, can be an expression or manifestation of religious extremism the equal—at least ideologically, if not always behaviorally—to any Islamic threat, perceived or real.

Arguably, the common basis for the two exemplary Islamophobic cases I focus on is the rejection of religious and cultural diversity in respect, specifically, to Islam and Muslims. So what light does the Swiss ban, and Breivik's actions, shed on our understanding of Islamophobia?

Rejection of Diversity: Minarets and Murder

The Swiss Ban

The process that led to the minaret ban commenced with a pre-referendum petition launched in May 2007.[19] Populist concerns were picked up and fanned into fires of fear by right-wing politicians eager for grass-roots support. Xenophobia and racism played a part in the negative discourse, alongside anxieties associated with immigration and asylum-seeker concerns, and diatribe about foreign-born criminals. However, for the most part, the attention of the angst was Islam itself. The minaret was the focal symbol so far as the discourse about Islam was concerned.[20] Construed as a symbolic motif of a presumably exclusivist and domineering religion, the response of the Swiss to an imagined Islamic take-over was to enact a domineering exclusivism of their own. So a blanket rejection of a material feature of the religion, rather little-found in Switzerland, was enacted. An architectural trope of Islam became the lightening rod of pent-up anxiety although, as Lienemann notes, the motives and arguments of the initiative broadly echo concerns and prejudices widely held throughout Western Europe, even now. The general question underlying much of the negative discourse, he suggests, is whether Islam, with its predominating legal perspective and approach, is in the end compatible with a free society.[21]

In particular, the minaret was portrayed as a symbol of aggression and power; an inherently negative symbolic edifice representing an inherent Muslim desire to live by—and impose on others—Shari'a law codes. Thus central to the anti-minaret argument was the claim that the building of minarets is itself an expression of Muslim pretensions of socio-political hegemony. This reference to minarets as symbolizing Muslim aggression—they were likened to, and portrayed as, menacing rockets—was quite widespread and utilized by some right-wing politicians. One object of the religion was seen to represent both piety and power—with power emerging as dominant, so provoking a fearful reaction. Muslims were portrayed invariably as religious fanatics; intolerant and unenlightened, as incapable of integration into the normal realms of Western society. As Muller and Tanner put it, the minaret was viewed as 'a symbol of a religio-political demand which wants to know nothing of fundamental religious freedom'.[22]

Lying behind many negative arguments and opinions supporting the ban was the reality that many Swiss held fears concerning Islam and its presumed challenge to Swiss, indeed Western, democracy. Some stated that the rising overt presence of Muslims led them to feel foreigners in their own land. One general anti-minaret argument was that the presence of Islam in Europe threatens the secular status-quo; therefore Islam should be either 'tamed' or rejected. But it is unlikely to be tamed, in the sense of becoming, like the Churches, secularized vis-à-vis relations with the State. So it must be rejected.[23] This led to the paradoxical enactment of a prohibition of further erections of 'a religious-political symbol of that which represents the rejection of religious toleration *thereby ensuring the freedom of belief for all*'.[24] The very presence of Islam was—and for many is still—regarded as threatening the religious freedoms of non-Muslims.

The Norwegian Nightmare

From the outset, Breivik's manifesto combines a certain form or understanding of Christianity with advocacy of military action and the defense of Europe that yields a vision of a 'new Templar terrorist organization, dedicated to fight Islam, save Europe and kill the traitorous "cultural Marxists" – that is, politicians on the left, their journalist protégés, academics in the humanities and social sciences, and anyone sympathetic to multiculturalism and feminism'.[25] Attacks on such targets are discussed in some detail. In the end it led him to murder innocent Norwegians in the cause of attempting to provoke a European-wide rejection of Islam. A generic fear of creeping 'Eurabia'[26] fueling concern at the rise of Islam threatening to replace church with mosque and imposing Shari'a law, dominated his thinking. Significantly, such concerns were—and are still—echoed by many parties of the Right within the European parliamentary system.[27] Thus there has emerged the rhetoric of an imperative to 'save Europe' and, in the process, eliminate the traitors who allow the entry of the Islamic Trojan horse. For Breivik this had become a matter of urgency. He declared multiculturalism to be 'the root cause of the ongoing Islamization which has resulted in the Islamic colonization of

Europe through demographic warfare (facilitated by our own leaders)'.[28] And he went on to add: 'Time is of the essence. We have only a few decades to consolidate a sufficient level of resistance before our major cities are completely demographically overwhelmed by Muslims'.

For Breivik, it is Christianity that has the necessary unifying power to stand up to the incursion of Islam. At the same time he declares the Church he loves 'does not exist anymore because it has been deconstructed' but, he avers, 'I know that it can be reformed and that it again will embrace and propagate principles of strength, honor and self-defense'.[29] He wishes to see the Christian Church reformed as a Eurocentric nationalist institution. He is also inclusive, or at least accepting, of distinctive European pre-Christian traditions such as Odinism; nevertheless he believes that Christianity is 'the only cultural platform that can unite all Europeans, which will be needed in the coming period during the third expulsion of the Muslims'. Indeed he declares:

> Only Europeans, in solidarity with each other, can solve our current problems. As for secularism, are there any strong uniting symbols at all? I think not. In order to protect your culture you need, at the very minimum, strong, uniting symbols representing your culture. In this context, the cross is ... unrivalled as it is the most potent European symbol.[30]

Breivik may be best described as a cultural Christian. His religious identity, such as it is, serves a greater cultural cause. He champions Christian values and the legacy of the Church only insofar as they are key cultural markers. He owns also a pagan North European Odinist identity. To this extent his extremism and exclusivism are not so much focused on the preservation of a particular religious identity against all 'others', but on the specific exclusion of a particular religio-cultural other: Islam. His is the rejection of all things Islamic. He manifests Islamophobia, the fearful rejection of Islam. It is his anti-Muslim stance that leads to a focused form of religious extremism rather than a religious fundamentalism that drives an extremism resulting in the rejection of Islam and Muslims. Nevertheless, there is still a correlation between perceptions of Islam as inherently extreme, so requiring to be rejected, and the level and nature of the rejection that is advocated and enacted. It is still within the orbit of religious extremism.

Reactive Co-Radicalization Elsewhere

The criminal actions of Breivik and the quixotic Swiss minaret ban are examples of 'reactive co-radicalization'. And, of course, they are not the only ones. We do not have to look far to find examples of an Islamophobia that give evidence of reactive co-radicalization at play, be it in Europe or North America, or elsewhere. Since the inauguration of Donald Trump as President of the USA, for instance, the American response in respect to Islamism as well as immigration more generally (although at times these two are conflated) is to shut down immigration from certain countries in order to exclude those regarded as suspect in some way. Or else, in various ways (such as the wall on the Mexican border; rejecting free trade deals; sanctioning those 'not friends' of America) to erect barriers of protection—in effect to retreat into fortress America. However, such responses to Islam and the perceived threat it evokes, amount to no more than a reactionary mirror-image to the driving ideology of ISIS, for example, which aims to create a fortress Islam. America today manifests many examples of Islamophobic extremism that are clearly in reaction to the perceived—as well as the real—threat of Islamic extremism.[31]

The evidence for a growing, deepening, Islamophobia world-wide is incontrovertible. The French 'Burkini' reaction is perhaps one of the more recent and putatively laughable, were it not so serious.[32] Nor we need to look too far to see such evidence in Australia, a close ally of America, especially in the realm of contemporary politics. The Australian Liberty Alliance, for example, presents an anti-Islam platform—'Islam is a problem and if we don't take steps to put laws in place to protect our culture and our society, then we are going to lose our freedom'.[33] The Restore Australia party would ban Islam entirely.[34] This party claims 'We're not racists', but it is rabidly Islamophobic. Its leader, Mike Holt, is quite open on the matter: 'We believe that Islam is not compatible with Australian society, and under our Constitution it is actually illegal for anyone to be a supporter of Islam'.[35] And groups such as the United Patriots Front and Reclaim Australia also see Islam as having no place in the country—where, according to the 2016 Census, Muslims make up only around 2.6% of the total population. It's all a bit like the Swiss, really; comedic if it were not so tragic, even sinister.

Apart from organized groups, there are also plenty of individuals deeply hostile to Muslims and all things Islamic, believing, along with Europeans of similar outlook—including Anders Breivik—that western societies are suffering from an Islamic 'invasion'. Aryan Nations Australia, with their 'White Pride—Aussie Wide' slogan, is 'worried about Islam immigration to Australia'.[36] And the Islamophobic temperature is kept up with public figures, such as Pauline Hansen, or Tony Abbot whom various sources cite as calling for the reform of Islam and for Muslims to conform with 'the Australian way of life', urging Muslims to 'reform' (which translates as: become secular and apathetic to religion, like us; or to become religiously liberal, like us) or otherwise, whether by implication or directly stated, to go away. Fear of the other—xenophobia—when directed at Muslims and Islam is Islamophobia and it has become a pressing challenge socially, culturally, religiously, and politically. With respect to religion it is often linked to the interrelationship of extremism and fundamentalism, to which we now turn.

Fundamentalism and Extremism

Recent discussions and analyzes of religious fundamentalism have elucidated the nature of underlying ideology and resultant behaviors. Anna Halafoff, in commenting on the reaction of religious extremists to diverse expressions of contemporary secular plurality, usefully notes the general fundamentalist belief to which many religious extremists, of varying ilk, subscribe; namely that 'humanity has lost its way and fallen into moral decay and materialism by disavowing ... [relevant religious] ... guidance in the pursuit of freedom'.[37] In my own analysis I have identified three interrelated sets or phases of fundamentalism, namely passive, assertive, and impositional.[38] Passive fundamentalism tends to 'mind its own business' so far as the rest of society is concerned. Assertive fundamentalism perhaps somewhat less so. But it is of the essence of impositional fundamentalism to impose its views and demand its programmatic vision be implemented. An impositional fundamentalism wants to see things change to fit its view of how things should be, and will take steps to make its views dominant and, if need be, act imposingly to bring about change—including fomenting revolution or enacting terrorism. It is not 'fundamentalism' itself that is the primary issue. Indeed, 'fundamentalism' is a contested term and can be perhaps better thought of as a synonym of 'religious absolutism'. Rather, the impositional dimension of fundamentalism, expressive of an absolutist form of religion, which gives the primary clue as to what is extreme and what is not.

Because Islam is perceived as something extreme by virtue of supposedly being *necessarily* impositional, reactions to it are deemed by some to be likewise necessarily extreme and impositionally applied. This is the paradox of reactive co-radicalization. Extreme right-wing Christian and quasi-Christian religio-political rhetoric, for instance, often regards Islam as an implacable threat fully deserving of all the opprobrium heaped upon it and so, furthermore, justifying any exclusionary, if not eliminative, actions that can be mounted against it. The criminal actions of Breivik and the quixotic Swiss minaret ban are examples of such reactive co-radicalization. The mutuality of radicalization yields the irony of an 'impositional extremism'—even elimination—being enacted against those perceived to be 'impositional extremists' and whose extremism and supposed impositional intentions are denounced. In the process, the perception of a religious 'other' as a threat yields a paradoxical extreme action that itself transgresses otherwise norms of behavior, value and religious narrative of the religion or culture that feels so threatened—in this case, societies, or groups within societies, perceiving themselves to be threatened by Islam. Arguably, in some contexts the vice versa holds, if only as a legacy from colonial times: Muslim societies in these cases may be fearful of the aggrandizing and impositional intentions of western secular, or Christian, societies.

Conclusion

As we advance into the twenty-first century it seems that horrifying headlines provide an incessant reminder of the widespread presence of extreme forms of Islam. And with the headlines there comes the inevitable result of much media commentary and, in consequence, too many people simplistically and mistakenly equate 'extreme' with 'mainstream'. They tar all Muslims with the same brush of hostile intent. Furthermore, they project a hostile response onto all Muslims, anywhere, without differentiation. This is the generalized fear of Muslims, Islamophobia. But Islamophobia names not just an attitudinal stance, it applies also to sets of enacted exclusionary reactions, often drawing on religious imagery for inspiration and justification. As an expression of fear of Islam, Islamophobia can come across as a form of extremism every bit as abhorrent and problematic as the Islamist extremism that ostensibly provoked it. I argue that the Islamophobic response to Islamic extremism, including a diffused yet palpable rising antipathy towards Islam and Muslims that is found within Western societies today—whether perceived to be secular or Judeo-Christian—points us to the paradox of reactionary extremism of reactive co-radicalization.

Reactive Co-Radicalization refers to the phenomenon of a perception of a religious 'other' as being an inherent threat whereby, in response, an extreme action is undertaken that, relative to the religion or cultural norms of those responding, is abnormal. However, this is not to say the action taken is entirely absent from within the range of possibilities that lie within the responding religion or culture; only that they are not normally invoked. For in and of themselves they are extreme: they transgress otherwise norms of behavior, value, and the religious narrative of the reacting group. To the extent there is a mutuality of radicalization, there is a resultant paradox. An 'impositional extremism'—even elimination—is enacted against, so imposed upon, those perceived to be 'impositional extremists' and whose very extremism and supposed impositional intentions are denounced and abjured by those acting against them.

What we are faced today in the so-called secular West is increasing evidence of extreme right-wing and quasi-Christian religio-political rhetoric abjuring Islam and Muslims. It is drifting ever more steadily toward the center. Former marginal views are becoming increasingly mainstream. Arguably, 'the center' is becoming radicalized, more extreme. Extreme denouncements, and reactionary calls advocating and justifying exclusionary or eliminative actions against the threatening 'other' of Islam, are increasingly tolerated. They are rarely challenged. They are becoming increasingly normal. Fear of the 'other', of difference and diversity, is the root problem. It lies at the heart of the mutuality of reactionary extremism of which Islamophobia is a prime example.

NOTES

1. Douglas Pratt, 'Islamophobia as Reactive Co-Radicalization', *Islam and Christian-Muslim Relations* 26, no. 2 (April, 2015): 205–218; Douglas Pratt and Rachel Woodlock, eds., *Fear of Muslims? International Perspectives on Islamophobia* (Cham: Springer, 2016).
2. Virginie Andre and Douglas Pratt, eds., *Religious Citizenships and Islamophobia* (London and New York: Routledge, 2016).

3. Virginie Andre, 'Neojihadism and YouTube: Patani Militant Propaganda Dissemination and Radicalization', *Asian Security* 8, no. 1 (2012): 27–53; Virginie Andre, 'The Janus Face of New Media Propaganda: The Case of Patani Neojihadist YouTube Warfare and Its Islamophobic Effect on Cyber-Actors', *Islam and Christian-Muslim Relations* 25, no. 3 (July, 2014): 335–356.
4. Hannah Beech, 'The Face of Buddhist Terror: How Militant Monks Are Fueling Antimuslim Violence in Asia', *Time*, July 1, 2013, http://content.time.com/time/magazine/article/0,9171,2146000,00.html, accessed March 26, 2018.
5. John Azumah, 'Boko Haram in Retrospect', *Islam and Christian-Muslim Relations* 26, no. 1 (October, 2015): 33–52.
6. See, for example, Enes Bayrakli and Farid Hafez, eds., *European Islamophobia Report 2016* (Istanbul, Cairo and Washington, DC: SETA, 2017); Derya Iner, ed., *Islamophobia in Australia* (Multi-Institutional PDF Report, July 2017).
7. Douglas Pratt, 'Reactive Co-Radicalization: Religious Extremism as Mutual Discontent', *Journal for the Academic Study of Religion* 28, no. 1 (2015): 3–23. See also Douglas Pratt, *Religion and Extremism: Rejecting Diversity* (London and New York: Bloomsbury, 2018).
8. Jean-Francois Mayer, 'In the Shadow of the Minaret: Origins and Implications of a Citizens' Initiative', in *The Swiss Minaret Ban: Islam in Question*, ed. Patrick Haenni and Stephane Lathion (Fribourg: Religiscope, 2011), 10.
9. Andrew Berwick (Anders Breivik), *2083: A European Declaration of Independence* (London: Self-Published PDF, 2011), 4.
10. Ibid., 8.
11. Ibid., 9.
12. Ibid., 8.
13. For a recent critical discussion see: Sindre Bangstad, *Anders Breivik and the Rise of Islamophobia* (London: Zed Books, 2014).
14. See, e.g., Jan Stark, 'Beyond 'Terrorism' and 'State Hegemony': Assessing the Islamist Mainstream in Egypt and Malaysia', *Third World Quarterly* 26, no. 2 (2005): 307–327.
15. Gary D. Bouma, *Australian Soul: Religion and Spirituality in the Twenty-First Century* (Melbourne: Cambridge University Press, 2006), 5.
16. See, for example, Perry Schmidt-Leukel, *God Beyond Boundaries: A Christian and Pluralist Theology of Religions* (Münster and New York: Waxmann, 2017).
17. See Douglas Pratt, 'Religious Plurality, Referential Realism and Paradigms of Pluralism', in *Frontiers of Diversity: Explorations in Contemporary*

Pluralism, ed. Avery Plaw (Amsterdam and New York: Rodopi, 2005), 191–209.
18. See Douglas Pratt, 'Religious Fundamentalism: A Paradigm for Terrorism?' *Australian Religion Studies Review* 20, no. 2 (2007): 195–215; Douglas Pratt, 'Religion and Terrorism: Christian Fundamentalism and Extremism', *Terrorism and Political Violence* 22, no. 3 (June, 2010): 438–456.
19. Douglas Pratt, 'Swiss Shock: Minaret Rejection, European Values, and the Challenge of Tolerant Neutrality', *Politics, Religion & Ideology* 14, no. 2 (July, 2013): 193–207.
20. J.-F. Mayer, 'In the Shadow of the Minaret', 8.
21. Wolfgang Lienemann, 'Argumente für ein Minaret-Verbot? Eine kritische Analyze', in *Streit um das Minarett: Zusammenleben in der religiöse pluralistischen Gesellschaft*, ed. Mathias Tanner, Felix Müller, Frank Mathwig, and Wolfgang Lienemann (Zürich: Theologischer Verlag, 2009), 135.
22. Felix Muller and Mathias Tanner, 'Muslime, Minarette und die Minarett-Initiative in der Schweiz: Grundlagen', in *Streit um das Minarett*, 40.
23. For a fuller discussion see Douglas Pratt, 'Swiss Shock', op. cit.
24. Muller and Mathias Tanner, 'Muslime, Minarette und die Minarett-Initiative', 40.
25. E. Asprem, 'The Birth of Counterjihadist Terrorism: Reflections on Some Unspoken Dimensions of 22 July 2011', *The Pomegranate* 13, no. 1 (2011): 18.
26. Cf. Bat Ye'or, *Eurabia: The Euro-Arab Axis* (Madison, NJ: Fairleigh Dickinson University Press, 2005).
27. Notably the Dutch PVV, the Sweden Democrats, the Norwegian Peoples' Party, the True Finns, and the Hungarian Jobbik Party.
28. A. Breivik, *A European Declaration*, 9.
29. Ibid., 1361.
30. Ibid.
31. The website of the Council for American-Islamic Relations (CAIR—www.cair.com) provides a constant stream of examples.
32. See, for example, Lizzie Dearden, 'Burkini Ban: Why Is France Arresting Muslim Women for Wearing Full-Body Swimwear and Why Are People so Angry?' *Independent*, August 24, 2016, https://www.independent.co.uk/news/world/europe/burkini-ban-why-is-france-arresting-muslim-women-for-wearing-full-body-swimwear-and-why-are-people-a7207971.html, accessed March 26, 2018.
33. Grant Taylor, 'Anti-Islam Party Takes First Steps', *The West Australian*, October 25, 2015, https://thewest.com.au/news/wa/anti-islam-party-takes-first-steps-ng-ya-131215, accessed February 11, 2016.

34. Bianca Hall, 'Restore Australia: The Party That Would Ban Islam', *The Age*, January 1, 2016, http://www.smh.com.au/federal-politics/political-news/restore-australia-the-party-that-would-ban-islam-20160101-glxsfh.html, accessed February 11, 2016.
35. Ibid.
36. Brendan Foster, 'Aryan Nations: Perth White Supremacist Group on Letterbox Recruitment Drive', February 9, 2016, http://www.watoday.com.au/wa-news/aryan-nations-white-supremacist-group-on-letterbox-recruitment-drive-in-perth-20160209-gmpsfj.html, accessed February 15, 2016.
37. Anna Halafoff, 'Riots, Mass Casualties, and Religious Hatred: Countering Anticosmopolitan Terror Through Intercultural and Interreligious Understanding', in *Controversies in Contemporary Religion: Education, Law, Politics, Society, and Spirituality*, ed. Paul Hedges (Santa Barbara, CA: Praeger), 297.
38. Douglas Pratt, 'Fundamentalism, Exclusivism and Religious Extremism', in *Understanding Interreligious Relations*, ed. D. Cheetham, G. D. Pratt, and D. Thomas (Oxford: Oxford University Press, 2013), 241–261.

CHAPTER 4

Marocanization of Dutch Islamophobia and Radicalization of Dutch Moroccans

Sam Cherribi

> When individuals define nationhood through ideology instead of rationality, the state no longer functions as 'the supreme instance' of authority. Instead, the state transforms into a pawn in a game of conflicts and factions. Aron, Raymond[1]

In the past two decades, there has been a substantial increase in the alienation of Muslim immigrants—with critics blaming them for everything from crime to economic instability—even though they have been living in the Netherlands since the 1950s. However, in the public discourse the evidential actions of this group appear to amount to a vague but visceral aura ascribed to them by naysayers.

Muslims have a high visibility in the Netherlands, even though there has been no significant population increase as in the case of Syrian refugees traveling to Germany in 2015. This prominence can be explained by three factors. First, Islam is an urban phenomenon in the Netherlands. More recently, several larger mosques have seen a substantial increase in attendance, especially among second-generation Turks and Moroccans who attend mosques regularly or at least once a week during Fridays

S. Cherribi (✉)
Emory University, Atlanta, GA, USA
e-mail: scherri@emory.edu

© The Author(s) 2019
J. L. Esposito and D. Iner (eds.), *Islamophobia and Radicalization*,
https://doi.org/10.1007/978-3-319-95237-6_4

congregational sermon. According to a survey done by the Central Economic Policy Analysis Bureau of the Netherlands, mosque attendance among second-generation Dutch-Turkish citizens declined from 25% in 1998 to 10% in 2002 and steadily increased to 35% in 2005, with a similar phenomenon evident with Moroccan-Dutch citizens. There was a decrease from 10% in 1998 to 5% in 2002 and a steady increase in attendance to 33% in 2005. After which the increase stabilized and remained at the same level of 35% for the Dutch-Turkish population and 33% for the Moroccan-Dutch population. The numbers indicate that the Turkish population is slightly more religious than the Moroccan population in the Netherlands. In 1998, it was a difference of 15% but after 2002 they nearly equalize.[2] Theoretically, both Muslim groups should suffer equally from islamophobia, but why are there more Dutch-Moroccans radicalized than Turkish-Dutch individuals? One of the explanatory variables is the extreme focus on the Morocanization of islamophobia in the Netherlands; a phenomenon which I attempt to explain in this chapter. The increase in radicalization coincided with the rise of Geert Wilders. Even though Geert Wilders created his own party on the backdrop of rejecting the candidacy of Turkey to be part of the EU, his discourse focused on Moroccan youth. Another interesting phenomenon is that mosque attendance dropped from 45% in 1998 to 32% in 2002, and for the Moroccan-Dutch first generation from to 34%. Since 2006, that figure has increased to the old level of 45% for both Turkish and Moroccan-Dutch populations. This trend can be explained by the fear of the stigma related to mosque attendance due to the media and political hyper-fixation on mosques and imams in that period.[3] After four consecutive years of decline, the increase started only in 2006 for both groups. This indicates that the stigma became normalized and that there was little hope of changing the negative perceptions on Islam and Muslims. This process resulted in the establishment of Muslims as permanent outsiders.

The second factor that explains the high visibility of Islam in the Netherlands is the medialization and politicization of the display of religious symbols such as the veil and Islamic garment.

The third factor is due to the radicalization of some of the Muslim youth in the Netherlands and Europe. In 2017, 138 young people went to Syria and Iraq, 107 males and 31 females. In 2015, the intelligence service AIVD estimated that the Netherlands counts 'several hundred' jihadists and several thousand sympathizers.[4] By 1 June 2017, approximately 280 people have left the Netherlands. The number of people from the Netherlands with "jihadist" intentions in Syria and Iraq is approximately 190. Of that amount, a total of 45 people died by mid-2017.[5] Dutch authorities are uncertain about the number of Dutch militants who have perished after the bombing of ISIS in Syria and Iraq. The European Union's anti-terrorism coordinator, Gilles de Kerchove, estimates that Europe has more than 50,000 radicalized persons.[6]

All of these three factors, particularly the extreme medialization, leads to voluntary and involuntary forms of conquest of visibility in the public space.[7] This causes individuals to overestimate the number of Muslims living in a state. In comparison with the growth of the total population, the estimated number of Muslims per country and the actual percentage of Muslim migrants and non-Muslim migrants are comparable to 2005 percentages.[8]

The Party for Freedom (PVV), founded by the anti-Islamic extremist Geert Wilders, was expected to be the largest political party in the Netherlands in 2017. While its share of power remains insignificant in the coalition-government, the impact that the PVV could have had on the elections in France and Germany is substantial. Wilders might have been able to establish the tone for the expansion of ultra-nationalism in Europe by amplifying the populist triumphs of Nigel Farage in the Brexit referendum and Donald Trump's anti-immigration and anti-Muslim policies. The defeat of the PVV was a result of four factors: an increased turnout due to hospitable weather, a substantial number of youth voting for the first time, the Dutch cabinet's decisive actions during the Turkish crisis four days prior to the election and Wilders' inability to convey new ideas beyond his 10-year-old anti-Islamic talking points during the televised debate.[9] At times, the debate between Wilders and Prime Minister Rutte was embarrassing for Wilders. When Rutte challenged him for specifics regarding his idea of the Quran Police, asking Wilders "Are you going to go door to door to ban the Quran?", Wilders repeatedly dodged the question. The question remained unanswered. Rutte intended to call Wilders' bluff and succeeded. Both candidates understand that it's a nonsensical idea because the Quran is readily available on the Internet, memorized and recited with no need for a physical copy. So what purpose will the Quran Police serve?

By envisioning himself as the Donald Trump of Europe, Geert Wilders mistakenly assumed that he would not need a successful campaign or concrete policies in order for victory to fall into his lap. Wilders is the "consummate opportunist", a longstanding member of the political establishment, whose ego constantly craves attention. The fear he sells is what sells Dutch political news. European populist parties at the extreme right discovered an ethnic and religious difference which they framed as race and as an expression of a complex reality. All of these categories of race, ethnicity and religion, specifically Islam, were simplified and put into one-size-fits-all categories. Despite the influence of the Forum of Democracy, Wilders succeeds in setting the tone in the media and in political debate. He is the source of the ripples in the media pond.

Previous literature analyzing Islamophobia in the Netherlands predominantly focuses on Geert Wilders, his successful political party Party for Freedom (PVV), and the media's representation of his anti-Islamic statements. A study by Meindert Fennema (*Geert Wilders, Tovenaarsleerling*, Uitgeverij Bert Bakker 2010) is one of the most comprehensive study of Wilders and the PVV, tracing back his ideological roots to the liberal party, the VVD, and its former leader Frits Bolkestein. Fennema argues that the release of the movie *Fitna*, a collage of negative media footage concerning Islam, was a turning point in the construction of Wilders as a champion for freedom against the 'expansion of Islamic settlements'. Koen Vossen examined the ideological developments of Geert Wilders, arguing that the far right Dutch leader abandoned neo-conservatism to garner support through national populism.[10] Vossen credited José Pedro Zuquete for originating the idea of the "Muslim take-over" which had the potential to give a new élan to a trans-European anti-Islam ideology. In *Youth and the Extreme Right*, Cas Mudde concluded that the far right in Europe functions as "a barometer for discontent" and that the manifestos and bill-proposals of the far right create an apartheid for citizens who aren't of Dutch origin.

Theoretical Framework

Abram de Swaan explains the mechanism of exclusion and inclusion of certain groups in society based on their social, linguistic, ethnic, or religious characteristics. De Swaan uses identification and dis-identification processes to describe in-group out-group dynamics. These processes led to the narrowing and enlarging of circles of identification in society and consequently altered the endorsement by the dominant group and the rejection of the dominated group of people. In other words, identification is "not an emotion, but rather a person's disposition to be affected by others with whom that person identifies".[11] Using this definition of identification, de Swaan connects both the figurational and reflexive sociological theories of Nobert Elias and Pierre Bourdieu, both of whom have a deep "parenté" with concepts such as dispositions and habitus.

The figurational sociology of Norbert Elias and especially his study, *The Established and the Outsiders,* explains the construction of guest-workers' outsiderness into inferior, dangerous groups of society. The reflexive sociology of Pierre Bourdieu examines how predispositions transform into durable dispositions through habitus. De Swaan's research allows researchers to observe and analyze why creation dispositions and exclusionary habitus persists in society.

The composite lens that de Swaan develops assists in our understanding of how Islam and Muslims are constructed as a "race" through inhabit stigmatized spaces. Stigmatization increases or decreases increases significantly in the times of pivotal events e.g. terrorist attacks such as the murder of Van Gogh, the Charlie Hebdo massacre, or even the influx of Muslims due to the Syrian crisis. De Swaan's theoretical framework allows researchers to understand pacification and de-pacification processes in order to trace the processes of stigmatization as a component of sociogenesis and psychogenesis in a given society. For example, Loic Wacquant practically applied de Swaan's theories in the hyper ghetto of Chicago.

Inspired by de Swaan, Elias and Bourdiet I explored in *In The House of War: Dutch Islam Observed*, three forms coercion of Europe's Muslim migrant community from below, from within, and from above.

Coercion from below is how one's migrant status affects common and even universal pressures—the pressure to make a living, to succeed in one's profession, to have a place in one's community, but the way that this coercion occurs among migrant imams and the influence that the imams consequently have throughout the European Muslim community is strongly significant to the issue of integration.

The second part of the trifecta, coercion from within refers to the pressures from within the Muslim European individual as well as that felt within his or her community. This coercive pressure is produced by the conflict of messages brought forth by the larger society and the Muslim religious establishment.

Coercion from above, the third part of the trifecta, is twofold. It is exerted both by official Islam, represented by embassies and government programs, and by radical unofficial Islam, represented by a message of

Muslim transnationalism and anti-western activism. Radical unofficial Islam uses official Islam—governments, civic organizations and their programs—as vehicles to gain access to poor, uneducated and isolated immigrants. For radical unofficial Islam, Europe is a hunting ground and its quarry is the disenfranchised seeking empowerment. This coercion is also brought to bear against well educated and affluent European Muslims through the Muslim migrant underclass, whose very presence at times makes the more economically advantaged or more literate feel guilt or estrangement. Within them the ancient question persists, "They are Muslims and I am Muslim, but surely we are entirely different individuals?".[12]

CAN ISLAM BE FRAMED AS RACE?

Beyond what JanMohamed call "fetishization" of racial discourse, Magali Bessone (2013) redefines race beyond the biological reality in order to grasp it as a "racialized social reality". This complex racialized reality, according to Luc Foisneau (2013), is that being black, white, or Arab in France is having a different social destiny and trajectory. Foisneau, who agrees with Bessone, sees that European countries have a thick screen in front of their eyes through which they look at society, ignoring the complex realities of race. He adds that it suffices to read surveys about the social exclusion and its victims to see the size of dysfunction in society. Racism in society is responsible for all forms of exclusion and social tensions. The merit of the work of Magali Bessone is to redefine race as a more inclusive notion in order to solve the enigma of exclusion. So the discourse of far-right introduces a process of rationalization in society and the discourse of Geert Wilders re-Islamizes this racialization process or even sometimes Moroccanize it. The efficiency of the exclusive discourse of Wilders lies in the fact that the visible minorities in large cities happen to be Moroccans and Muslims. The interesting thing is he never mentions the Turks by the names and just calls them Muslims. Even though Turkey and the debate about its accession to the European Union was the watershed moment between him and his former Liberal party, the VVD. His stance against Turkey led to the creation of his own party, the PVV. It is perhaps because Moroccan youth figures more in crime and maybe also because Turkey is a member of NATO and has a stronger economy than many European countries while still a potential member of the European Union. Moreover, since Wilders limits his discourse to nonspecific Muslims outside of the Netherlands, Wilders' marocanization of Islamophobia is exclusively intended for Dutch internal consumption.

CHARACTERISTICS OF DUTCH ISLAMOPHOBIA

What makes the Dutch Islamophobia different from other forms of Islamophobia in politics can be summarized in one major distinct difference. The party (PVV) that thrives on Islamophobia is tolerated by almost all political parties, not only in terms of co-singing motions and amendments in Parliament or municipalities (see www.tweedekamer.nl). If in Belgium, a cordon sanitaire, a kind of official boycott has been imposed for years on Vlaams Belang and its predecessor Vlaams Blok, and in France, Le Front National is stigmatized by all other parties, the Partij voor de Vrijheid (Party for Freedom) is used as *buitenboordmotor*[13] or as an outboard engine to support certain coalitions. Also, if the former leader of the far right party Centrum Democraten was not taken seriously, the leader of the Party for Freedom, Geert Wilders, is building on the aura of Pim Fortuyn which propels him to national fame in addition to the fact Wilders was *woordvoeder sociale zaken*, spokesman for social affairs during his time with the VVD party which gave him a standing in the political arena. He is also very distinguished looking with blond dyed hair.

ISIS-Thugs

The mayor of The Hague (Josias van Aartsen) actually was the party leader that ousted Geert Wilders from his own caucus in Parliament in 2004/2005. The mayor issued a protest ban after riots in the Schilderswijk (a nationally stigmatized neighborhood in the Dutch political capital, The Hague) between pro- and contra Gaza-riots. According to the PVV, some of the protesters 'chanting slogans that are pro-ISIS' (The Islamic State in Iraq and Syria). The story became contested in the news because of a right winged framing of the issue. De Telegraaf, which takes the same position on issues of talk radio show hosts in the US such as Rush Limbaugh and Sean Hannity, framed the issue.

After these protests, the mayor issued a protest ban for the neighborhood. Leon de Jong, the PVV spokesman and leader in the municipal council, said 'the mayor kneels for Isis-tugs, Islam and jihad' and he added that the ethnic neighborhood the Schilderswijk forms the caliphate of the thugs in the Netherlands. The PVV wants to respect the right to protest 'except for the ISIS-thugs'.

However, the PVV itself wanted to organize its own march in the ethnic neighborhood in order to protest the presence of what they call the fundamentalist Islam in the Netherlands. After stirring a lot of controversy in the news, the PVV for security reasons put the demonstration on hold.[14] Muslim leaders saw the marsh as a provocation in a neighborhood where a Muslim majority exists. The Muslim leaders rejected any link to fundamentalist Islam or the radical jihadi group ISIS. The situation became more complex when right-wing and lefty groups wanted to claim part of the Transvaal neighborhood to protest. The mayor Van Aartsen postponed the decision.

Road to Salvation: Hope for the Muslims!

Wilders sees one solution to the problem of the Moroccan-problem in the Netherlands if the Dutch Moroccans voted for his party. He believes that the way to integration has a tiny chance of success if the Moroccans choose to vote for the PVV and "repudiate Islam".

However, Dutchness is not accessible to Muslims, who are permanent outsiders according to the PVV's logic. Blinded by short-term political gain, the PVV cannot acknowledge the downside to its exclusionary politics, which concerns the Dutch history and civilization process. This downside can be summed up in two negative outcomes. The first is disidentification with the Dutch past and the second is disidentification with the long tradition of tolerance since Spinoza, which occurs through the PVV's agitating and self-branding as an anti-Islam party. This intentional destruction of the Dutch history of tolerance is not limited to the Netherlands but is also exported internationally as an Islamophobia model, through the promotion and creation of anti-Islam parties including the PVV.

In sum, Wilders thrives on cutting any links to the great traditions of Islam in the Netherlands. The Dutch University of Leiden hosts treasures of Islamic civilization and Indonesia, the largest Islamic country was once part of the Dutch empire. Christiaan Snouck Hurgronje, the erudite Dutch scholar of Oriental cultures and languages and Advisor on Native Affairs, believed in the integration of Islam in the modern world (Cherribi 2010). Wilders denies any link by doing two things:

According to some investigative journalists (NRC Handelsblad) Wilders forgets his own Indonesian heritage and by selecting a former professor Hans Jansen, an Arabist form the University of Leiden to join his caucus in the European Parliament. Hans Jansen doesn't hide his essentialist interpretation of the large Islamic tradition by reducing the large diverse corpus of Muslim traditions to the contested notion of jihad. Also Wilders denies any contribution of Moroccans to the wellbeing of the Netherlands. Many Moroccan soldiers of the French army during the Second World War fought for the Netherlands against Nazi Germany. Many Moroccan tombs, in Capelle (Zeeland), are the visible archives of their heroic contribution to the Netherlands.

These basic elements of Dutch history facilitate an understanding of how the PVV has transformed the Dutch mindset and political landscape. Many scholars have sought to explain how one of the most tolerant countries produced one of the most rabid anti-Islamic parties in the world. Due to the propagation of this party-model into Europe, the United States, and Australia, this ideological metamorphosis has surpassed national boundaries and has attracted global visibility. The reasons underlying this international outreach to the English-speaking world are self-evident; with the loss of New Amsterdam (New York), the Dutch traditionally supported the United States, even in their policies towards the European Union (Paul Scheffer) argued for American force within the EU through NATO. In addition, since the massive migration after the potato-plague, Dutch writers, actors, painters and artists generally view the United States as the ultimate place to seek fame and notoriety. The most recent example is Ayan Hirsi Ali, who was drawn to the spotlights of American public life after a career in parliament. Her close colleague Geert Wilders, the leader of the PVV, followed in Hirsi Ali's footsteps to promote an anti-Islam propaganda in the United States. Similarly to Hirsi Ali, Wilders wrote a pamphlet in English (Hirsi Ali wrote 'Infidel' and Geert Wilders wrote 'Marked for Death: Islam's War Against the West and Me'). Together with their mastery of the English language, they successfully garnered an international audience; unlike Pim Fortuyn, whose lack of English fluency caused a fight with BBC's John Simpson. By contrast, Geert Wilders, who is fluent in both English and German, actively seeks media appearance and the limelight of the Western public outside the Netherlands.

In the words of Entman and Rojecki, the boundaries that Wilders creates through his frames initiate a chasm. Wilders translates his racist ideology into anti-Muslim outcomes.[15] Similar to race, Islam in Europe is 'peculiarly visual'.[16]

Wilders is highly mediatized; therefore, his impact on society is substantial. For example, Fatima Elatik, the first veiled former alderman in the city of Amsterdam, described how abjected Wilders made her feel through her Facebook account. During a televised discussion with the Dutch-Moroccan mayor of Rotterdam, Wilders extensively discussed his parents' fears in coming to the Netherlands as guest workers and even went as far to outline the fears that Dutch-Moroccans must feel. The media's influence on culture and society, and on attitudes has been widely documented.[17]

Whereas typically it is difficult to understand media frames, to decipher racist or Islamophobic codes, and to generate meanings from hidden messages, Wilders and his party simply and boldly communicate their intolerant messages for mass consumption. Considering that people have a tendency to remember negative messages and information,[18] we could assume that the exaggerated negative images, frames and sound bites of Wilders contribute to the construction of Muslims as a permanent out-group. Wilders bases the PVV anti-Muslim discourse on the idea that Muslim European citizens don't contribute to European societies and cultures. In the 'Outsider', Paul Sneiderman argues that it is not the frequency of the negative frames that have an effect but their consistency.[19]

Many studies have confirmed that negative messages against Muslims appear consistently in Dutch media (De Vreeze et al. 2011; Koopmans 2015). These general messages magnify distortions of Islam and Muslims. More specifically to the PVV, Wilders frames party discourse to propagate Islam as a foreign religion with alien followers who wear offbeat clothing and accessories. Wilders and PVV politicians depict Muslims as terrorists, colonists, veiled or under the burqa. Wilders' discourse supplies enough stereotypes that it creates a new cultural and political pattern of dealing with Muslims and justifies their exclusion. In addition, Wilders' discourse aims to limit 'interpersonal contact' between Muslims and non-Muslims, prevent Muslim access to the job market, and to prioritize mobility in order to racially cleanse Muslims from the Netherlands and Europe. Moreover, Wilders has promised to make the Netherlands leave the European Union, provided he is still in power, if Turkey becomes a member.[20]

Wilders has distorted the ethnic, cultural, and social harmony of the Netherlands. However, this disharmony began much earlier and took a clear anti-Islamic form during Pim Fortuyn, who was benign in comparison to Wilders. Wilders called for 'fewer Moroccans' and even confirmed in a tweet to the Dutch media, after a televised debate with the mayor of Rotterdam, that he is working on it. Wilders transformed the legacy of tolerance in the Netherlands, which is the most tolerant nation in the world according to Russell Shorto, into a country that wrestles with its own identity. In addition to grappling with the pressures of globalization and the enlargement of the European Union, the Netherlands has become torn by an internal and artificial divide between its citizens based on a religion which functions as a race boundary.

Research demonstrates that positive framing can enhance the well-being of society and 'nurture a virtuous circle of respect, empathy, and generosity to replace the vicious circle of suspicion, separation, and stinginess.[21]

'Thinking stereotypically is not only an easy habit to fall into, it is a normal way of thinking; in essence, stereotypes are schemas, short-cut mechanisms for processing what would otherwise be an overload of information. Gandhi reminds us that stereotypes are very sticky. Overturning them involves a substantial commitment and resolve on the part of the individual, and it may require the rebuilding of a large part of the individuals' cognitive structures due to the multiple links that a particular racial stereotype may have within that structure".[22] Wilders has "polluted the Netherlands' entire political field with stereotypes.[23]

FRAMING FATIGUE: BOOMERANG OF "FEWER MOROCCANS"

When the media feels that incitation to hatred can turn into potential physical elimination 'fewer Moroccans', restraint is advised. When words start to have fascist connotations, a kind of authoritarian bite, such as 'I will make it happen' that goal of having fewer Moroccans if Wilders party is voted in. It was embarrassing for the media to work on a déjà-vu from the Second World War when members of the Jewish community were deported to the concentration camps. Hatred is tolerated but not suggesting extermination. Otherwise, what is the meaning of fixing the call to fewer Moroccans? To their credit, even some politicians of the PVV took distance of the statements of Wilders about 'less Moroccans'.

Some members of the European Parliament couldn't deal with the discrimination level that the words of Wilders contain. The words had fascist resonances. How would Wilders achieve the goal of 'less Moroccans'? By deporting them, by putting them in prison or by what other means does he have in mind?

The impact of Wilders' words such as 'fewer Moroccans' on Moroccan youth and Muslim children is enormous. Many stories were reported of little children scared to death to be deported or to be killed reported Fatima Elatik, former alderman of district *Oost* in Amsterdam, on her Facebook page. The reaction of the Dutch media to Wilders 'fewer Moroccans', including in de populist newspaper De Telegraaf, was more robust than during the year that followed the killing of Van Gogh. The statements of Geert Wilders were critically covered by the Dutch media. It seems like the Dutch media learned from the criticism they were subjected to after the period Fortuyn and after the killing of Theo van Gogh. It was less complacent. The statement about 'less Moroccans' triggered more critics than ever. But it is not the critical tone about Wilders that counts, his almost daily appearances and coverage in the media; the media hangs at his lips. Wilders succeeds to set the tone in the media and political debate. Wilders continues to make waves and the headlines. It is almost like the media is a secret admirer of somebody who helps the media industry generate more readership and income. So the category Muslims and Moroccans are becoming interchangeable in this discourse. These categories are stigmatized to death and refer to an underclass in society, not defined by race but defined by religion. So religion, but also ethnicity and country origin, becomes substitute to racial characteristics.

The discourse of Wilders turns the existing pre-dispositions, possible discrimination on basis of the visibility of Muslims and Moroccans into permanent dispositions in the public sphere. These durable dispositions don't function as racial labels but function as mechanisms of exclusion and shame. Being Muslim or Moroccan is something to be ashamed of. Being Moroccan in the time of Wilders, in the Netherlands is belonging to the lowest of the low ranks in society. The discourse of Wilders legitimizes and reproduces segregation into a society based on religion and country-origin. So, the neighborhood *Schilderswijk* in The Hague becomes quickly labeled as the center of the Islamic caliphate something mythical and imaginary that draws its saliency from the news in the Middle East mainly after the disintegration of Iraq and the start of the civil war that is ravaging Syria. Every neighborhood with a Muslim majority or ethnic majority is a potential territory for jihadists, according to the PVV. Also Schilderswijk becomes the new Gaza of the political capital of the Netherlands according to the terminology of the PVV.

This authoritarian drift on the level of the speech doesn't bode well for the future of democracy. If citizenship is inclusive, then all citizens should be equal; nobody should be excluded from belonging to the Dutch 'nation'. Moroccans and Muslims in the Netherlands are just the name of the hatred phenomenon that is widespread in Europe. In some places they are called *Roma* or *Beurs* in the banlieus of France, or *Türken* in Germany, and even in Scandinavia, where everything is perfectly organized, far right parties rose after they discovered the new migrants.

What characterizes the new far right in Europe is the touch of erudite exclusive populism with leaders having a kind of charisma like the former Austrian leader Jörg Haider, the Belgian Philip Dewinter of Vlaams Belang, the French Marine le Pen of the National Front and the Dutch Geert Wilders of the PVV. European populist parties at the extreme right discovered an ethnic-religious difference that they framed as race and as an expression of a complex reality. All these categories of race, ethnicity, religion and specifically Islam, were simplified and put in one size fits all categories. This means that they are not ready for assimilation as minorities. Because of their religious and ethnic belonging they will remain outsiders forever. The US, for example, is much more pronounced about its secularity being inclusive of all religions; therefore, the US accepts religious pluralism as a fact of life. Geert Wilders, who made a furor in European media with his short documentary Fitna, didn't receive much attention in the US. It could be concluded by drawing on the work of Michele Lamont in her comparative study about US vs. France, the Dignity of the Working Man, that it's easier to be Muslim in the US than Muslim in Europe. According to Essed and Hoving, "the Netherlands echoes, if not leads a wider European trend, where offensive statements about Muslims are an everyday phenomenon.[24] The authors argue 'the moral rejection of racism seems to be losing ground in Europe'.[25]

Since it is difficult to establish a link between Islamophobia and radicalization, the trifecta of coercion seeks to determine the implications of the Islamophobia experienced by Muslims in the Netherlands.[26] Islamophobia may contribute to radicalization but it is not the determining factor.[27] However, highly exclusive native acculturation can generate reactive co-radicalization similar to the Breivik case that Nussbaum argued (Pratt 2015: 216).

By analogy, I concur that the corollary of Islamophobia is 'reactionary extremism.' In other words, radicalization occurs with both the dominant and dominated, as an intended and unintended byproduct of the far right and anti-Islam messages. Far right active Islamophobia may cause individuals to be susceptible to extreme behavior, such as joining ISIS or imitating mass killers such as Anders Breivik. Due to the lack of data based on empirical research, researchers should establish these behavioral connections using research fieldwork.

In order to demonstrate that the Netherlands is still a civilized country, Paul Schnabel argued that no Moroccans were "lynched" after the killing of Van Gogh.[28]

Marion van San (2015) concludes that the rhetoric of the PVV and government-sponsored practices of social exclusion such as the headscarf ban, ban on ritual circumcision, etc. has been a major causal factor in radicalization. However, there are unexplained pull factors that make Moroccan youths feel more attracted to the conflict in Syria than Turkish youths. Radicalization is not only a result of social exclusion but instead due to innumerable social, cultural, and political confounding variables that together lead to radicalization and disavowal of the host state. In that sense the identification and disidentification processes are fully at work.

Notes

1. Aron, Raymond (Polémiques); Les Essais, LXXI (Gallimard, 1955: 108).
2. Accessed January 25, 2018, http://www.pewforum.org/2017/11/29/europes-growing-muslim-population/—"Europe's Growing Muslim Population," http://www.pewresearch.org/fact-tank/2017/11/30/qa-the-challenges-of-estimating-the-size-of-europes-muslim-population/—"Q&A: The Challenges of Estimating the Size of Europe's

Muslim Population," https://nos.nl/artikel/2163084-het-aantal-moslims-stijgt-maar-met-hoeveel.html.
3. Cherribi (2010).
4. Accessed January 27, 2018, https://www.nctv.nl/organisatie/ct/dtn/uitreizigers-terugkeerders.aspx.
5. Ibid.
6. Ibid.
7. Bozarslan (2011) and Mudde (2014).
8. Bosma (2011).
9. Accessed April 14, 2017, https://nos.nl/artikel/2162992-felle-confrontaties-rutte-en-wilders-in-debat.html.
10. Vossen (2013: 184).
11. de Swaan (1997: 25).
12. Cherribi (2010: 5).
13. Term used by Frits Bolkestein former Euro Commissioner and former leader of the Conservative Liberal Party (VVD) in interview in the political talk show Buitenhof in 2011 (VPRO TV).
14. Accessed August 19, 2014. Nieuwe mars in Schilderswijk is erg riskant, De Telegraaf, August 13, 2014.
15. Entman and Rojecki (2000: VII).
16. Ibid.: XV.
17. Poole (2012) and Cherribi (2010).
18. Entman and Rojecki (2000: 6).
19. Paul Sniderman et al. (2000).
20. Accessed January 20, 2018. NRC (Dossier Wilders 2018), https://www.nrc.nl/dossier/proces-wilders/.
21. Entman and Rojecki (2000: 12).
22. Ibid.: 93.
23. Ibid.: 95. Extreme framing can lead to an extreme cultural reaction. The following rap song is one example: http://www.telegraaf.nl/binnenland/403, http://www.bing.com/videos/search?q=mosheb%2c+wilders&qpvt=Mosheb%2c+Wilders&FORM=VDRE#view=detail&mid=47FBB9E7209A69E5CB4A47FBB9E7209A69E5CB4A-Research should be conducted to measure the level of mistrust within Dutch society concerning interactions between Muslims and non-Muslims. 4140/_Mosheb_tegen_beveiliging_Wilders__.html+.
24. Essed and Hoving (2014–2019).
25. Ibid.
26. Cherribi, op.cit.
27. Koopman, op.cit.
28. Herman Vuijstje (Op-ed: Wat ons bindt, De Rode Hoed/VU podium, 2008).

PART II

Crosspollination

CHAPTER 5

Interweaving Islamophobia with Radicalism: Feeding the Radicals with the Anti-Halal Debate

Derya Iner

The halal debate in Australia has escalated following a series of organized anti-Islam and anti-Muslim campaigns in the public and social media since 2014. These multifaceted accusations provide a prominent case study for the analysis of the interaction between radicalization and Islamophobia. Through an in-depth analysis of radicalism and Islamophobia discourse and how it is reproduced in different platforms, including the halal debate in Australia, this chapter will explore the presence of Islamophobia in radicalism discourse and likewise, is the existence of radicalism in Islamophobia discourse.

Background of the Anti-Halal Debates in Australia

The years 2014–2015 saw a significant rise in the specific targeting of Australian Muslims' consumer practices and their religious dietary regulations. Anti-halal campaigners used diverse arguments and speculations, organized nationwide rallies, conducted social media campaigns and

D. Iner (✉)
Charles Sturt University, Sydney, NSW, Australia
e-mail: diner@csu.edu.au

© The Author(s) 2019
J. L. Esposito and D. Iner (eds.), *Islamophobia and Radicalization*,
https://doi.org/10.1007/978-3-319-95237-6_5

drew on sympathetic far-right groups and political parties to pressure the government into removing, or at least limiting, halal food production and certification. While anti-halal campaigns were prevalent in the media and public discourse, politicians like the Senator for South Australia, Cory Bernardi, the Queensland Senator and founder of the One Nation Party Pauline Hanson as well as the Senator for Tasmania (2014–2017) Jacqui Lambie accused the halal certifiers of funding terrorism and called for a senate investigation into halal meat. As a result, a submission was made to Parliament on the 13 May 2015. Although the inquiry was seemingly on third-party food certification, the target was halal.

The massive social media campaign among the Islamophobes bore fruit: of the 1492 submissions,[1] only 1.1% directly related to third-party certification and only 2.2% were positive in their responses to halal certification. The Australian Muslim response to the senate inquiry was largely silent with 0.4% individual and 0.06% institutional level Muslim representation. While the senate inquiry gave Islamophobes a supposedly 'legitimate' platform to raise their anti-Islamic sentiments, the Muslim community remained largely silent. The suggested links between terrorism and the anti-halal debate will be discussed further at the end of the first part of this chapter.

ISLAMOPHOBIA IN RADICALISM DISCOURSE

Islamophobia operates in radicalism discourse by labeling all Muslims as terrorists or as potential terrorists. Prior to analyzing this resurgent discourse within the context of the halal debate, it is essential to dissect this strong association that is continually and collectively reinforced by the political discourse, media and academia.

Political Discourse

Where Muslims sit in the political discourse is important in terms of understanding how Muslims are positioned within the Australian national discourse, legislation and the public opinion.[2] The political bias against Muslims in the West is on the rise due to far-right political discrimination. Their unapologetic rhetoric against Islam and Muslims is a concern due to the legitimization of Muslims' defamation in the political and public arena.

The connection between terrorism and Islam/Muslims is one of the most prevalent and damaging tactics employed by far-right politicians and their voters in the West. For instance, in his first address to Congress on February 28, 2016, Trump promised to take strong measures against radical Islamist terrorism and a week later, he announced his second executive order that called for the ban of people entering the United States from six Muslim countries.³ In doing so, Trump publicly equated terrorism with Muslims. His most influential advisors added to the Islamophobic rhetoric. Lt. Gen. Michael Flynn publicly stated that Islam was not a religion and Stephan Bannon called it the religion of submission.⁴ Bannon also accused American Muslims of seeking to create an "Islamic State of America."⁵

Similar sentiments were observed within Australia's shores through various political parties including used Islam and Muslims for their fear-mongering politics by equating Muslims and Islam with terrorism and threats to national security.⁶ One ALA director declared that all Muslims and faces of Islam are dangerous for Australia⁷ while the leader of the One Nation Party, Pauline Hanson, compared Islam to a disease which Australians need to vaccinate themselves against.⁸

The far-right direction of these politically 'legitimized' and suggestive comments can be seen in the way they that describe Islam and Muslims as a contagion that irreparably endangers the Australian way of life.⁹ During his time as Prime Minister, Tony Abbot publicly referred to Muslims at least 40 times.¹⁰ In all these instances, the references were linked to terrorism. Abbott made no attempt to include them as Australian citizens living in, and contributing to, mainstream society. Three months after leaving office, Abbott publicly and openly shamed Islam for enabling people to kill in the name of God. In another comment, Abbott stated that Australians "pussyfoot around the fact many passages of the Muslim holy book command things that are completely incompatible with modern Western life."¹¹

In the same year another Liberal Party minister, Josh Frydenberg, blatantly claimed that terrorism is "a problem within Islam".¹² Following an attack on Maryland's police station by a mentally sick elderly man in 2016, another Liberal Party MP, George Christensen, quickly connected the alleged "terrorist attack" to Islam stating that only an "idiot" would argue the absence of a link with Islam.¹³ The impulsive nature and frequency of such comments in the public political discourse led the head of the Australian Security Intelligence Organization, Chief Duncan Lewis, to warn the conservative-liberal MPs about their comments vilifying Islam and Muslims.¹⁴

The official bias extended to the government's refugee policy which saw a clear preference for Christian refugees over Muslim ones.[15] The unarticulated bias behind this decision was bluntly expressed by Pauline Hanson and her One Nation party members who linked Muslims refugees to terrorism.[16]

Media Discourse

Politics has been the main drive and primary source of data for the mainstream media. The biased political approach to Muslims, namely their direct and frequent association with terrorism and securitization, was amplified and disseminated to the public through various media outlets. Coupled with the media's own prejudices, the negative portrayal of Islam and Muslims peaked. One Path media corporate observed five media outlets run by Murdoch and Fox groups during 2017 in Australia and found that 3000 articles referred to Islam or Muslims alongside words like violence, extremism, terrorism or radical. Likewise, over 8 articles per day defamed Muslims in the Murdoch press. Muslims who make up only 2.6% of the Australian population were significantly overrepresented in media and 'tagged' with terrorism and violence.[17] There was a repetitive pattern, as pointed out by studies that looked at the previous years' media discourse in Australia, showing the same disproportionate representation of Muslims and in relation to violence and terrorism.[18]

The essential problem is the lack of a clear distinction between ordinary Muslims and terrorists.[19] The skewed but strong terrorist-Muslim/Islam associations have seen an increase in the number of Islamophobic incidents directed at ordinary local Muslims following international, and locally irrelevant, Islamist terrorist attacks.[20]

Academic Discourse

Explicit connections between terrorism and Islam/Muslims, which is an important pillar of Islamophobia and common rhetoric in the media and politics, has also been approved by radical and extremist literature. Most of the publications on radicalism and terrorism have used violent extremism and terrorism interchangeably with Jihadi or Salafi terrorism, which is a subcategory of generic terrorism.[21] They overlook the fact that terrorism is not specific to one particular religious ideology and can be identified in different religions, worldviews and ideologies both in the past and present.[22]

In the aftermath of 9/11, Walter Laqueur differentiated this "new terrorism" from its counterpart which was rooted in nationalism, communism or fascism and reduced the new terrorism to Islamist terrorism.[23] He espoused that this new type of terrorism did not require explanation beyond blaming an evil ideology that is called "Islamic fundamentalist violence."[24] By the early 2000s, terrorism became synonymous with Muslims and was reproduced systematically in public discourses?[25] Despite its generic title, *Religious Radicalization and Violent Extremism*, this literature review of 310 publications which was published in 2012, focused solely on Islamist versions of radicalization. The review focused the field of study on the "Muslim population" rather than terrorists and terrorist suspects:

> We have not examined other forms of 'extremism' such as that of the far-right, except where there was direct relevance to the radicalisation process or where there was some valuable crossover in programmes and interventions concerning prevention, or other applicable joint learning. This narrows down the field of study to a focus on the (mostly) Muslim population in the West who are subject to radicalisation that leads to violence and Jihadist terrorism. (p. 6)

A significant methodological flaw is identifying the shared features of terrorists and introducing those indicators as if they were the main factors for committing violence. Arun Kundnani finds this mismatch among the analyses of influential terrorism experts including Mark Sageman, Quintan Wiktorowicz and Walter Laqueur. The presentation of indicators as the main drive behind violent extremism not only conceals the main factors but also places entire Muslim communities under suspicion because of common indicators like religion, grievances, ideology, social networks and sociopolitical disadvantages.

Kundnani also questions the validity of the above-mentioned indicators and argues that even if a few Muslims adopt exclusivist ideologies, this does not necessarily make them prone to violence. What drives people to commit acts of violence and gravitate towards certain social groups requires further study. Rather than approaching these indicators as causes and correlating them with the risk of terrorism, Kundnani suggests using control groups to assess the role of these indicators in encouraging violent extremism.[26]

Goli and Rezaei's criteria for assessing radicalization are even more problematic as they suggest a direct link between Muslims and radicalization. Their two of the four assessment questions are about being Muslim and developing a comprehensive understanding of the religion.[27] Their descriptors for radicalism include: "(Being) Less trustful of Danish media; more likely to want to marry only another Muslim; more likely to have become more religious within the past three years; and more committed to religious duties like paying Zakat and Khoms, (and) daily prayer."[28] Making individuals target because of their religion fits well into the description of Islamophobia and this particular example shows how Islamophobia survives in Radicalization.[29] This tendency, i.e. perceiving Muslims as radicals or terrorist suspects can also be seen in the 2006 FBI report on *The Radicalization Process: From Conversion to Jihad*, which eventually cause the massive surveillance of Muslims in the United States.[30] The direct targets of the countering violent extremism programs were the Muslim community,[31] especially the young Muslim men who were perceived to be vulnerable to radicalization.[32]

More than a decade after 9/11, the terrorism can be assessed as worsening but in the meantime bettering. It is worsening because activist Muslims like Muslim Brotherhood is associated with terrorism.[33] The systematic production of biased knowledge against Muslims is similarly in force by the so-called "misinformation experts" and especially in the securitization and terrorism field.[34]

Contrarily, another trend in the field tends to critically review the post-9/11 literature and its aftershocks penetrated into countering the terrorism measures. Eventually, recent academia is alert to the existing biased patterns in the literature[35] while Islamophobia in academic is getting more organized and globalized.

Ordinary Muslims' Connection to Terrorism in the Halal Debate

Anti halal submissions (out of around 1500 submissions, 1389 were available to the public and only 2.2% were positive about halal) reflect the anti-halal campaigners' complaint regarding 'halal.' Half of all respondents (50.3%) called for clearer labeling. It is well within consumer rights to know the source of a product and make a conscious choice when purchasing goods. Yet the actions followed by identifying the halal manufacturers are observed to be boycotting and defaming those companies. The Conservative Member of Parliament Kirralie Smith' Halal Choices Australia website,[36] Facebook groups like Boycott Halal (97 K followers) and Boycott Halal Certification in Australia (89 K followers) mobilized people to react and even insult the halal manufacturers. For instance, in addition to criticizing Bega for opting for halal certification, the Australia First Party (AFP) falsely accused the CEO of Bega Cheese, Von Ryn, of taking trips to Thailand for the purposes relating to pedophilia.[37]

There were overtly biased submissions that defamed Islam and Muslims and perceived halal certification as a means of funding Islam (48%), Sharia Law (26%), Islamization (20%) while refusing to pay so-called religious tax (40%) that helps in Islamizing Australia.[38]

The submissions also argued for the financial transparency of the halal certifiers (32%) and funding terrorism (26%). Kylie Hawson, in her submission (No. 464), claimed like many others that "The money is transferred to charity organizations that are known fronts for terrorist organizations." Going through all the submissions, Etri and Yucel observed that above-mentioned claims "demonstrate a high level of mistrust towards Muslims living in Australia, particularly halal certifiers. (…) Such arguments demonstrate a high level of fear and anxiety towards Muslim ownership of businesses [as well]."[39] Supporting terrorism by buying or manufacturing halal was officially falsified by ASIO. Nevertheless, anti-halal campaigners continued to use this argument frequently.

The halal method of slaughtering animals was also used to revive associations between ordinary Muslims and so-called Islamic violence and Muslim brutality. As concluded by Etri and Yucel "Perpetuating the myth of animal cruelty is an example of subtle anti-Muslim prejudice as it uses 'the values and norms' of Australian society in an attempt to indirectly argue that barbaric practices are innate to the Islamic faith." [40]

The intense and relentless public scrutiny and backlash resulting from the anti-halal campaigners saw a number of halal producing manufacturers opt out of halal certification. Anti-halal campaigners' massive boycotting campaign targeted Cadbury's, Sanitarium, Byron Bay Cookies, Four'N Twenty and Kellogg's. A "buy-cott" campaign was also initiated by former One Nation candidate Mike Holt. He instructed consumers to buy a Cadbury product, open the package, and then ask for a refund—on the grounds that eating halal-certified food offends their beliefs.⁴¹ A small South Australian company, Fleurieu Milk and Yoghurt abandoned the halal certification in 2014 while Kellogg and Sanitarium dropped it in 2016.⁴²

This intense revulsion for halal raises interesting questions regarding changes in the 'visibility' of Muslims and Islamic religiosity that are now being associated with terrorism not through the face veil, long beard and robes (and so called Salafi Islam) but with the increase in halal-certified Australian products in the aisles of Australian supermarkets.

Radicalism in Islamophobia: A Dismissed Radicalism

Contrary to the noticeable Islamophobia in radicalism discourse, negligence of radicalism engrained in some levels of Islamophobic performances dismisses far-right violent extremism. The double standard in the perception of supposed Islamist and Islamophobic extremism leads to a skewed view that overestimates Islamist terrorism while underestimating Islamophobic terrorism. This was indeed evident in the anti-halal debate, which will be discussed at the end of this section.

One illusion is the harmless face of Islamophobia. While local and global Islamist terrorism has left deep imprints in the public psyche, speaking in the aftermath of London attack 2017, Abbott unnecessarily compared Islamist terrorism in this context with Islamophobia stating that "Islamophobia has not killed anyone."⁴³ Abbott's frustration did not allow him to make an accurate assessment. Ironically, this statement was made in the same month that saw an Islamophobic extremist murder two male bystanders who were defending two Muslim girls against the perpetrator. The murderer's ideological motive was evident as he expressed his pleasure and proudly associated his murder with so-called patriotism.⁴⁴ Islamophobic violent extremism was in force in the same year in Canada. Five out of fifty-three Muslims were killed on January 29, 2017 in the Quebec City mosque by a young man, who was angry at the President Trudeau's welcome to the Syrian refugees.⁴⁵ In October 2016, three men were arrested in Kansas for plotting to bomb an apartment complex where Somalian refugees reside as well as a mosque. He used four cars laden with explosives.⁴⁶ A man whose anti-Islamic posts were found on social media killed three young Muslims in Chapel Hill, NC in 2015. The examples of Muslims stabbed to death and mosques damaged by firebombs are not rare. Moreover, the Center for

Investigative Reporting found that the incidents plotted by right-wing extremists in the United States were behind nearly twice as many when compared with their Islamist counterparts between 2008 and 2016. Indeed, the majority were acts of terrorist violence that involved deaths, injuries and damaged property.[47] All of these examples make Abbott's statement about the harmless face of Islamophobia highly questionable and dangerous.

Abbott's comparison opens up another discussion. What is terrorism and what constitutes an act of terror? There is no 'official' definition of terrorism in the West and even the United Nations cannot agree on one of over 200 definitions that are documented… These definitions highlight the fact that terrorism is an illegitimate act against a state, a method of violence or threat of violence, a tactic used against civilians, that aims to effect change by creating fear and aimed at a political, religious or ideological outcome.[48] The political definitions used for legislative purposes by the different departments in the West, particularly in the United States, UK and Australia[49] define terrorism in their own terms but highlight the political, religious or ideological cause behind the crime. Targeting non-combatants is made clear in all the three cases and harming even one individual is considered to be an act of terror. Both academic and political definitions of terrorism make the ideological component of a crime quintessential in terms of assessing whether it is a terrorist act or not.

In that regard, accuracy in assessing the motivation behind an act of terror requires an unbiased, transparent and considerably diligent procedure. However, predisposed approaches embedded in the racialized criminology,[50] quick assessments and overgeneralizations make the result doubtful in some cases. This section of the chapter reflects on the disparities in handling violent extremism and terrorism in Islamist and Islamophobic cases (i.e. far-right extremism) and argues the overestimation of Islamist extremism and underestimation of Islamophobia. The disparity can be better captured by comparing the assessments of the two types of extremism based on the following criteria: (a) Ideological vs. Mental drives, (b) Organizational vs. Individual crimes, and (c) All are harmful vs. all are harmless generalizations.

When an act is self-evident, it may not require an assessment. There is a general consensus that the violent crimes of organizations like Al Qaida, ISIS and Boko Haram warrant the terrorist label. Yet, what if a mentally ill local person claims to be affiliated with a global terrorist organization? Or, what if an ideologically motivated terrorist pretends to be mentally sick and independent from any violent extremist group? This gray area requires a meticulous and transparent investigation to be able to assess the number, nature and implications of the crimes in order to inform the public accurately and thereby avoid unnecessary social panics or unnecessary denial of certain extremist groups.

Ideological vs. Mental Drives

A quick overview of sources highlights the repetitive patterns especially the racialization of crimes reinforcing the Muslim/Arab/terrorist "Middle Eastern" of Islamic faith paradigm.[51] The public is always insinuated in the first instance of a violent crime that the perpetrator is expected to be a Middle Eastern looking Muslim man. This was massively documented in the first hours of the Oklahoma bombing, which was indeed committed by a young white American Christian man.

Muslim convicts' violent crimes are quickly assessed to be ideological whereas their non-Muslim counterparts' crimes are not labeled in the same way. Instead, their mental disorders are always brought to the foreground as an excuse to distance their violence from terrorism. The mental health excuse was in force even in those cases in which the perpetrator expressed his ideological motive behind his violent crime. For instance, the Quebec Mosque shooter expressed that he plotted the shooting after hearing the Canadian President's welcome to the refugees. Yet, his mental disorder at the court was addressed as a driving force for wanting to kill anybody, not necessarily Muslims.[52] In doing so, the ideological motive behind his terrorism was deliberately diluted. It was due to President Trudeau's explicit reference to him as a terrorist, that the convict received a life sentence for his terrorist attack. Nevertheless, the incident is still addressed in the media and remained in public psyche as the "Quebec shooting" rather than an act of terrorism.

Likewise, Anders Breivik is publicly addressed as a mass-killer rather than a terrorist, despite his ideological motive for killing 77 people. His psychiatric disorders are addressed as the driving factor behind his violence.[53] Similarly, the assassination of Jo Cox, the British Labor MP in June 2016 was referred to as an act of a 'crazed loner' and a 'loner with a history of mental illness' rather than recognizing his self-evident links with the extreme right.[54] In another case, Larry McQuilliams fired more than 100 rounds at government buildings that included the Police

Headquarters and the Mexican Consulate in Austin, Texas in November 2014, news media commentators quickly focused on the question of his mental illness.[55] In stark contrast, the mental disorders of Muslim convicts committing violent crimes were not counted to divert their stories from terrorism to mentally sick loner's individual acts.

In this regard, the blurred line between the two types based on the convict's Muslim or non-Muslim background not only misinforms the public and judiciary but also unnecessarily inflates Islamist terrorism while unnecessarily underestimating the non-Islamic and Islamophobic form of terrorism.

Organizational vs. Individual Crimes

Another significant factor in terrorism cases is the assumed link with the global terrorist organizations. Islamist terrorists are always introduced to the public as participants in a broader, global terrorist network, however, no evidence is included to support the claims. It is difficult to locate to an example of a loner Muslim violent extremist or terrorist in the existing public discourse. In the case of violent actions committed by Muslims, what determines those crimes to be Islamist terrorism remains in the gray area unless they openly declare an association with a terrorist group. In the cases when a declaration has been made, the organizational side of the crime can be still doubted when the convict is mentally sick and lacking supporting evidence. For instance, uttering the words "God is great" while committing a crime does not automatically make the action committed, part of a broader terrorist organization. This mismatch only helps inflate terrorist organizations and their supposed sphere of influence. Counterterrorism expert David Kilculen writes on this under the terms 'aggregation and disaggregation' to interrogate "Who do we help terrorist groups project an aggregated image of global strength and unity when the opposite is actually truer?"[56]

Contrary to their Islamist counterparts, most of the Islamophobic extremists and terrorists were introduced to the public as if they were lone wolves. Yet the *Lone Wolves* report analyzing about 40 far-right extremist individuals' cases debunks the lone wolf myth and concludes that the cases in the report "demonstrate conclusively that far right terrorists are not lone wolves but are connected with, influenced by and often helped by organisations whose beliefs they share."[57] What is interesting here is that most of them were arrested by "luck." For instance, when the police went to David Tovey's home for a report on a graffiti incident and to the home of Martyn Gillard for his racist comments on social media, they were found preparing violent attacks with explosive materials at home.[58]

The reluctance to categorize far-right extremist as terrorists and their crimes as organizational was evident in the trial of a British National Party member, Tony Lecomber, who attempted to blow up the offices of a leftwing political party in the 1980s. Although his house was full of grenades, petrol bombs and detonators, he was sentenced to three years because the judge denied his act to be organizational, nor an act of terrorism, stating that "You are not a terrorist in the normal sense of the word, nor were you acting on behalf of some political group."[59]

The disparity is still in force since similar types of violent extremism cases beginning from the interference of the police till the court are handled differently and represented by media disproportionately based on the perpetrator's Muslim/non-Muslim background. The recent report released by *The Equal Treatment?* analyzes similar types of ideological crimes committed by Muslim and non-Muslim convicts in the United States and finds that Muslim perpetrators received four times the average sentence as their non-Muslim counterparts for attempted plots of similar conduct (211 vs. 53).[60]

Similarly, in the print media, Muslim-perceived perpetrators received twice more coverage than their non-Muslim counterparts. In cases of foiled plots, Muslim convicts received seven and a half times more media coverage.[61] Another survey in the United States also reported 5 times more media coverage of terrorism if committed by Muslims.[62]

The inaccurate handling of terrorism by the media according to the UNESCO's report helps feed the following myths: "Western" countries are the most affected by terrorism, Western Europe has never been more affected by terrorism than today, Fear of terrorism is rational—terrorism is likely to kill you, Refugees and recent migrants bring terrorism, People in many "Western" cities are living in permanent warzones.[63]

There is no doubt that these myths legitimize Islamophobic sentiments while further fueling Islamophobic extremism. For instance, Mohamed Osman Mohamud was provided with financial, logistical and motivational support by FBI agents and thereby trapped into be arrested as a terrorist. Another Oregan youth, Cody Seth, launched a homemade firebomb into the mosque two days after Mohamud's arrest and learning that Mohamud sometimes prayed in that mosque. Crowford introduced

Mohamud in his Facebook post as a "really bad guy" who went to the mosque right in front of Crowford's house. Another discrepancy in this particular case was Mohamud was sentenced to 30 years because of playing the roles of terrorist within the FBI's stage setting while Crawford's history of mental illness led him to be sentenced to five years' probation, which he considered "a total victory" for himself as he "kicked the federal government's ass in court."[64]

All Harmful vs. All Harmless

Although there are nuances among the varying levels of radicalism that range from ideological sympathy to violent extremist action, all the ranges of extremism for Muslims are leveled in the public mind to one simple category, either being a terrorist or suspected of a terrorist act. In contrast, similarly diverse levels of Islamophobic radicalism are reduced to the action of a civic citizen who has freedom of speech and the right to disclose one's dislike.

Muslim individuals arrested in sting operations are portrayed as either terrorists or supporters of terrorism. All we know from the publicized Sydney and Brisbane raids of 2015, the biggest counter-terrorism operation in Australia's history which saw 800 police officers deployed, is that only a few arrests were made,[65] and that the level of extremism or level of support or the intention to perform terrorist acts is still anonymous to the public.

Although arrests can be claimed to be not for arrest but for "disruption" of what the police perceived as a plot in development, the overarching question still applies: Why do Australian (and in the wider sense Western) police and intelligence only seem to use terrorism legislation in cases of Islamic people being involved? Murders and attacks by far right individuals are usually treated under 'biased crime' or 'hate crime' or 'fixated person,' but Muslims are almost invariably treated under 'counter terrorism' legislation.

Instead of making the suspects' varying levels of extremism clear to the public, there seems to be an extra effort to fit the suspects into the present "sting" operations' theme. One ironic example among the quickly mismatched terrorism stories is the raid at the house of Mustafa Dirani's parents, where a plastic 'sword of Ali' decoration was found by the police. Removing the sword from the wall during the raid, "The media were told, amid hysteria among beheadings, that a sword had been found." [66] Ironically, the 'sword of Ali' was a Shiite house decoration and had nothing to do with ISIS since the Shiites are the archenemy of ISIS.[67]

Furthermore, while varying levels of extremism are quickly transformed into terrorism or being suspect of terrorism in the portrayal of those string operations in media, not many far-right extremists are associated with violent extremism and terrorism. Similarly, no sting operation is aimed at any far-right group and far-right terrorists. As the Lone Wolves report documented, most of the far-right violent extremists were found coincidentally.[68] This reinforced the idea that all levels of Islamic extremism are harmful whereas all levels of Islamophobic extremism is harmless.

A similar message is consistently given to the public by dismissing the nuances among the sub-categories of the Islamist and Islamophobic extremism and labeling all of them as dangerous. For instance, nuances among Islamist and Salafi ideologies are dismissed and all are associated directly with violent extremism. All the groups who express different views from those espoused by Western governments are perceived as a potential threat. For instance, although Salafi Islam identified as the source of violent extremism in terrorism literature,[69] a thorough investigation by the University of Maryland's Terrorism studies debunked this monolithic public image of Salafism. The study categorized Salafis as violent and non-violent streams while addressing Salafis as "highly fractured and often [in] fight with each other" (STARR report).[70] It is unrealistic to expect such a diversified ideology in dispute within itself can manufacture uniform products, i.e. terrorists or terrorist suspects.

Placing all the supporters of Salafi Islam and reactionary Islamist ideologies into one "terrorist" box is problematic as it overgeneralizes and inflates the number of violent extremists and perpetuates an unwarranted public fear. Furthermore, this skewed representation heightens the tension and hatred against Muslims who are already targets of Islamophobes' terrorism discourse.

While the officially unproven Islamic ideologies are branded as Salafi, Jihadi or Islamist, bigoted anti-Muslim people are not openly and directly addressed as Islamophobes in the public discourse. Islamophobic groups are always promoted under different banners and in the way that they like to introduce themselves to the public such as anti-halal campaigners, anti-mosque campaigners, anti-burqa campaigners and so forth... Moreover, in concealing their hatred against Islam and Muslims through their use of various banners and by using seemingly patriotic arguments (such as saving, securing and striving for the nation), Islamophobes are not seen as posing threat to the nation with their discriminative and intolerant views.

There is radicalism in Islamophobia. The lack of substantial criminological cases does not reduce the abundance of Islamophobic extremes. The number of convicts is relatively small due to the lack of monitoring, positive bias, negligence and the skewed perception of a threat.

Nevertheless, in the absence of surveillance, monitoring, reporting and penalty which are generously offered to the Islamists, Islamophobic extremism in the cyber world is evident and common. Being uncontrolled on cyberspace increases and normalizes Islamophobic brutality. The Islamophobia in Australia Report highlighted that more than half of the online incidents (53%) reported in the Islamophobia Register Australia were found to be in the severest level, which is in the level of wanting to harm and encouraging others to incite violence against Muslims.[71]

Radicalism in Islamophobia and the Halal Case

The public recognizes this campaign due to the Senate's public inquiry that was concluded with around 1500 submissions to the Parliament. The senate inquiry gave the public an impression that anti-halal campaigners are democratic and erudite citizens who express their legitimate fears and concerns about halal through a democratic platform.

However, the level of hate among the Islamophobes was also diverse. The anti-halal campaigners' antagonism was evident in their rallies when they clashed with anti-racist groups as they found no Muslim to clash with. The irrational mobs had brawls with anti-racist Australians and caused injuries despite police intervention.

Unlike the Islamic radicals who are often registered due to police scrutiny, not many violent extremists were able to be identified. On the far-right, the extremist Philp Galea was found in possession of a knife at the Bendigo mosque protest and a flare at another event. Upon further investigation, he was found possessing five teasers and 360 grams of mercury—which can be used to make explosives—along with information on his computer about confecting explosives and an 'extensive' amount of 'extreme' material linked with far-right groups. He was sentenced to one month in prison.[72] Galea was a member of Reclaim Australia which objects to so-called "Islamization" by protesting halal and mosques and the other Islamic images. This was the first time an Islamophobic extremist was sentenced according to the Australian anti-terrorism laws in August 2016.

Anti-halal campaigners' extremist versions were more observable on social media since they were neither monitored nor charged with any offense. One forerunner of the anti-halal campaign, Senator Cory Bernardi recently (April 16, 2018) described Muslim halal certifiers as 'cockroaches' who are running an extortion racket on the nation's food suppliers.[73] Bernardi's hate was so extreme he resorted to dehumanization and disgust which is indeed perceived by terrorism experts[74] at a severe level which is prerequisite feeling for being able to harm the other.

Moreover, despite the traumatizing effect of the ISIS beheadings in the public psyche especially in 2014–2015 when anti-halal campaigns peaked in Australia, the online hate incidents reported to the Islamophobia Register found that halal related death threats, i.e. killing Muslims by halal slaughtering, doubled.[75] This is an indication of not only the severity of Islamophobic hate but also the impact of anti-halal debate in heightening violent extremist sentiment among Islamophobes and the broader Australian community. In addition to killing Muslims by halal slaughtering, other horrifying expressions were posted in the context of the halal food debate. One Islamophobe, frustrated with seeing halal everywhere, suggested through his Facebook page that all Muslims be placed in gas chambers for a Muslim version of the holocaust.[76]

These online death threats were posted in the year Australia witnessed discussions on amending a key part of the nation's racial discrimination laws by suggesting to make it unlawful for someone to publicly "offend, insult, humiliate or intimidate" a person or a group of people. Attorney-General George Brandis critiqued the proposal saying that people have "a right to be bigot." This has been interpreted by the opposing MPs as giving "the green light to racist hate speech in Australia."[77] Islamophobes in Australia used the hate speech right to the extent that posting death threats to Muslims on social media.

Conclusion and Implications

There is Islamophobia in Radicalism that causes overestimation of Islamist terrorism while putting ordinary Muslims under the suspect category. This was evident even in the anti-halal debates by accusing the halal certifiers, manufacturers and consumers with funding and supporting terrorism overseas.

Similarly, there is Radicalism in the Islamophobia discourse, yet its negligence causes underestimation of Islamophobic violent extremism. In the case of anti-halal debates, although varying levels of extremism (including violent extremism) are observed and documented, the public recalls the anti-halal debaters with their submissions to public inquiry rather than death threats by "halal slaughtering" Muslims.

What turns a crime into terrorism is the ideological motive behind the crime according to the Western governments' definitions of terrorism. Hence, it is quintessential to accurately, transparently and deliberately assess the gray areas when an act is not self-evidently a terrorist act. Otherwise, quick mismatches with implicit biases will cause (a) inflating Islamist terrorism and deflating Islamophobic terrorism, (b) Social panicking on Islamist terrorism and social denial of Islamophobic terrorism, (c) ordinary Muslims to feel under siege but extremist Islamophobes to increase recklessness, and (d) all the aforementioned implications would affect criminology and the justice system in favor of Islamophobic convicts and disfavor of Islamist or Muslim convicts.

Notes

1. Australian Senate, "Third Party Certification of Food," Parliament of Australia, December 1, 2015, http://www.aph.gov.au/Parliamentary_Business/Committees/Senate/Economics/Food_Cert_Schemes/Report.
2. Jennifer Cheng, *Anti-Racist Discourse on Muslims in the Australian Parliament* (Sydney: John Benjamins Publishing, 2017).
3. These countries ironically did not include the birthplaces of the 9/11 hijackers and the forerunners of Al Qaida, i.e. Osama bin Laden and Ayman Al Zawahiri.
4. David Neiwert, "Home Is Where the Hate Is," *The Investigative Fund*, June 22, 2017, 4 https://www.theinvestigativefund.org/investigation/2017/06/22/home-hate/.
5. Ibid., 4.
6. Linda Briskman and Susie Latham, "Political Islamophobia," in *Islamophobia in Australia 2014–2016*, ed. Derya Iner (Sydney: Charles Sturt University, 2017), 17.
7. Shahram Akbarzadeh, "The Muslim Question in Australia: Islamophobia and Muslim Alienation," *Journal of Muslim Minority Affairs* 36, no. 3 (2016): 4.
8. Amy Remeikis, "Pauline Hanson Says Islam is a Disease Australia Needs to 'Vaccinate'," *Sydney Morning Herald*, March 24, 2017, https://www.

smh.com.au/politics/federal/pauline-hanson-says-islam-is-a-disease-australia-needs-to-vaccinate-20170324-gv5w7z.html.
9. Akbarzadeh, "The Muslim Question," 4.
10. Ibid.
11. Sharri Markson, "Tony Abbott: Australia is 'Pussyfooting' Around Radical Islamism, Calls for Special Terror Courts," *Daily Telegraph*, June 1, 2017, https://www.dailytelegraph.com.au/news/nsw/tony-abbott-australia-is-pussyfooting-around-radical-islamism-calls-for-special-terror-courts/news-story/8be5a32fef96b0a1420d824fe9c76303.
12. Rosie Lewis, "Josh Frydenberg Blames 'Problem Within Islam' for Terror Attacks," *The Australian*, November 29, 2015, https://www.theaustralian.com.au/national-affairs/paris-attacks-grand-mufti-in-graphic-leadership-failure/news-story/5e9fa96d29dafa65a167c970f8ad7ccf.
13. Jared Owens, "George Christensen Under Fire Over 'Terror' Label for Merrylands Attack," *The Australian*, July 22, 2016, https://www.theaustralian.com.au/national-affairs/george-christensen-under-fire-over-terror-label-for-merrylands-attack/news-story/9438773b9b520eb3c652a9991c77b0ec.
14. Mark Kenny, "Liberal Divisions After ASIO Chief Duncan Lewis 'Intervenes' on MPs' Islam Comments," *The Sunday Morning Herald*, December 17, 2015, https://www.smh.com.au/politics/federal/liberal-divisions-after-asio-chief-duncan-lewis-intervenes-on-mps-islam-comments-20151217-glpp8x.html.
15. A. Odysseus Patrick, "Australia's Immoral Preference for Christian Refugees," *The New York Times*, May 3, 2017, https://www.nytimes.com/2017/05/03/opinion/australias-immoral-preference-for-christian-refugees.html.
16. Kate McRa, "Linking Refugees to Terrorism: Cofveve [sic] Pauline Hanson Style," *SBS*, June 6, 2017, https://www.sbs.com.au/comedy/article/2017/06/06/linking-refugees-terrorism-cofveve-pauline-hanson-style.
17. "Islam in the Media 2017," *OnePath Network*, February 18, 2018, https://onepathnetwork.com/islam-in-the-media-2017/.
18. Iner, *Islamophobia in Australia*; Kabir, Nahid. "Representation of Islam and Muslims in the Australian Media," *Journal of Muslim Minority Affairs* 26, no. 3 (2006): 313–328; Kabir, Nahid. "Media is One-Sided in Australia: The Muslim Youth Perspective," *Journal of Children and Media* 2, no. 3 (2008): 267–281; and Halim Rane, Jacqui Ewart, and John Martinkus, *Media Framing of the Muslim World: Conflicts, Crises and Contexts* (Palgrave Macmillan, 2014).
19. Matthews, "The Media and Islamophobia in Australia," in *Islamophobia in Australia*.

20. Iner, *Islamophobia in Australia*, 54.
21. P. French, "What Do Islamist Extremists Believe? Salafi-Jihadism by Shiraz Maher and Crusade and Jihad by Malcolm Lambert—Review," *The Guardian*, March 25, 2016, https://www.theguardian.com/books/2016/mar/24/salafi-jihadism-shiraz-maher-crusade-jihad-malcolm-lambert-review-patrick-french.
22. David Neiwert, "Home Is Where the Hate Is,"; "Correcting Media Myths About Terrorism," *United Nations Educational, Scientific and Cultural Organisation (UNESCO)*, April 12, 2017, https://en.unesco.org/news/correcting-media-myths-about-terrorism; Arie Perliger, "Comparative Framework for Understanding Jewish and Christian Violent Fundamentalism," *Religions* no. 6 (August 31, 2015).
23. Arun Kundnani, "Radicalisation: The Journey of a Concept," *Race & Class* 54, no. 2 (2012).
24. Ibid., 7.
25. Ibid., 10.
26. Ibid., 10.
27. Marco Goli and Shahamak Rezaei, "House of War: Islamic Radicalisation in Denmark," Centre for Studies in Islamism and Radicalisation (CIR), Department of Political Science, Aarhus University, Denmark, 2010, p. 48, http://tinyurl.com/cqrqpvd (www.ps.au.dk/fileadmin/site_files/filer_statskundskab/subsites/cir/Rapport_2FINAL.pdf).
28. Randy Borum, "Radicalization into Violent Extremism II: A Review of Conceptual Models and Empirical Research".
29. Ibid.
30. Federal Bureau of Investigations, *The Radicalization Process: From Conversion to Jihad* (FBI, 2006), http://cryptome.org/fbi-jihad.pdf.
31. Adrian Cherney and Kristina Murphy, "Being a 'Suspect Community' in a Post 9/11 World—The Impact of the War on Terror on Muslim Communities in Australia," *Australian & New Zealand Journal of Criminology* 49, no. 4 (2016); Anne Aly and Jason-Leigh Striegher, "Examining the Role of Religion in Radicalization to Violent Islamist Extremism," *Studies in Conflict & Terrorism* 35, no. 12 (2012).
32. Poynting, "The Islamophobic Crimes of the Past and Present," in *Islamophobia in Australia*.
33. The two bills were introduced in the Senate and the House of Representatives to designate the Muslim Brother as a terrorist organization in 2017 Raymond Tanter and Edward Stafford "Designating the Muslim Brotherhood as a Terrorist Organization Is a Bad Idea," i, March 3, 2017, http://foreignpolicy.com/2017/03/03/designating-the-muslim-brotherhood-as-a-terrorist-organization-is-a-bad-idea/.

34. Steven Emerson of the Investigative Project on Terrorism, Frank Gaffney Center of the Security Policy, Robert Spencer of Jihad Watch & Stop Islamization of America, Frank Gaffney of the Center for Security Policy Daniel Pipes at the Middle East Forum and David Yerushalmi of the Society of Americans for National Existence reinforced the "muslim terrorism" idea in their publications. Wajahat Ali, et al., Fear, Inc., *The Roots of the Islamophobia Network in America* (Center for American Progress, 2011).
35. One section of this book is indeed dedicated to this topic with the contribution of this kind of terrorism experts. Also, for instance, the Australian experts who prepared the Australian Government Attorney-General's book entitled *Preventing Violent Extremism and Radicalisation in Australia* defines the stages of radicalization and violent extremism definitions of radicalization stages are generic and as inclusive as possible in the provided examples to avoid singling out one particular religion, race or culture.
36. "Byron Company Suffers Halal Anzac Biscuit Backlash," *ABC News*, October 23, 2014, http://www.abc.net.au/news/2014-10-23/anzac-biscuit-halal-backlash/5835792.
37. John Hood, "Bega Cheese Goes Halal to Fund Islam, Sharia and Invite More Muslims and Their Mosques," *Australian First Party*, March 30, 2017, http://australiafirstparty.net/bega-cheese-goes-halal-to-fund-islam-sharia-and-invite-more-muslims-and-their-mosques/.
38. Manal and Yucel, "Halal Certification and Islamophobia: A Critical Analysis of Submissions Regarding the Review of Third Party Certification of Food in Australia Inquiry," *Australian Journal of Islamic Studies* 1, no. 1 (2016), 15.
39. Ibid., 16.
40. Ibid., 21.
41. Michael Safi, "Food and Drink Manufacturers 'Have No Plans' to Ditch Halal Certification," *The Guardian*, November 11, 2014, https://www.theguardian.com/australia-news/2014/nov/11/food-and-drink-manufacturers-have-no-plans-to-ditch-halal-certification.
42. Andrea Hogan, "Kellogg's and Sanitarium Drop Halal Certification," *Australian Food News*, July 19, 2017, http://www.ausfoodnews.com.au/2017/07/19/kelloggs-and-sanitarium-drop-halal-certification.html.
43. Philip Coorey, "Tony Abbott Targets Muslims, Malcolm Turnbull Blames Social Media," *Financial Review*, July 5, 2017, http://www.afr.com/news/politics/tony-abbott-targets-muslims-malcolm-turnbull-blames-social-media-20170604-gwkcbf#ixzz5EOJdNFDU.
44. The perpetrator said: "I'm gonna say that on the stand. I'm a patriot, and I hope everyone I stabbed died." qtd in M. Park and S. Becker,

"Portland Train Suspect: 'I Hope Everyone I Stabbed Died'," *CNN*, May 31, 2017, https://edition.cnn.com/2017/05/31/us/portland-train-stabbing-what-happened/index.html.
45. Leyland Cecco, "Canada Mosque Shooter Says He Was Motivated by Trudeau Welcoming Refugees," *The Guardian*, Saturday April 14, 2018, 05.19 a.m. AEST, https://www.theguardian.com/world/2018/apr/13/canada-mosque-shooter-alexandre-bissonnette-trudeau-trump-refugees-travel-ban.
46. Kan Witchita, "3 Men Convicted in Kansas Plot to Bomb Somali Refugees," *NBC News*, April 19, 2018, https://www.nbcnews.com/news/us-news/3-men-convicted-kansas-plot-bomb-somali-refugees-n867201.
47. David Neiwert, "Home Is Where the Hate Is."
48. For details see Richard Rubenstein, Martha Crenshaw, Wilhelm Reich, Walter Laquer, Brigitte L. Nacos's definitions.
49. Edward Halibozek, Andy Jones, and Gerald L. Kovacich, *The Corporate Security Professional's Handbook on Terrorism* (Butterworth-Heinemann, 2007), 6; J. R. Greene, *Encyclopedia of Police Science: 2-Volume Set* (Taylor & Francis, 2006), 1263; and Susan Robinson and Tracy Cussen, *The Criminology and Criminal Justice Companion* (Macmillan International Higher Education), 145.
50. Scott Poynting, "The Islamophpobic Crimes of the Past and Present," in *Islamophobia in Australia*.
51. Scott Poynting and Victoria Mason, "The Resistible Rise of Islamophobia: Anti-Muslim Racism in the UK and Australia Before 11 September 2001," *Journal of Sociology* 43, no. 1 (2007); Iner, *Islamophobia in Australia*, 23.
52. Julia Page, "Mosque Shooter Shows Potential for Rehabilitation, Quebec City Court Hears," April 24, 2018, http://www.cbc.ca/news/canada/montreal/mosque-shooter-alexandre-bissonnette-day-nine-sentencing-1.4632952.
53. Clare Allely, "The Psychiatric Disorders that Might Have Driven Anders Breivik to Kill," *Independent UK*, Monday November 7, 2016, https://www.independent.co.uk/life-style/health-and-families/features/the-psychiatric-disorders-that-might-have-made-anders-breivik-into-a-mass-murderer-a7402126.html.
54. Sam Tonkin, "Inside the Lair of a Killer: How A Quiet and Unassuming Loner, 53, Plotted a Murder that Shocked the World from a Two-bed Semi-Filled with Nazi Souvenirs, Far-Right Books," *Daily Mail UK*, November 23, 2016, http://www.dailymail.co.uk/news/article-3961010/Inside-lair-political-assassin-quiet-unassuming-loner-53-plotted-murder-Jo-Cox.html.

55. Scott Shane, "Homegrown Extremists Tied to Deadlier Toll Than Jihadists in U.S. Since 9/11," *New York Times*, June 24, 2015. https://www.nytimes.com/2015/06/25/us/tally-of-attacks-in-us-challenges-perceptions-of-top-terror-threat.html.
56. David Kilcullen, *Blood Year: Islamic State and the Failures of the War on Terror* (Black Inc., 2016).
57. Gerry Gable and Paul Jackson, "Lone Wolves: Myth or Reality?" (2011), 7. http://nectar.northampton.ac.uk/6014/1/Gable20116014.pdf.
58. Ibid., 7.
59. Ibid., 6.
60. Rao, Shenkman, et al., *Equal Treatment? Measuring the Legal and Media Response to Ideologically Motivated Violence in the United States*.
61. Ibid., 2.
62. Benjamin Kentish, "Terror Attacks Receive Five Times More Media Coverage If Perpetrator is Muslim," *Independent*, July 3, 2017, https://www.independent.co.uk/news/world-0/terror-attacks-media-coverage-muslim-islamist-white-racism-islamophobia-study-georgia-state-a7820726.html.
63. "Correcting Media Myths About Terrorism," United Nations Educational, Scientific and Cultural Organisation (UNESCO), April 12, 2017, https://en.unesco.org/news/correcting-media-myths-about-terrorism.
64. David Neiwert, "Home Is Where the Hate Is," 6–8.
65. "Anti-Terror Operation in Sydney and Brisbane 'Thwarted' Beheading Plot," *ABC News*, September 18, 2014, http://www.abc.net.au/news/2014-09-18/anti-terror-police-mount-large-scale-raids-in-sydney-brisbane/5752002.
66. Anthony Colangelo, "Shooter Links to Mosque, Islamist Group Probed," *The New Daily*, October 5, 2015, https://thenewdaily.com.au/news/national/2015/10/05/police-probe-shooter-links-mosque-islamist-group/.
67. Poynting, "The Islamophobic Crimes of the Past and Present," in *Islamophobia in Australia*.
68. Gable and Jackson, *Lone Wolf*, 6.
69. Akimi Scarcella, Ruairi Page, and Vivek Furtado, "Terrorism, Radicalisation, Extremism, Authoritarianism and Fundamentalism: A Systematic Review of the Quality and Psychometric Properties of Assessments," *PLoS One* 11, no. 12 (2016).
70. N/A, "Debates Among Salafi Muslims About Use of Violence," National Consortium for the Study of Terrorism and Responses to Terrorism (START), May 2017, https://www.start.umd.edu/pubs/START_Debates AmongSalafiMuslimsAboutViolence_SummaryReport_May2017.pdf.

71. Iner, *Islamophobia in Australia*, 67.
72. Scott, *Islamopbhobic Crimes in Islamophobia in Australia*, 26.
73. Boycott Halal Certification in Australia Facebook page. https://www.facebook.com/permalink.php?story_fbid=1658840564200728&id=693361674081960.
74. Willem Koomen and Joop Van Der Pligt, *The Psychology of Radicalization and Terrorism* (Routledge, 2015).
75. Iner, *Islamophobia in Australia*, 58.
76. Ibid., 71.
77. Emma Griffiths, "George Brandis Defends 'Right to Be a Bigot' Amid Government Plan to Amend Racial Discrimination Act," *ABC*, March 24, 2014, http://www.abc.net.au/news/2014-03-24/brandis-defends-right-to-be-a-bigot/5341552.

CHAPTER 6

Can Islamophobia in the Media Serve Islamic State Propaganda? The Australian Case, 2014–2015

Nahid Afrose Kabir

INTRODUCTION

Muslim Australians are a diverse group of people. In 2016, Australian Muslims comprised 2.6% of the Australian population.[1] The Muslim unemployment level was two times higher than the national total despite Muslims' higher average education level. Since the 9/11 Twin Towers attacks, Muslims have received more attention than any other religious groups in the media and in parliamentary politics (relating to immigration, policing, national security and integration).[2] Some participants in my broader study on young Australian Muslims' identity that I conducted in 2006–2007 expressed their frustration, anger and sadness about the Australian media's representation of Islam and Muslims.[3] For example, Fatima, a 17-year-old girl of Iraqi origin, commented:

N. A. Kabir (✉)
BRAC University, Dhaka, Bangladesh
e-mail: Nahid.Kabir@unisa.edu.au

N. A. Kabir
University of South Australia, Adelaide, Australia

> I just hate the media, I hate it. For example, what I think is that people shouldn't blame us Muslims for everything that happens around them such as London bombings, as soon as they hear a bomb they say: "Oh it's terrorists, it's the Muslims" ... The fact of what they say, like you know "get out of our country". (Interview, Melbourne, 2007)

Fatima discussed the repercussions that mainstream Muslims generally face after any acts of violence. Some non-Muslims yell at Muslims to get out of their country. Marium, a 17-year-old of Albanian background who migrated to Australia at the age of 10, stated:

> Whenever something happens, as soon as they find out the religion of the person they put over all Muslims, which is not fair because I might not have done that, and many Albanians might not have done that. We have suffered so much as well from the Christians but none of our Muslims go and say, "This Christian he's doing this!", but they're criticizing all the Muslims because of one person done something. They should say that person in particular, not put all the Muslims because they are bringing shame to all of us. (Interview, Melbourne, 2007)

In 1999, Serbian authorities (predominantly Orthodox Christians) conducted ethnic cleansing against Kosovar Albanians. Reflecting on that context, Marium said the media never labelled the perpetrators as Christians.[4] Researchers have observed that in times of crisis some Western media lump Muslims together as though they are one politically relevant monolithic group. Significantly, the media imply that this group poses a threat to national security.[5] For example, in the Australian, British and American contexts, in the mainstream print media, any isolated Muslim issue is presented under the label or headline of "Muslims", thereby putting all Muslims under one banner.[6] Positive stories about Muslims are blurred by sensationalist headlines. But there have been very few studies that have examined whether there is any correlation between Islamophobia and radicalization, particularly, whether negative media representation of Muslims can inadvertently be a pathway to radicalization.

Shryock observed that the term Islamophobia can be applied to any setting where people hate Muslims, or fear Islam. Islamophobia can lead to acts such as mosque vandalism, and hate crimes against people who are perceived as Muslims. It can also lead to sensationalist press coverage of the "Muslim threat" or the "Muslim problem", racial profiling and surveillance of Muslim communities, electoral smear campaigns against Muslims, discrimination in the job market and vilification in public spaces.[7]

On the other hand, Borum observed that radicalization is driven and sustained by multiple factors. Casual factors include broad grievances (such as Islamophobia) that "push" individuals towards a radical ideology and more specific "pull" factors (extremists ideology) that attract them.[8] Goli and Rezaei found that radical Muslims among other things were more dissatisfied with life in general, more preoccupied with international conflicts affecting Muslim countries, lonelier, more likely to have experienced discrimination, and less trustful of the media.[9]

Under the circumstances, if Islamophobia means marginalization of Muslims through prejudice and discrimination in the wider society and media representation of Islam/Muslims as the "Other", then it can be a contributing factor in some young Muslims' alienation from the mainstream society. It can then make them susceptible to radicalization.

Since 2014, with the emergence of the Islamic State of Iraq and the Levant (ISIL), media coverage of Islam and Muslims has reached another level. The media is saturated with coverage of ISIL, and Islam and Muslims through headlines, images and letters to the editor. In this chapter, I examine whether the intense print media coverage of Islam and Muslims can inadvertently assist ISIL propaganda and have an impact on young Australian Muslims, creating a pathway to radicalization. I examine two News Corp papers, *The Australian* and *The Advertiser*, from August 2014 to January 2015. First, I discuss my research methodology. Secondly, I briefly discuss the background to this study. I examine the national and international events that have put mainstream Australian Muslims in the limelight as the "Other". Thirdly, I analyse reporting on Islam and Muslims in selected print media from 1 August 2014 to 31 January 2015. Fourthly, in the discussion section, I discuss how Islamophobia in the media can be a pathway to radicalization. Finally, I conclude that media stereotypes of Islam/Muslims may further alienate vulnerable Muslim youth which can open their pathway to radicalization. They will thereby serve Islamic State propaganda.

Research Methodology

For this chapter, I conducted research on the newspapers *The Australian* and *The Advertiser* from 1 August 2014 to 31 January 2015. I applied thematic content and critical discourse analysis to study both newspapers' representations of Islam and Muslims.[10] I researched both the hard copy and the online editions of the newspapers. In the hard copies, I looked at the images, headlines, news content, and letters to the editor that used the labels "Islam" or "Muslim", or whose subject matter related to Muslims, for example, the *burka*. Then I downloaded the same news items from the database available via NewsBank Inc. Access World News through the University of South Australia library. Through a computer search for the words "Islam", "Muslims", "Jihad", "Koran/Quran" and "*burka/burqa*", I secured the approximate number of times each word was used.

Using content analysis, I examined how *The Australian* and *The Advertiser* newspapers represented news about Muslims through their headlines, whether the news item was placed on the front page, whether its placement was on the top of the page, and how negative and positive Muslim news was conveyed to the readers. I also tried to make sense of the language of the news reporting through its headlines and images. For example, I assessed whether the newspapers were simply trying to convey the message that the rise of the Islamic State and its atrocities were a matter of concern to all Australians (including Muslims) or whether they implied there was a division between "Us" and "Them" with an Islamophobic tone. The content analysis method assisted me not only to find the similarities and differences between the newspapers but also to identify nuances in their respective languages. The critical discourse analysis of the letters to the editors assisted me to understand the impact of the news content on the readers. I wanted to find out through the language used on the letters page whether the tone of some readers was also Islamophobic.

Background

With the advent of the Islamic State, Australian Muslims have been drawing more media attention. As of 6 June 2015, it was estimated that 110 Australians (approximately 0.02% of the total Muslim population) were fighting for the Islamic State and other extremist groups in Syria and Iraq. About 160 Australians (approximately 0.03% of the total Muslim population) were suspected by the Australian Security Intelligence Organisation to be actively supporting the Islamic State in Australia.[11] In addition to the ongoing news on the Islamic State, from August 2014 to January 2015 a series of events took place that affected Muslims in Australia.

In August 2014, Prime Minister Tony Abbott announced that the Australian government would introduce a series of counter-terrorism measures to give security agencies the resources and legislative powers to combat home-grown terrorism and to punish Australians who participate in overseas terrorist activities. The Muslim community denounced these proposed "anti-terror" laws because giving excessive power to law enforcement agencies would be an infringement of civil liberties. Muslim leaders were also critical of Mr Abbott's divisive comments when he said, "Everyone has got to be on team Australia", and "you don't migrate to this country unless you want to join our team".[12]

In September 2014, politicians such as Liberal Senator for South Australia Cory Bernardi; Liberal National Member of Parliament for Queensland George Christensen, and Independent Senator for Tasmania Jacqui Lambie called for the *burka* to be banned from Parliament House as a security measure.[13] However, Greens Senator for Tasmania Christine Milne criticized this proposal, saying it would turn Muslim women into "second-class citizens" by putting them away somewhere they could not be seen or heard.[14] In the same month, the terror alert was lifted to high after 180 police raided nine homes across Brisbane in a counter-terrorism operation. It aimed to stop would-be foreign fighters from travelling to Syria.[15] About a week later, more than 800 officers from law enforcement agencies launched dawn raids at a series of properties across Sydney, which led to the arrest of 15 men and women.[16] The heavy-handedness of the law enforcement agencies and the media presence during the raids were criticized by some Muslims.[17]

On 23 September 2014, an Australian Muslim of Afghan heritage, Numan Haider, aged 18, was shot dead after he stabbed two officers from the Joint Counter Terrorism Team in Melbourne. On 22 October 2014, Michael Zehaf-Bibeau, a Canadian Muslim convert, opened fire at Canada's national parliament and killed two Canadian soldiers.

On 15–16 December 2014, Man Haron Monis held hostage some customers and employees of a Lindt Chocolate Café located at Martin Place in Sydney. After a 16-hour siege, police stormed the café. Hostage

Tori Johnson was killed by Monis and hostage Katrina Dawson was killed by a police bullet ricochet in the subsequent raid. Monis was also killed.

In Paris on 7 January 2015 two brothers, Saïd and Chérif Kouachi, forced their way into the offices of the French satirical weekly newspaper *Charlie Hebdo* in Paris and killed 12 people. A third killer, Amedy Coulibaly, killed four Jewish people in a kosher supermarket in Paris.

Against the backdrop of these political and terrorist incidents, I discuss my observations about the print media in the next section.

THE *AUSTRALIAN* AND THE *ADVERTISER*, 1 AUGUST 2014–31 JANUARY 2015

The Australian is a broadsheet national newspaper published in Sydney from Monday to Saturday. *The Advertiser* is a daily tabloid-format local newspaper published in Adelaide. It is currently printed daily from Monday to Saturday. Both newspapers are publications of News Corp Australia. However, *The Australian* had more coverage of Islamic/Muslim topics than *The Advertiser*. For this study, I examined *The Australian* because it is a national newspaper. At the time of this research, I lived in Adelaide. Therefore, I selected the local newspaper, *The Advertiser*, and compared its news representation of Islam and Muslim with *The Australian*.

Table 6.1 shows the number of times certain words were mentioned in *The Australian*: Islam (1106); Muslim (756); jihad (238); Koran (57) and *burka* (121) were used more frequently compared to *The Advertiser*: Islam (240); Muslim (209); jihad (74); Koran (24) and *burka* (33). The

Table 6.1 Media representation of Islamic/Muslim topics, August 2014–January 2015

Category	The Australian	The Advertiser
Mention of Islam	Approx 1106 (including Islamic: 611; Islamist: 116)	Approx 240 (including Islamic: 153; Islamist: 7)
Mention of Muslim	Approx 756	Approx 209
Mention of jihad	Approx 238 (including jihadi: 164; jihadist: 120)	Approx 74 (including jihadi: 59; jihadist: 34)
Mention of Koran/Quran	Approx 57	Approx 24
Mention of *burka/burqa*	Approx 121 (spelt *burka*)	Approx 33 (spelt *burqa*)

Table 6.2 Australian Newspaper Readership, 12 months, March 2014–March 2015

Newspapers	R'ship ('000s) Monday–Friday March 2014	R'ship ('000s) Monday–Friday March 2015	R'ship ('000s) Saturday March 2014	R'ship ('000s) Saturday March 2015
The Australian (National)	356	334	727	664
The Advertiser (South Australia)	379	334	488	391

Source Roy Morgan Research ("Australian Newspaper Readership, 12 months, March 2014–March 2015," accessed March 28, 2018, http://www.roymorgan.com)

Australian, being the national broadsheet newspaper, is likely to incorporate more national and international news coverage. However, as the next Table 6.2 shows, *The Australian* is not faring better commercially. For commercial reasons *The Australian* appears be more desperate to sensationalize its news items through headlines, images and content. Under the circumstances, Muslim news could be a convenient target.

Table 6.2 shows that *The Australian*'s readership is less for per state/territories than *The Advertiser*'s if its total number is divided by eight (as it is circulated in six states and two territories).

Comparison Between the Two Newspapers

In the six months from August 2014 to January 2015, *The Australian* had most news coverage of the Islamic State and the associated terror raids on page 1. The information provided by *The Australian* was newsworthy but sometimes the images of beheading and terrorists posing with guns were confronting. Sometimes its reporting may have given unnecessary publicity to terrorists. For example, on 23 September 2014, *The Australian* had a headline on its front page, "ISIS Urges Local Terror Attacks". It was associated with the image of Islamic State spokesman Abu Mohammad al-Adnani al-Shami holding a rifle, who stated:

> If you can kill a disbelieving American or European – especially the spiteful and filthy French – or an Australian, or a Canadian, or any other disbeliever from the disbelievers waging war, including the citizens of the countries that entered into a coalition against the Islamic State, then rely upon Allah, and kill him in any manner or way however it may be. Do not ask for anyone's advice and do not seek anyone's verdict.

The *Advertiser* did not generally publish such statements with massive headlines on the Islamic State or the terror raids on its front page. Perhaps, *The Advertiser* did not aim to sensationalize Muslim news as *The Australian*.

On the *burka* issue, both *The Australian* and *The Advertiser* published photos of women wearing *burkas* on their front pages.[18] But the presentation of the news in *The Australian* was more sensationalist than in *The Advertiser*. On 3 October 2014, *The Australian* published a photo on its front page of a woman wearing the full *burka* (with only her eyes showing). Above the photo was a small headline, "PM Urges Rethink on Burka 'Segregation'". But on the left-hand side of the *burka* woman's image was a much bigger headline with a different report, "Fear of Jihadi Bomb Makers". At first glance, it could appear to the reader that women who wear the full *burka* could all be "bomb makers". On page 5 of the same issue was a positive article, "Thousands of Women Unite with Muslim Sister", which reported that many non-Muslim women including the presenter of Channel 10 show *Studio 10*, Jessica Rowe, wore the *hijab* (head scarf) to support Muslim women. But this positive note was blurred by the representation of the *burka*-wearing Muslim woman on page 1.

On Sydney's Martin Place siege, both the newspapers published relevant images and headlines on their front pages. On the *Charlie Hebdo* incident, both newspapers also had relevant images and headlines on their front pages. However, *The Australian* had more confronting headlines, reporting and images. For example, on 9 January 2015 there was a big headline on the front page of *The Australian*, "Islamists at 'War with the World'". While on the same day the headline on the front page of *The Advertiser* was, "12 Dead in Paris Attack".

On some occasions, *The Australian* has presented good news about Muslims alongside negative news. For example, on 10–11 January 2015 on page 10, Natasha Robinson's report "We're all Fighting 'Disease': Imam" reported that Imam Abdul Azim Afifi, the President of the National Imams Council, expressed his condemnation of the murders in Paris. But underneath the imam's big image and photo caption, "Imam Abdul Azim Afifi: 'We Support All People That Love Peace and Freedom'", was another headline (for a report continued from p. 1), "How Sydney Siege Gunman Beat Me, Terrified the Kids: Ex-wife". It was a report about Haron Monis. The positive story about Imam Afifi and his image could become blurred in readers' minds with the Sydney siege gunman's story. It could create doubt about whether imams can be trusted.

Similarly, during the *Charlie Hebdo* incident, a young Muslim, aged 24, Lassana Bathily, helped save some Jewish people during a siege by Amedy Coulibaly in a kosher market. But his news and image did not receive a big space on the front page of *The Australian*. It was mentioned briefly on page 1. Lassana Bathily's news received space on page 5, under the headline, "'Nice' Muslim Boy who Helped Shoppers Hide".[19] However, underneath this good news was a report on Hayat Boumeddienne, terrorist Coulibaly's wife, with an image of her wearing a full *burka* and wielding a crossbow.[20] Once again *The Australian* blurred the good news about Bathily with negative news. On 22 January 2015 on page 8, *The Australian* reported under the headline "Muslim Hero Given Citizenship", that Bathily was hailed as a hero and the French government granted him citizenship. It was associated with the smiling image of Bathily. It is unfortunate that the positive report of Bathily did not appear on the front page. The front page news headlines and reports generally draw readers' attention. Bathily's news on the front page of the newspaper would have revealed that many Muslims are law-abiding people.

After the *Charlie Hebdo* tragedy, the front cover of the first edition of *Charlie Hebdo* featured a cartoon depicting Prophet Muhammad (Peace Be Upon Him) crying and holding up a sign which stated: "*Je suis Charlie*" (I am Charlie). A headline above read: "*Tout est pardonne*" (All is forgiven).[21] *The Australian* was quick to report on the tensions sparked by this new depiction of Prophet Muhammad (PBUH) in Muslim countries and within the Australian Muslim community. For example, some protestors in Turkey were angry at the publication of cartoons from the *Charlie Hebdo* issue. *The Australian* was quick to publish the image of the protestors.[22] *The Australian* also hastily reported the national incidents. For example, a Muslim leader Keysar Trad held up the *Charlie Hebdo* magazine cover, defending its depiction of a crying Mohammed. But the Islamic Council of Victoria held that any depiction of Prophet Muhammad (PBUH) was deeply offensive and the right to free speech came with responsibilities.[23] Through its selective reporting, *The Australian* revealed the "Muslim problem" that Muslims either protest or disagree on issues raised by the West.

On 30 January 2015, *The Australian* and *The Advertiser* reported how the Sydney siege perpetrator Monis told the Lindt Cafe manager

Tori Johnson to call the emergency number 000 and pass on the message that "Australia is under attack by Islamic State". For this report on the Sydney siege, *The Australian* chose the sensationalist headline on its front page "Australia is Under Attack by Islamic State" (continued on p. 6). *The Advertiser* published a similar report but it chose a different headline, "Executed in the Act of Cold-Blooded Evil", on pages 4 and 5. In the same issue, there was another headline in *The Australian*, "Islamic State Vows to Kill Pilot" (p. 7). It reported that Islamic State militants vowed to execute a Jordanian pilot if an Iraqi woman on death row in Jordan was not handed over.

The later reporting (p. 7) was relevant with an appropriate headline on the Islamic State. But the choice of words "Islamic State" to report on the Sydney siege is questionable because the perpetrator Monis was a lone wolf with no connection to the Islamic State. *The Australian*'s constant headlines on the Islamic State could scare readers on the one hand and, on the other, terrorists want publicity, and the newspaper provided it.

Islam/Muslims Labelled

On 9 August 2014 on page 8, under the headline "We'll Fight Islam 100 Years", *The Australian* reported Defence and Strategic Analyst Peter Leahy's comments that Australia should prepare itself for a 100-year war against radical Islam that will be fought at home and in foreign lands. On 11 August 2014 on page 1, there were images of Australian-born Khaled Sharrouf, aged 23, and allegedly his 7-year old son holding a decapitated head and machine guns. On page 2, under the headlines "Ex-army Chief's Call to Arms Rejected" and "Muslims Slam 100-Year War Call", it reported that Islamic community leaders and the Labor Party had criticized Peter Leahy's provocative warning as "ludicrous, inflammatory and counter-productive". Muslim leaders said that young Muslims may think that the community does not want them. It will push young Muslims further away. There was another news article on page 2 concerning the persecution of Christians in the Islamic State of Iraq. It reported that there used to be a million Christians in Iraq and now there are around 100,000 left.[24]

The news on Muslims/Islam/radical Islam, Khaled Sharrouf's son holding a severed head and machine guns, and the persecution of Christians in Iraq sparked concerns from some readers. This was expressed on the letters page under the headline "Photo Showed the Reality of Islamist Behaviour" on 12 August 2014, page 13. Letter 1 had a demanding tone: "Muslims throughout the world must make every effort to dissociate themselves from these fanatical Islamists ... Those who hijack Islam or any other religion for wicked purposes have no place in *our* society". Letter 2 appeared sarcastic: "I await with interest Islam's reaction to the photo of one of its young adherents proudly holding the severed head ... the religion of peace".

Letter 3 provided an ultimatum, "Until Muslims learn to live in this century instead of the seventh, and come to terms with democracy, their objections to *our* defence against the enemy within and without will be treated in the manner it deserves". The reader continued, "Of course, if they don't care to live in the country that gave them shelter, they have a recourse". Letters 4 and 5 were critical of Muslims' silence: "If there are any moderate Muslims in Australia, where are they? They should be screaming at radicals to stop". Letter 5: "It's time to stop pussy-footing around with the Muslim community. Muslims should stand up and condemn the atrocities".[25]

Interestingly, the letter that needed to be highlighted on the letters page with a bigger headline on 12 August 2014 should have been Peter Leahy's letter where he clarified that his concern was only with radical Islam. Leahy also said that *The Australian*'s headline "We'll Fight Islam 100 Years" (9 August) had totally misrepresented his views.[26]

A similar tone of labelling all Muslims as the "Other" appeared in *The Advertiser* after Numan Haider's case in Melbourne. But the rhetoric in the letters pages on 25 and 26 September 2014, page 22, focused on Muslim parents and integration. Letter 1 blamed Muslim parents: "Why are Muslim parents in Australia allowing their sons and daughters to be instructed in the poisonous distortion of their religion?" Letter 2 pointed out that Muslims do not integrate: "The main reason Muslims have not integrated is that they are forbidden to intermarry". Letter 3 raised doubts about Australian Muslims' loyalty: "The fact that Australian girls could be sent overseas to marry Islamic extremists raises two points. First, are they true Australians? Second, why the hell doesn't this country demand that to live here abide by *our* rules?"

Analyst Richardson observed that letters are usually written in response to previous articles in the newspapers. Letters are normally published on the basis of the "arguer, audience and argument", which serves the purpose of both the producer (the press) and the consumers (readers).²⁷ Wahl-Jorgenson found that editors apply four rules to select letters for publication: brevity (direct and to the point), relevance (on current events), entertainment (involving emotions), and authority (from cultural capital authority).²⁸ So if the newspapers choose to highlight issues involving Muslims, then it is obvious that readers will respond from their emotions and cultural capital.

Terror Raid Controversy

After the September 2014 terror raids, some letters published in *The Australian* on 19 September 2014 implied that Muslims are a problem and they do not integrate. They criticized Muslims who rallied against the terror raids.²⁹ Over the next few days, the letters page in *The Australian* had a similar tone. *The Australian* also published a letter by a Muslim woman, Naureen Choudhry, who was critical of Islamists. Two readers appreciated Naureen for her outspoken stance.³⁰ On 24 September 2014 on page 16, two readers in *The Advertiser* were critical of the ABC television show *Q&A*, stating that ABC presenter Tony Jones had given a lot of time to "Muslim women" and "Muslims" who were critical of the heavy-handedness of the terror raids.

Western democratic societies cherish their liberty of freedom of speech but when some Muslims exercise their rights of protest or freedom of speech in criticizing government policies it is frowned upon by some members of the wider society (also exemplified by the readers of *The Advertiser*).

Burka Controversy

The *burka* controversy once again brought out attitudes of "us" and "them". In *The Australian*, two readers commenting on the *burka* referred to assimilation and integration, for example, "'when in Rome' adage" and "We should liberate newcomers to Australia by inclusion and assimilation".³¹ On 25 September 2014 on page 22, one reader in *The Advertiser* used the label "*Sharia*" and supported Jacqui Lambie's statement, stating, "Senator Lambie says that those who wish to impose sharia in Australia should pack their bags and leave the country. She is quite right but too generous – I would actually urge deportation". The *burka* controversy continued in *The Advertiser* for some time; however, there were also some positive comments, such as from one reader who said,

"Stop vilifying Muslim women for their choice of clothing". This reader asked the parliament to introduce a "hi-tech ID method" for security.[32]

Christians' Versus Muslims Dichotomy

In August 2014, after news of beheadings by the Islamic State, Muslims were criticized by a number of readers. For example, a reader in *The Australian* commented, "The Muslim faith calls on its followers to spread Islam and its teachings and to despise and enslave those who do not recognise the rule of Allah ... It is written in the Koran, the manual Islamists use to guide their lives".[33] Another reader said that though he was an atheist he found in the Bible "some concepts of love". He questioned, "A reading of the Koran provides me no such references. When will the Muslims get their new testament?"[34] After the terror raid in September 2014, there was mention on the letter page of *The Australian* that the Quran "is not open to historical criticism in the same way that the Bible has been".[35] One reader commented, "Jesus commands his followers to belief and repentance, good works and love. This is why we don't have terrorist threats from Christians. But we have plenty from Islamists".[36]

After the *Charlie Hebdo* incident, on 16 January 2015 Muslims were again mentioned in *The Australian*. One reader was critical of Muslims for being too sensitive about the cartoon of Prophet Muhammad (PBUH). He argued that "the Koran was written about 300 years after Mohammed died, so no one who wrote this holy book would have known what his face looked like".[37] So how could Muslims react to the sketch of a man with a turban and a beard?[38] A few days later, another reader was critical of Saudi Arabia. He asked if Jews lived safe and free in Saudi Arabia or whether Christianity was allowed the freedom that Islam has in Christian countries, and if women will ever have equal rights.[39]

A similar critical tone appeared in *The Advertiser*. On 13 November 2014 on page 22, the editorial of *The Advertiser*, "Crusaders Set Example of National Spirit", praised Dr Gill Hicks for her determination to work with the Muslim communities in New South Wales and Victoria and find an alternative narrative to the jihadist rhetoric used by the Islamic State to recruit young people. At the 7/7 London bombings, Dr Hicks luckily survived though she lost both her legs. While the content of the editorial was positive, the use of the word "Crusader" in the headline implied that Christianity is superior.

On 22 December 2014 on page 18, a reader in *The Advertiser* mentioned how under the banner of religion 2 innocent lives in Sydney and 132 children's lives in Pakistan were lost. He did not mention Islam, but he was referring to the Martin Place siege and a Taliban attack on a school in Pakistan. He also said that Australia's refugee policy was highly questionable. He asserted, "It's about time we re-read the Ten Commandments". Another reader was critical of Islam as a "religion of peace" given the many atrocities committed by Muslim extremists, for example, in Nigeria and Pakistan. Also, "millions of Muslims are welcomed into so-called Christian countries and receive benefits there, in the Middle East (and elsewhere) where Islam rules, millions of Christians ... have been persecuted, murdered, and expelled by ISIS ... from their homeland for many centuries".

On 24 December 2014 on page 20, one reader in *The Advertiser* indicated his view that Islam is the worst religion compared to other religions or groups when he said that "perverted Christianity has killed between 1 and 3 million people from the Crusades to the IRA, black oppression, etc.". But over the same period people killed "in the name of mainstream Islam ... 80 million Hindus, 60 million Christians". He continued, "Purchase a copy of the Qur'an and a copy of the Bible. Read, compare, and ask yourself: 'which is the religion of love?' and 'which is the religion of misogyny, intolerance and incitement to violence'? The answers are pretty obvious".

The *Charlie Hebdo* killings brought out emotions in both newspapers. On 12 January 2015 on page 16, a reader of *The Advertiser* was critical of the silence of Muslim leaders over the "acts of indiscriminate murder of innocent men, women and children in the name of Allah and his prophet Mohammed". On 15 January 2015 on page 20, another reader doubted if Islam was a religion of peace when he said, "The Koran contains readings that justify the believer's violence towards non-Muslims, who are considered infidels". He also provided the example of Boko Haram in Nigeria. Other comments published on 16 January 2015 on page 24 included "Islam is in desperate need of enlightenment".

Positive/Rational Coverage

There has been some positive media coverage of Muslims in Australia. For example, during the *burka* controversy, one reader wrote to *The Australian* about her experiences during her teaching career, noting that all Muslim students she met were "polite, respectful, hardworking, modest, pious and grateful for the opportunity to learn. They are a wonderful example to the whole school community".[40] An even more positive tone appeared in *The Advertiser*. For example, after the Sydney siege, an article in *The Advertiser* praised the "#illridewithyou" campaign, initiated by non-Muslim Australians, which went viral. Many Australians offered to accompany Muslims in public places to protect them from a possible backlash. The campaign was also critical of the "Idiot racists who predictably – flooded online to blame all Muslims for the actions of one abhorrent man".[41] *The Advertiser* also published a letter from a Muslim woman who was appreciative of the Australian society's support in the wake of the Sydney siege. She wrote, "There was no 'us versus them' rhetoric. Instead, Muslim Australians have been made to feel valued as members of the same Australian family".[42]

Some readers of *The Advertiser* wrote letters that were considered and rational in tone. For example, one reader was critical of conservative columnist Andrew Bolt and reminded him of the Muslim victims of atrocities carried out by non-Muslims such as Buddhists in Myanmar, Hindus during the 2002 Gujarat riots, Orthodox Jews in Israel, and born-again Christians in the United States.[43] Another reader asked society to stop demonizing Muslims. They reminded other readers that extremism in Ireland, the IRA, the Ulster Defence Force and the Rev Ian Paisley were never about religion, but always about power and money.[44]

After the *Charlie Hebdo* incident a reader in *The Advertiser* was critical of "misguided Muslims" who were doing "exactly the opposite of the Koran's teachings".[45] Referring to the cartoon showing Prophet Muhammad (PBUH) weeping after the *Charlie Hebdo* killings, a reader said Prophet Muhammad (PBUH) must have wept because of what "those terrorists, extremists posing as Muslims, are doing to the religion he created".[46]

Discussion

My research on *The Australian* and *The Advertiser* from August 2014 to January 2015 found that *The Australian* had more coverage on Muslim-related topics than *The Advertiser* (see Table 6.1). Both newspapers are publications of News Corp Australia. *The Australian*, being the national broadsheet newspaper, is likely to incorporate more national and international news coverage. But *The Australian*'s readership is a much smaller proportion of its target audience than *The Advertiser*'s (Table 6.2). For commercial reasons, *The Australian* may have been desperate to increase its sales and readership through sensationalist news about Muslims.

It is important that the news media keeps its readers updated on world events, but sensationalist news can create fear among its readers. It can thereby generate Islamophobia at the societal level as revealed by the readers' letters to the editors.[47] That Islamophobia can have an impact on the already marginalized young Muslim Australians. Studies have found that radical Muslims are generally more dissatisfied with life, more preoccupied with international conflicts affecting Muslim countries, lonelier, more likely to have experienced discrimination, and less trustful of the media.[48] As discussed earlier that radicalization can be driven and sustained by multiple factors. Causal factors include broad grievances, for example Islamophobia, that "push" individuals towards a radical ideology and more specific "pull" factors such as the message of welcome from the radical groups that attract them.[49] Foy observed that the Islamic State through its online *Dabiq* magazine has been constantly sending information to its (Muslim) readers alleging that Western governments do not help their Muslim citizens in times of crises.[50]

Richardson observed that both the media and politicians are giving terrorists what they desire most: "three Rs: Revenge, Renown, Reaction".[51] When the media publicizes terrorist acts, it gives the terrorists both reaction and renown. While examining the Western media coverage of the Islamic State, Williams observed that the Islamic State is desperate to recruit young Muslims from Western countries. The Western media's reporting of news about the Islamic State (through headlines and images) has been instilling fear among the mainstream population, leading to Islamophobia and division between Muslims and non-Muslims.[52] Williams suggested that the Western media should use less sensationalist and divisive rhetoric, including when reporting the views of political leaders and media representatives. Williams noted that the Western media should exercise restraint in its reporting, like the *Guardian* newspaper, which has taken a stance not to glamorize perpetrators of terrorism through videos and inflammatory rhetoric.[53]

Yet the conventional reporting of the Australian print media continued. A recent research on five Australian newspapers in the entire year of 2017 found that almost 3000 articles associated Islam or Muslim with words such as violence, extremism, terrorism or radical. As a usual practice, *The Australian* had far more negative coverage on Islam on its front page compared to *The Advertiser*. Analyst observed that *The Australian's* media talk about Islam and Muslim is "disproportionate, divisive and dangerous". Therefore, there is a need for ethical journalism.[54]

Conclusion

In this chapter, I have examined whether the print media is Islamophobic and if its sensationalist representation of Muslim news can serve Islamic State propaganda. I conclude that the selective representation of news and images by *The Australian* (as compared to the *Advertiser*) can be considered Islamophobic. The media's sensationalist representation of Muslim news or Islamic State news creates further division between Muslims and non-Muslims (as revealed in the letters page). It reinforces Islamic State propaganda which is trying to recruit young Muslims by saying that Western governments "do not care" and "turn their back" on their own (Muslim) citizens.[55]

In this chapter and in my other studies on young Australian, British and American Muslims, I found Muslim youth and young adults were frustrated with the Western media's representation of Islam and Muslims. If Islamophobic reporting in the news media continues, there will be further social division, which will make young Muslims feel more marginalized and unsupported in Australia. This will make them more willing to listen to the appeals of the Islamic State. The Islamic State is desperate to recruit young Muslims, and Islamophobic media coverage is making young Australian Muslims more inclined to abandon their host country and join the Islamic State or other radical groups that make them feel welcome at least on the surface. By supporting or joining radical groups such as the Islamic State, marginalized Muslim youths may think that they can fight against the injustices of the West. Therefore, the sensationalist representation of Muslim news is inadvertently serving Islamic State propaganda.

Notes

1. See Australian Bureau of Statistics, 2016 Census: Religion, June 27, 2017, Media Release, http://www.abs.gov.au, accessed March 28, 2018.
2. Nahid Kabir, *Muslims in Australia: Immigration, Race Relations and Cultural History* (London: Routledge, 2005).

3. Nahid Kabir, "Media is One-Sided in Australia: The Muslim Youth Perspective," *Journal of Children and Media* 2, no. 3 (2008): 267–281.
4. US Department of State, "Ethnic Cleansing in Kosovo: An Accounting," 1999, http://www.state.gov/, accessed March 28, 2018.
5. Zachariah Matthews, "The Media and Islamophobia in Australia" in Islamophobia in Australia (Report), ed. Derya Iner (Charles Sturt University 2017), pp. 27–36; Peter Gottschalk and Gabriel Greenberg, "From Muhammad to Obama: Caricatures, Cartoons, and Stereotypes of Muslims," in *Islamophobia: The Challenge of Pluralism in the 21st Century*, ed. John L. Esposito and Ibrahim Kalin (New York: Oxford University Press, 2011), pp. 191–209; Saifuddin Ahmed and Jorg Matthes, "Media Representation of Muslims and Islam from 2000 to 2015: A Meta-Analysis," *The International Communication Gazette* 79, no. 3 (2017): 219–244; and Jacqui Ewart, Adrian Cherney, and Kristina Murphy, "News Media Coverage of Islam and Muslims in Australia: An Opinion Survey Among Australian Muslims," *Journal of Muslim Minority Affairs* 37, no. 2 (2017): 147–163.
6. Nahid Kabir, "Representation of Islam and Muslims in the Australian Media, 2001–2005," *Journal of Muslim Minority Affairs* 26, no. 3 (2006): 313–328; Nahid Afrose Kabir, *Young British Muslims: Identity, Culture, Politics and the Media* (Edinburgh: Edinburgh University Press, 2012), pp. 112–142; Nahid Afrose Kabir, *Young American Muslims: Dynamics of Identity* (Edinburgh: Edinburgh University Press, 2014), pp. 114–147; and Nahid Afrose Kabir, *Muslim Americans: Debating the Notions of American and Un-American* (London: Routledge, 2017), pp. 119–154.
7. Andrew Shryock, ed., *Islamophobia/Islamophilia: Beyond the Politics of Enemy and Friend* (Bloomington, IN: Indiana University Press, 2010), p. 2.
8. Randy Borum, "Radicalization into Violent Extremism II: A Review of Conceptual Models and Empirical Research," *Journal of Strategic Security* 4, no. 4 (2011): 37–62, see pp. 54–57.
9. Marco Goli and Shahamak Rezaei, *House of War: Islamic Radicalisation in Denmark* (Aarhus, Denmark: Centre for Studies in Islamism and Radicalisation, Aarhus University), accessed March 28, 2018, http://pure.au.dk/portal/files/32769733/Rapport_2FINAL.pdf.
10. John E. Richardson, *Analysing Newspapers: An Approach from Critical Discourse Analysis* (New York: Palgrave Macmillan, 2007); Nathan Young, "Working the Fringes: The Role of Letters to the Editor in Advancing Non-Standard Media Narratives About Climate Change," *Public Understanding of Science* 22, no. 4 (2013): 1–17.
11. Cameron Stewart, "Half of All Terrorists Hit by Citizenship Changes," *The Weekend Australian*, June 6–7, 2015, p. 1.

12. "Islamic Council Pulls Out of Talks," *The Advocate*, August 20, 2014, p. 15.
13. Editorial, "Burka Debate a Sideshow to Serious Security Issues," *The Australian*, October 3, 2014, p. 15.
14. Tory Shepherd, "Parliament's 'Bigoted' Burqa Box Condemned," *The Advertiser*, October 3, 2014, p. 4.
15. *The Australian*, September 12, 2014, p. 6.
16. Paul Maley and Dan Box, "Islamic State Horror Hits Home," *The Australian*, September 19, 2014, p. 1.
17. Randa Abdel-Fattah, "Be Alert But Not Alarmed," *Q&A*, Australian Broadcasting Corporation, September 22, 2014.
18. Tory Shepherd, "Free to Wear This Head Dress—But Only Behind Glass," *The Advertiser*, October 3, 2014, p. 1; "PM Urges Rethink on Burka 'Segregation,'" *The Advertiser*, October 3, 2014, p. 1.
19. Tony Allen-Mills, "'Nice' Muslim Boy Who Helped Shoppers Hide," *The Australian*, January 12, 2015, p. 6.
20. "Coulibaly's Wife Reported to Have Crossed into Syria," *The Australian*, January 12, 2015, p. 6.
21. Matthew Knott and Lucy Battersby, "Huge Demand for Hebdo Special Issue," *Canberra Times*, January 14, 2015, p. 5.
22. *The Australian*, January 16, 2015, p. 7.
23. Pia Akerman, "Muslim Community Splits Over Leader's Defence of Mag," *The Australian*, January 17, 2015, p. 8.
24. Gina Rushton, "Christian Exodus as Radicals Attack," *The Australian*, August 11, 2014, p. 2.
25. Last post, Letters to the Editor, *The Australian*, August 12, 2014, p. 13.
26. Peter Leahy, "Leahy's Concern is Solely with the Radical Islamists," Letters to the Editor, *The Australian*, August 12, 2014, p. 13.
27. John E. Richardson, *Analysing Newspapers: An Approach from Critical Discourse Analysis* (New York: Palgrave Macmillan, 2007), pp. 151–176.
28. Karin Wahl-Jorgenson, "Understanding the Conditions for Public Discourse: Four Rules for Selecting Letters to the Editor," *Journalism Studies* 3, no. 1 (2002): 69–81.
29. Letters to the Editor, "Muslim Countries Are Most at Risk from Islamists," *The Australian*, September 19, 2014, p. 15.
30. Letters to the Editor, *The Australian*, September 22 and 23, 2014, pp. 11, 13.
31. "Wearing the Burka Inhibits Inclusion and Assimilation," Letters to the Editor, *The Australian*, October 8, 2014, p. 11.
32. "Text Talk," *The Advertiser*, October 8, 2014, p. 8.
33. "Where Is the Aid from Wealthy Muslim Nations?," Letters to the Editor, *The Australian*, August 15, 2014, p. 11.
34. "Last Post," Letters to the Editor, *The Australian*, August 15, 2014, p. 11.

35. "Muslim Countries Are Most Risk from Islamists," Letters to the Editor, *The Australian*, September 19, 2014, p. 15.
36. "Perpetrators Should Not Be Portrayed as Victims," Letters to the Editor, *The Australian*, September 25, 2014, p. 13.
37. "Religion and Ethnicity Should Be Kept Separate," Letters to the Editor, *The Australian*, January 16, 2015, p. 11.
38. Ibid.
39. "Soft on Saudi Arabia," Letters to the Editor, *The Australian*, January 28, 2015, p. 11.
40. "Last Post," *The Australian*, October 2, 2014, p. 13.
41. Tory Shepherd, "There is a Clear Connection Between Poverty, Conflict-Riven States and Terrorism," *The Advertiser*, December 17, 2014, p. 24.
42. Letters to the Editor, *The Advertiser*, December 18, 2014, p. 22.
43. Ibid.
44. Letters to the Editor, *The Advertiser*, December 24, 2014, p. 20.
45. Letters to the Editor, *The Advertiser*, January 14, 2015, p. 16.
46. Ibid.
47. Iner, ed., Islamophobia in Australia, op. cit.
48. Goli and Rezaei, *House of War*, op. cit.
49. Randy Borum, "Radicalization into Violent Extremism II," op. cit. p. 57.
50. Kelli Foy, "Framing Hostage Negotiations: Analysing the Discourse of the US Government and the Islamic State," *Critical Studies on Terrorism*, 8, no. 3 (2015): 516–531, see pp. 522–523.
51. Louise Richardson, *What Terrorists Want: Understanding the Threat* (London: John Murray Publishers, 2006), pp. 95–132.
52. Lauren Williams, Islamic State Propaganda and the Mainstream Media, Report (Sydney: Lowy Institute, 2016), p. 6.
53. Ibid., p. 8.
54. *Islam in the Media 2017* (One Path Network.com), February 18, 2018, pp. 6 and 21.
55. Kelli Foy, "Framing Hostage Negotiations: Analysing the Discourse of the US Government and the Islamic State," *Critical Studies on Terrorism*, 8, no. 3 (2015): 516–531, see p. 522

CHAPTER 7

Muslim Civil Society Under Attack: The European Foundation for Democracy's Role in Defaming and Delegitimizing Muslim Civil Society

Farid Hafez

This article deals with the impact of one of the main drivers of what has been called the "Organized Islamophobia Network" (OIN) in the USA or "Islamophobic elite movements from above". It is one of the first studies to look at European based think tanks and their role in defining and excluding Muslim civil society organizations. It specifically looks at how the Brussels-based think tank "European Foundation for Democracy" (EFD), which has a transatlantic relationship, systematically produces knowledge to define vocal and representative actors of the Muslim civil society as potentially radical and Islamist, which then should lead to state and civil society exclusion. The strategy of constructing Muslim Brotherhood-affiliations to the aforementioned actors is analyzed as part of a larger strategy of defamation and delegitimization. Two cases, Austria and Sweden, are analyzed in detail.

F. Hafez (✉)
University of Salzburg, Salzburg, Austria
e-mail: farid.hafez@sbg.ac.at

F. Hafez
The Bridge Initiative, Georgetown University, Washington, DC, USA

© The Author(s) 2019
J. L. Esposito and D. Iner (eds.), *Islamophobia and Radicalization*,
https://doi.org/10.1007/978-3-319-95237-6_7

Islamophobic Social Movements from Above

The analysis of think tanks in the production and dissemination of Islamophobia has for a long time been focused mainly on the USA. The Center for American Progress analyzed what has later become known as the "Islamophobia Network" in 2011[1] and 2015.[2] These and other analyzes[3] were primarily focusing on the network that fuels Islamophobia and their respective funding structures. Nothing similarly comprehensive has been produced for Europe so far. One of the reasons for this might be that while in the United States with a weak federal government, philanthropy has a long tradition and is crucial also for the political landscape, domestically as much as for international affairs, think tanks play a significant weaker role in Europe, although one might argue that their relevance is increasing.

The first attempt to fill this gap has been the collective work edited by Narzanin Massoumi, Tom Mills and David Miller.[4] In their critique of some of the literature of Islamophobia Studies, they propose to shift the focus for understanding Islamophobia to what they call the "five pillars of Islamophobia", which represent five social actors or five social movements that produce ideas and practices that disadvantage Muslims: the state, neoconservative movements, parts of the Zionist movements, the counterjihad movement[5] and the far right, as well as elements of liberal, left, secular and feminist movements.[6] Their theoretical contribution lies in making social movement theory fruitful in understanding these five driving factors of Islamophobia. While the US reports were primarily produced for policy making and advocacy, Massoumi et al. offer a much more theory-based work that also mentions European think tanks, but does not offer an in-depth analysis of their work.

Next to the state, which for them makes the "backbone" of Islamophobia, Massoumi et al. see elite social movements or movements from above as groups that try to influence state policies and bring about change in accordance with the ideologies around which they cohere. Their elitism is reflected in their privileged access to political decision-making and financial resources. They remind us that while most of the social movement theory literature focuses on movements from below, the analysis of elite movements is sparse.[7]

As part of the neoconservative movement, they identify think tanks as "elite elements of social movements from above"[8] and argue that it is them, who are playing a key role in the production of Islamophobia in the UK and elsewhere. Massoumi et al. suggest—drawing on scholarship by Cox and Nilsen as well as Boies and Pichardo—turning our attention to four questions to differentiate between "social movements from below" and "from above": (1) Their emergence, meaning "from what milieu, social and political struggles, crises"[9] these movements emerged. (2) Their organizational form and political location, meaning if they are movements on the streets or in the corridors of power, their membership structure. (3) Their strategy and goals and (4) The outcomes, meaning intended as well as unintended outcomes.[10]

In this article I intend to present a first analysis of the Brussels-based think tank EFD and the role of its team in defining the landscape of organized Muslim civil society actors. The next section connects the work at hand to the existing scholarship and is followed by a short description of the EFD. Then, I turn to an analysis of the EFD's team in their endeavor to defame and delegitimize Muslim civil society actors, before I turn to a more detailed analysis of two cases, Austria and Sweden. The last section gives an overview of the conclusions.

A Transatlantic Network

While the transatlantic exchange, especially in case of the so-called counterjihad movement, a movement that dedicates itself to countering an alleged "Islamization of the West"[11] and the far-right political parties and movements[12] have been analyzed in many works, there is not much literature dedicated to Islamophobic think tanks. Sarah Marusek has offered a first study in Massoumi et al. on the transatlantic Islamophobic network.[13] Marusek searched through the annual tax documents of registered charities and foundations in the United States and UK to understand the funding of these organizations, while putting emphasis on the US funders of these institutions. In her analysis, the Foundation for Defense of Democracy (FDD) ranks among the ten most influential in media and policy debates. According to the Center for American Progress, Anchorage Charitable Foundation and William Rosenwald Family Fund, which gave a total of $2,818,229 from 2001 to 2008, and is thus among the top seven funders of the Islamophobia Network.[14] Amongst its recipients is the FDD, together with the Hoover Institution, the Hudson Institute, the American Enterprise Institute, and the Jewish Institute for National Security Affairs. The director of the Future Terrorism Project at FDD in D.C. was its senior fellow Walid

Phares, who also acts as an "expert" lecturer on "Islamist Jihadism" for the Centre for Counterintelligence and Security Studies. Phares was a spokesman for the mostly Christian Lebanese Front, which was responsible for the Sabra and Shatila massacres of Muslims during the September 1982 Lebanese Civil War.[15]

Amongst the think tanks that are funded by the same persons that fund these neoconservative think tanks outside of the USA, she mentions the EFD in Brussels, the Henry Jackson Society (HJS) in London, NGO Monitor in Jerusalem and UN Watch in Geneva.[16] While Marusek does not argue that all of these organizations are peddling an Islamophobic agenda, she argues that their shared funders suggest a shared milieu. She states that the Washington D.C.-based FDD has organizational as well as financial ties to the EFD. Marusek quotes Eli Clifton, who called the FDD "Washington's premiere hawkish think tank".[17] There are numerous relations between central persons of the FDD and the Islamophobic network that produce and disseminate Islamophobia such as the HJS, Nina Rosenwald, R. James Woolsey and Matthew Levit, as Marusek reveals in her analysis.[18]

Between 2009 and 2013, Marcus Foundation gave $12,155,000 to different organizations, amongst them the EFD. The EFD was also granted funds by Paul E. Singer Foundation, which gave a total of $1,475,000 to EFD, NGO Monitor as well as the highly Islamophobic MEMRI.[19] Singer is listed as the second largest conservative donor in the United States and gave a total of $23.5 million to Republican causes in 2016, while Marcus gave a total of $13.5 million.[20] While many donors of Israeli settlement do not donate to Islamophobic networks, Marcus and Singer fund both.[21] Bernard Marcus, who funds both occupation and/or settlement, serves as director of the FDD. In 1991 Marcus co-founded the Israel Democracy Institute.[22]

European Foundation for Democracy's Islamophobes

The EFD was founded by Roberta Bonazzi in 2005. A political scientist, her personal expertise focuses on prevention of radicalization, foreign policy, democratic reforms and extremism.[23] She is linked to conservative personalities such as of the National Review.[24] The EFD describes itself as a policy institute that works with civil society, academic, government and other stakeholders on the "prevention of radicalization".[25] Beyond conferences, panel debates, workshops, policy briefings, advocacy work and publications, the EFD has also established a "Network for a New European Generation" to empower leaders who are working with—and within—communities of Muslim heritage in Europe to engage in radicalization prevention initiatives. Affiliates are from France, Italy, Germany, Sweden, the UK and Ireland.[26]

Amongst its team, there range numerous so-called "experts" on radicalization of Muslims. Switzerland-based Elham Manea, Italy-based Valentina Colombo, US-based Lorenzo Vidino, Germany-based Ahmad Mansour, Sweden-based Magnus Norell, amongst others. Some of them will be featured in the case studies. A central aim of the experts, who are widely interviewed and featured in international media across Europe, is to warn of not only violent extremism, but what they call "non-violent extremism". During the panel "Antidotes to Islamist Extremism" at the European Parliament on May 2, 2017, director Bonazzi explained this approach: According to her, the "key challenge" in the work with Muslim civil society is to "identify the right partners". She argued: "For too long, we have seen the wrong organizations being empowered being funded by national governments and European institutions […] For too long we have seen that ideological groups have become the official representatives […] ignoring the diversity we have within Islam […] Some ideological organizations have taken over the whole debate".[27] As a consequence, she opts for better screening and vetting of these Muslim organizations. This is part of a larger tendency of the War on Terror and the subsequent introduction of countering extremism programs, where a broadening of the notion of terrorism encapsulates non-violent extremism.[28] With Salman Sayyid's introduction of a post-positivist, post-orientalist, and decolonial perspective on Islamophobia,[29] the latter is less about the essentialist concepts that are used to describe them than the challenge of being Muslim today is that there is no epistemological or political space for the identity.[30] In this reading, Islamophobia is a form of epistemological racism, as another decolonial thinker, Ramón Grosfoguel, argues.[31] For Sayyid, central to Islamophobia is to discipline and regulate the Muslim subject, which is construed as posing a threat to the political order and especially white privilege. Hence, ,the Muslim question', which is being construed by Western political actors, is paving the way for cultural, governmental, and epistemological interventions[32] Through these lenses, I argue, the War on Terror or Countering Extremism-programs can all be seen as a means to narrow the space in which it is possible to be Muslim.

Defaming and Delegitimating Active Muslim Citizenship: The "Muslim Brotherhood"-Allegation

In an analysis of two Muslim civil society organizations in the UK, Shenaz Bunglawala shows how the state deployed offensive and defensive strategies to expand and maintain the position of domination and subsequently mark these organizations as illegitimate. Bunglawala argues:

> If earlier counter-terrorism strategies were marked by a focus on violent extremism and the conferring by the state of 'legitimacy' on Muslim civil society actors through (dis)engagement, the current drive to tackle 'non-violent extremism' and the expansion of the state's repertoire of disciplinary measures has left Muslim civil society actors not merely struggling to assert 'contested' practice but to engage in contestation at all.[33]

One possible means to exclude Muslim organizations from the field of civil society is to mark them as supporting non-violent extremism or representing or even being affiliated with some political Islam/radical/Islamist groups or patterns of thought. Using these fuzzy notions that are elastic in their use, it is easy to quickly mark an oppositional organization as being a threat to the society. In the USA, conservative politicians such as Senator Ted Cruz introduced the "Muslim Brotherhood Terrorist Designation Act of 2017", although with little success. Most Washington D.C.-based think tanks argued against such a designation amongst others because it is legally difficult to argue for such a designation.[34] One reason is also, because many Muslim Brotherhood-affiliated political parties are participating in many parliaments in Muslim majority countries. According to then spokesman of the Council on American-Islamic Relations (CAIR), Corey Saylor, such an Act would have severe domestic impact: "The designation is more about domestic control of American Muslims than national security. It would open the gate to an anti-Muslim witch-hunt. As in the past, such a campaign would see witch-hunters smearing and defaming their political opposition and scapegoating an entire minority".[35] According to Arsalan Iftikhar, "Anti-Muslim activists and the Islamophobia industry have long used the 'Muslim Brotherhood' label as a very sloppy shorthand to refer to all American Muslim civic organizations, politicians and government officials with whom they disagree".[36] He reminds us that these labels were not only used against Muslim civil society actors, but indeed against

Muslim as well as Non-Muslim opponents to the conservatives. The most descriptive example is the US conservative Islamophobia network's campaign against Barack Obama in spreading the conspiracy theory that he was not only Muslim, but that he was planning to create a global caliphate together with the Muslim Brotherhood.[37] Similar to the conspiracy of a Jewish world domination, the usefulness of the alleged takeover of the world by the Muslim Brotherhood is that real facts are mixed with sheer imagination. Obviously, the Muslim Brotherhood is real and not an invention. And because it has become a global movement with strong as well as loose affiliations and impacted the Islamic discourse at large, it makes it easy to link any possible Muslim organization to them. While single Jewish families such as Rockefeller and Rothschild were in fact owning banks, this is neither a proof that every Jew takes part in a this wealth, nor is it a proof that these families rule the world as it is claimed by anti-Semitic conspiracists. Similarly, while the Muslim Brotherhood is an influential organization that originated in Egypt has branches all over the world and its impact goes beyond its formal organization, it is neither a very powerful organization beyond few Muslim majority countries (and persecuted in many countries like Egypt), nor has it a strong hold in Europe. But it is real and this makes it easy for conspirators to use it for spreading theories about world domination attempts. These theories are so wide spread that even high government representatives such as the president of the Czech Republic, Milos Zeman, argued the influx of refugees into Europe in 2015 was masterminded by Egypt's Muslim Brotherhood.[38]

A trait of most of the experts of the EFD team is their focus on the Muslim Brotherhood and claiming its influence in nearly every Muslim Civil Organization that plays a significant role in the respective nation state. During the above mentioned event in the European Parliament with EFD director Roberta Bonazzi, many argued that so-called Salafists and the Muslim Brotherhood are "relevant examples, stressing that those share the same goals of ISIS, i.e. the creation of an Islamic state, only differing as to the means of achieving it".[39] This assertion allows for the widening of the Muslim threat, including not only violent extremists, but putting potentially every Muslim civil society organization under suspicion.

EFD senior fellow Valentina Colombo argues in an article published by the right-wing think tank "The Gatestone Institute" that the Muslim Brotherhood is even connected to terrorist organizations.[40] As she said in another piece: "Islamist movements have different tactics… but their goal is always the same: Get in and impose sharia law to establish an Islamic state".[41] And senior fellow Lorenzo Vidino already declared in 2005 before joining EFD in other conservative think tanks:

> What most European politicians fail to understand is that by meeting with radical organizations, they empower them and grant the Muslim Brotherhood legitimacy. There is an implied endorsement to any meeting, especially when the same politicians ignore moderate voices that do not have access to generous Saudi funding. This creates a self-perpetuating cycle of radicalization because the greater the political legitimacy of the Muslim Brotherhood, the more opportunity it and its proxy groups will have to influence and radicalize various European Muslim communities.[42]

Using again vague notions such as "radicalization", Vidino declares that Europe's leading Muslim civil society organizations all as connected to the Muslim Brotherhood. In another piece published by one of the conservative think tanks, Hudson Institute, Vidino concludes: "It is not unreasonable to assume, therefore, that should it become convenient for them to do so, the ever-flexible Brotherhood would embrace violent tactics in the West as well".[43]

Also, other EFD fellows regularly warn of a threat by Muslims by expanding the notion of "radical": In an op-ed in the center-right, liberal-conservative German newspaper *Frankfurter Allgemeine Zeitung (FAZ)*, Mansour argues that there are three groups of radicalization: At the top, it is Al Qaida and Daesh, followed by the Muslim Brotherhood including Erdogan, and then by the "Generation Allah", who might be prone to this radical version of Islam.[44] These "experts" regularly overstate f.i. when stating that a child wearing a headscarf is an "abuse" and calls for a general ban of the headscarf for pedagogues and teachers.[45] EFD fellow Mansour is also available to call to designate Muslim civil society actors—especially young and vocal ones—as radical and connected to MB ideology.[46]

A similar strategy can be found with the Italy-based EFD fellow Valentina Colombo. She regularly writes about the MB in Italy. If one believes her, the MB was "silently carrying out its invasion even in Milan's local election" in 2016, where a young Muslim, Maryan Ismail, ran for elections for the Milanese left.[47] She regularly warns of the alleged influence of the MB in Italy. According to her, "the Muslim Brotherhood is 'infiltrating' European societies in order to conquer the world ideologically and politically".[48] Hence, only the means, but not the goals would differ from Al Qaida or Daesh.

EFD fellow Colombo also argues in German newspapers that one of the most vocal and known Muslim representatives in media, Ayman Mazyek of the Zentralrat der Muslime would have an ideological affinity to the MB. She explains that the MB's aim is to seek power and fully integrate in the institutions and become a political reference.[49] Also EFD fellow Vidino gives his opinion on the MB in London,[50] the "Muslim world",[51] and the West in general.[52]

In the following section, I will show, what role EFD fellows play in the defamation strategies of Muslim civil societies and what patterns we can conclude from that based on two cases, Austria and Sweden.

CASE STUDIES

Austria

Austria is an interesting case to study, since it is a country with a genuine legal tradition of incorporating Islam as a religion and the respective Islamic Religious Community as an official religious community that serves as an interlocutor for the stare to take care of the affairs of Muslim religious lives. Hence, Austria was for a long time well known for its comparable tolerant church-state relation in regard to Muslims. Islam and the Islamic Religious Community were legally recognized in 1912. In 1979, the constitution of the Islamic Religious Community in Austria (*Islamische Glaubensgemeinschaft in Österreich*) was approved based on the recognition of Islam in 1912 and is today one of 17 legally recognized churches. As a consequence to this legal recognition, Islamic religious classes are provided in public school for Muslim pupils as is the case with other legally recognized churches. Also, the Islamic Religious Community has pastoral service in the military and prison. All of these services are organized by the Islamic Religious Community and funded by the state. Its representatives are regularly included in policy-making issues pertaining their religious life.[53] Since nearly all different strands of Islamic organizations are part of the Islamic Religious Community, Austria serves as an ideal example for a country with a tradition of great tolerance. Among them are also smaller Muslim Brotherhood-influenced

Arab organizations, while the majority of mostly but not only Turkish-origin organizations represent other institutions.[54]

But with the implementation of the new Islam Act in 2015, this legal framework from 1912 risked to become replaced by a new one that identified Muslims as a security threat and no more as an equal religious voice within the landscape of Austria's diverse religious communities. When the protest of the Muslim civil society started to form,[55] soon the opposition was declared "radical" by certain news media.[56] Amongst the most influential Muslim organizations next to the Islamic Religious Community is the Austrian Muslim Youth, an organization created in 1996 by young Muslims of different ethnicities, which shifted its focus on domestic issues of young people. Like with other youth organizations, the Austrian state with its highly institutionalized corporatism system funds its volunteer youth work. Also, the Austrian Muslim Youth is part of the Austrian Federal Youth Council and also elected amongst its leadership.[57] It traditionally had a communication channel to all political parties and was widely seen as a moderate voice of Muslims and progressive force fostering education, feminism, and political participation.

But after the government had published its draft for a new Islam Act in late 2014, and the Austrian Muslim Youth started a campaign consisting of several press conferences and a citizenship initiative that mobilized more than 20,000 voters against the new Act, media for the first time turned against them. The first attacks were clear in their message, but not openly definable in terms of the sources. Tabloid press headlined "Radicals Hijack Muslim Youth. Muslim Brotherhood out of Social Democrats. Hate Campaign against Islam Act".[58] The first articles mentioned that their informants would be "parts of the government" that would not want to be mentioned. Another tabloid press headlined "Instead of fighting Radicalisation. Uproar in Muslim youth because of Posting". Numerous such articles were spread following the protest organized by the youth organization.[59] But the most important role was played by a senior fellow of the EFD, Lorenzo Vidino. In an interview with the daily *Kurier* that argued that "there are hints that suggest that the Austrian Muslim Youth belongs to the Muslim Brotherhood", Vidino argued that "there are strong relations to people, who are influenced by the Muslim Brotherhood".[60] Therefore, Vidino sees the Austrian Muslim Youth as "ideologically within this milieu". At the same time he states that it is "difficult to characterize somebody simply as a Muslim Brother".[61] Based on this statement, numerous newspapers took the information and argued that the Austrian Muslim Youth had ideological and organizational relations to the Muslim Brotherhood. While in fact Vidino, who with his publication only said that the Austrian Muslim Youth had relations to people who in turn have relations to other people from the Muslim Brotherhood. But since Vidino, who is widely published on the Muslim Brotherhood especially in the West, including publication houses like Cambridge University Press, his statement is taken as one of an "expert".

While the Austrian Muslim Youth took legal action against most newspapers like weekly *Profil*, daily *Heute*,[62] and succeeded,[63] this statement of Vidino was hard to sue, since he never really said that the Austrian Muslim Youth was part of the Muslim Brotherhood, which the youth organization had spurned. Also, the proceedings took their time and some of them are still ongoing. Hence, the allegation against the Austrian Muslim Youth to be connected to the Muslim Brotherhood has been perpetuated again and again.

Shortly before the federal elections in October 2017, Lorenzo Vidino published a report entitled "The Muslim Brotherhood in Austria",[64] funded by the ministry of interior, the Austrian Integration Fund (basically an outsourced section of the ministry of integration and foreign affairs), the Federal Office for the Protection of the Constitution and the University of Vienna. Looking at these institutions, I argue that it was mainly an initiative supported by the Christian Conservative People's Party (ÖVP) under the leadership of the current chancellor Sebastian Kurz, who was also the main actor for the amended Islam Act of 2015. Kurz became famous for co-opting the anti-Muslim positions of the right-wing populist FPÖ like for instance claiming the general shut down of Muslim kindergartens.[65] In this report, Vidino accuses the most important Muslim voices as having "some ties to the Brotherhood". And the Brotherhood, according to him, endangers social cohesion, since it aims to create a "parallel society". Clearly, with Vidino's flexible definition of who belongs to the Brotherhood, not only are members named, but every potentially relevant Muslim activist in the broadest sense is potentially under attack, from the president of the Islamic Religious Community to the only Muslim member of the Viennese Council with a link to the Muslim community. More importantly, Vidino's report serves to target potentially every Muslim organization. While Vidino from a distance in Washington D.C. and Brussels is only giving hints, his commentators back in Austria are speaking out more openly to ban the Muslim Brotherhood in Europe and thus support investigation of anyone allegedly associated with this group.[66] With this broad definition, they clearly target most Muslim institutions and hence Islam itself. Since the report was published shortly before the elections on October 15 and was overshadowed by a journalist's investigation story on dirty campaigning,[67] there has been little obvious resonance to this report, which might still come, since the new coalition of the People's Party and the right-wing FPÖ has taken a harsher stance towards fighting "political Islam".[68]

Sweden

In Sweden, religious freedom has been guaranteed since 1951 in the Federal constitution. Muslims organize various welfare, religious and cultural activities under the laws of association. The Swedish Commission for Government Support to Religious Communities (SST) under the Ministry of Culture provides religious minorities with state funding in different categories. In 2008, there were five Muslim organisations that were provided by state funds from the federal government; the ISS (Islamiska Shia-Samfundeni Sverige—Islamic Shi'a Community of Sweden),[69] the oldest organisation, Förenade Islamiska Församlingari Sverige (Union of Islamic Congregations in Sweden, FIFS, which was set up in 1974,[70] a split off founded in 1982, the Swedish Muslim Union (Sveriges Muslimska Förbund, SMF). These two organizations are also cooperating under the roof of Swedish Islamic Religious Community (*Sveriges Muslimska Råd*, SMR). In the beginning of the 1980s, the Union of Islamic Cultural Centres (Islamiska Kulturcenterunionen, IKUS), which is influenced by the Süleymanci movement, was established. Also, the Swedish Islamic Assemblies (*Svenska Islamiska Församlingar*, SIF), established in 2002, is funded.[71] As in most other European countries, there also exist Muslim youth movements such as the most significant in Sweden, the Young Muslims of Sweden (Sveriges Unga Muslimer, SUM).[72] It receives funds from MUCF (Swedish Agency for Youth and Civil Society).[73] The SUM was founded in 1990 and is often seen as a promoter of what has been called a "Blue-and-Yellow" Islam (representing the colors of the Swedish national flag) encouraging Muslims to find ways to live their faith as Swedish people, while participating in the society.[74]

In Sweden, EFD senior fellow Magnus Norell published a similar report entitled "The Muslim Brotherhood in Sweden" together with Aje Carlbom and Pierre Durrani, the latter having a Bachelor degree and claiming to be a former member of the Muslim Brotherhood and thus claiming to possess "considerable inside information".[75] The report was published in February 2017 by the Swedish Civil Contingencies Agency (Myndigheten för samhällsskydd och beredskap, MSB), which is a Swedish administrative authority, organized under the Ministry of Defence and responsible for public safety, risk management and civil defense.[76]

The report was also published in English by the Clarion Project.[77] This is amongst the most Islamophobic think tanks with funding connections to the most Islamophobic actors such as Frank Gaffney and Daniel Pipes.[78] Based in New York City, the Clarion Project amongst others produced several anti-Muslim films like "Obsession: Radical Islam's War Against the West" and "The Third Jihad". The first was distributed to more than 28 million swing-state voters before the 2008 presidential election.

The report is based on a study held from November to December 2016. According to it, on one side the Muslim Brotherhood has infiltrated the Swedish society and its political parties since the 1970's, while on the other side, the authors argue that the MB strives to become the representatives of the Muslim minorities to the authorities. The authors assert that the MB is creating a "parallel society" to Islamize Sweden. Next to a detailed critique by Torbjörn Jerlerup,[79] 22 Swedish academic scholars in religious studies published a reaction to the report, in which they criticized it fundamentally as unserious.[80] According to them, the claim to see the MB as a "unified and organized, but secretive, powerful and 'spiritual brotherhood' with a clear political agenda" is lacking every empirical evidence. While—in contrast to the vast literature on the MB in general and the MB in Sweden—the organization is even characterized as an anti-democratic, violent and society-destructive organization, the authors also ignore intra-Muslim divisions and struggles. The critics do not argue that there "maybe individuals and maybe also organizations in Sweden who have sympathies with and/or direct links with the Muslim Brotherhood",[81] but see no value in the produced report. According to the report, many Muslim civil society organizations such as Studieförbundet Ibn Rushd, SMU, and Islamiska Förbundet i Sverige

(IFIS) are Swedish associations of the MB.[82] According to the authors, also the SMR[83] and the SMF are ideologically related to the MB.[84]

In other writings, Norell even goes several steps further in his assessment of the MB: "Segregation is promoted for the reason of maintaining control".[85] According to him, "the end-goal is the same whether you advocate a non-militant strategy (which the Brotherhood usually does in Europe) or a more militant activist strategy".[86] He argues that for the MB, it is important to establish "a parallel 'Islamic civil society' with its own schools, kindergartens, hospitals, cultural centers, mosques, and other types of institutions" referring to the notion of "a 'soft' apartheid-thinking that Muslims and non-Muslims should live in two different worlds". The dangerous consequences, which he derives from that is "decreased trust and social disintegration of society at large."[87]

While also serious scholars like Göran Larsson, who criticized the report, hold that some organizations like the SMF and the FIFS (both under SMR) are influenced in ideological terms by the Muslim Brotherhood movement,[88] the aimed policy impact as reflected in the writings of EFD scholar Norell is to exclude organized efforts of Muslims, the Muslim civil society landscape, in general from the political field. The state agency MSB quietly distanced itself by stating that "it does not back the report",[89] which did not qualify as "research".[90] Nevertheless, the Swedish Youth Agency MUCF rejected the SUM's application for government grants based on the "findings". Since grants can only be obtained if an organization respects democracy, MUCF declined SUM's proposal for 2017 due to its alleged "links with the Muslim Brotherhood". SUM took MUCF to court and in November, 2017, the Administrative Court of Appeal upheld SUM's complaint.[91]

Conclusion

Clearly, we can speak of the EFD as an elite social movement from above. As a think tank that is funded by wealthy donors, it emerges, and its followers are embedded, in a politically conservative milieu. EFD fellows are located in the corridors of power. Their experts produce knowledge for highly subsidized state institutions, as both case studies show. Hence, they obviously have a privileged access to political decision-making and financial resources, although one may argue that anti-racist organizations are also funded in different European countries such as Austria and Sweden. They intend to influence policy making on federal government level as well as in the European Union. While think tanks and philanthropy is less spread and developed in Europe compared to the US, it is surely interesting to further investigate if the significant role of think tanks in the production of Islamophobia can also be observed within other political fields or if this is a development sui generis.

In this article, I showed that the EFD as a Brussels-based think tank with transatlantic relations systematically produces knowledge about Muslims that follows a strategy of defamation and delegitimization. It especially draws on the allegation of a connection between visible Muslim civil society actors and the Muslim Brotherhood. The conspiracy lies not only in the construction of a connection, but rather in the accusation of a unified agenda of social destructiveness and world domination, a planned Islamization of Europe. To be clear: Neither is the Muslim Brotherhood a phantom or non-existent and of no impact. The Muslim Brotherhood—in ideological terms—is one of the most powerful Islamist organizations, but one that has also evolved around time and circumstances and is everything but static and homogenous. But I claim that the EFD fellows are not really interested in understanding the Muslim Brotherhood's impact, but are rather following a strategy of defamation and delegitimization of Muslim civil society organizations. Most of the attacked actors are not affiliated to the Muslim Brotherhood but are rather known to be the most vocal Muslim voice in media, important stakeholders, or often represent the younger generation that actively supports political participation and citizenship. It is an attempt by the Islamophobes to narrow down the epistemological and political space for the Muslim subject in European nation states or in the West at large.

As we can see, the discourse on terrorism and extremism/radicalism is used against vocal Muslims and organizations to dismantle, disable and discharge from the civic and political activism, because Islamophobia as a form of epistemological racism does not allow the Muslim subject to even have a voice. The only voices being heard are the "native informants",[92] who confirm and reproduce Islamophobia. When Muslim organizations are defamed and delegitimized, their space of action becomes severely reduced, as both cases reveal. In the Swedish case, the Swedish Agency for Youth and Civil Society stopped funding the Muslim youth organization following the publication of the report. In the Austrian case, media attacks on the Muslim youth organization impacted the way the organization could navigate following these accusations. Having to defend themselves and by that investing financial and human resources to challenge these allegations in court, media and political circles, they were interrupted in their civil society activism. There is a great need to provide more in-depth analyses on the role of think tanks in Europe regarding the role it plays in the production of Islamophobia and specifically in defamation and delegitimization of Muslim civil society actors. Also, the attempt to create an alternative Muslim identity by these think tanks, which I just implied but have not delved deeply in this article, is important to examine more.[93]

Notes

1. W. Ali, E. Clifton, M. Duss, L. Fang, S. Keyes, and F. Shakir, "Fear, Inc. The Roots of the Islamophobia Network in America," Center for American Progress, August 2011, https://cdn.americanprogress.org/wp-content/uploads/issues/2011/08/pdf/islamophobia.pdf.
2. M. Duss, Y. Taeb, K. Gude, and K. Sofer, "Fear, Inc. 2.0. The Islamophobia Network's Efforts to Manufacture Hate in America," Center for American Progress, February 2015, https://cdn.americanprogress.org/wp-content/uploads/2015/02/FearInc-report2.11.pdf.
3. Confronting Fear: Islamophobia and Its Impact in the U.S. 2013–2015, UC Berkeley, http://www.islamophobia.org/images/ConfrontingFear/Final-Report.pdf.
4. N. Massoumi, T. Mills, and D. Miller, *What Is Islamophobia? Racism, Social Movements, and the State* (London: Pluto Press, 2017).
5. The Counter-Jihad Movement is made up of mixed and disparate people and organisation who agree that the Western civilisation is under attack by Islam. Important counter-jihad organisations or anti-Muslim websites, news portals according to HOPE *not hate*. See N. Lowles and J. Muhall (2015). The Counter Jihad Movement, published by HOPE not HATE; L. Benjamin. "Why We Fight: Understanding the Counter-Jihad Movement." *Religion Compass* 10, no. 10 (2016): 257–265.
6. N. Massoumi, T. Mills, and D. Miller, "Islamophobia, Social Movements and the State: For a Movement-Centered Approach," in *What Is Islamophobia? Racism, Social Movements, and the State*, ed. N. Massoumi, T. Mills, and D. Miller (London: Pluto Press, 2017), 4.
7. Ibid., 17–19.
8. N. Massoumi, T. Mills, and D. Miller, "The Neoconservative Movement: Think Tanks as Elite Elements of Social Movements from Above," in *What Is Islamophobia? Racism, Social Movements, and the State*, ed. N. Massoumi, T. Mills, and D. Miller (London: Pluto Press, 2017), 215.
9. Ibid., 216.

10. Ibid.
11. T. Archer, "Breivik's Mindset: The Counterjihad and the New Transatlantic Anti-Muslim Right," in *Extreme Right Wing Political Violence and Terrorism*, eds. M. Taylor, P. M. Currie, and Donald Holbrook (New York: Bloomsbury Publishing USA, 2013), 169–185.
12. F. Hafez, "Shifting Borders: Islamophobia as Common Ground for Building Pan-European Right-Wing Unity," *Patterns of Prejudice* 48, no. 5 (2014): 479–499.
13. S. Marusek, "The Transatlantic Network: Funding Islamophobia and Israeli Settlement," in *What Is Islamophobia?*, ed. N. Massoumi, et al. (2017), 186–214.
14. Wajahat Ali et al., "Fear, Inc. 1," 14–15.
15. Ibid.
16. S. Marusek, "The Transatlantic Network," in *What Is Islamophobia?*, ed. N. Massoumi, et al. (2017), 187–190.
17. Ibid., 191.
18. Ibid., 194–196.
19. Ibid., 197.
20. Ibid., 198.
21. Ibid., 203.
22. Ibid., 204.
23. "Experts: Roberta Bonazzi," European Foundation for Democracy, 2018, http://europeandemocracy.eu/expert/roberta/.
24. C. D. May, "Muslims Attacked!," *National Review*, 12 January 2012, http://www.nationalreview.com/article/287918/muslims-attacked-clifford-d-may.
25. "About Us," European Foundation for Democracy, 2018, http://europeandemocracy.eu/about-us/.
26. Ibid.
27. Pearl TV Channel, "'Antidotes to Islamist Extremism'—European Parliament on 2nd May 2017—Panel 3," YouTube, May 20, 2017, https://www.youtube.com/watch?v=N_9dJBzuMGQ.
28. S. Bunglawala, "The 'War on Terror' and the Attack on Muslim Civil Society," in *What Is Islamophobia?*, ed. N. Massoumi, et al., (2017), 101.
29. S. Sayyid, *Recalling the Caliphate. Decolinization and World Order* (London: C. Hurst & Co. Publishers, 2014), 8.
30. F. Hafez, "Schulen der Islamophobieforschung: Vorurteil, Rassismus und dekoloniales Denken," *Islamophobia Studies Yearbook* 8 (2017): 9–29.
31. R. Grosfoguel, "Epistemic Islamophobia and Colonial Social Sciences." *Human Architecture* 8, no. 2 (2010): 29–38.
32. Ibid., 3.

33. S. Bunglawala, "The 'War on Terror'," in *What Is Islamophobia?*, ed. N. Massoumi, et al., (2017), 99.
34. R. Tanter and E. Stafford, "Designating the Muslim Brotherhood as a Terrorist Organization Is a Bad Idea," March 3, 2017, http://foreignpolicy.com/2017/03/03/designating-the-muslim-brotherhood-as-a-terrorist-organization-is-a-bad-idea/.
35. A. Iftikhar, Protocols of the Elders of Mecca, *The Islamic Monthly*, December 18, 2017, https://www.theislamicmonthly.com/protocols-elder.
36. Ibid.
37. F. Hafez, "Islamophobe Weltverschwörungstheorien," *Journal für Psychologie* 21, no. 1 (2013): 1–22.
38. AFP, "Integrating Muslims into Europe Is 'Impossible', Says Czech President," *The Guardian*, January 18, 2016, https://www.theguardian.com/world/2016/jan/18/integrating-muslims-into-europe-is-impossible-says-czech-president.
39. EU Reporter Correspondent, "Ideology: The Driving Force Behind #Radicalization?," Eureporter, March 1, 2017, https://www.eureporter.co/frontpage/2017/03/01/ideology-the-driving-force-behind-radicalization/.
40. V. Colombo, "The Muslim Brotherhood and Terrorist Organizations," Gatestone, May 6, 2014, https://www.gatestoneinstitute.org/4297/muslim-brotherhood-ansar-bayt-al-maqdis.
41. V. Colombo, "The Muslim Brotherhood's 'Peaceful Conquest'," Gatestone, May 28, 2014, https://www.gatestoneinstitute.org/4299/muslim-brotherhood-peaceful-conquest.
42. L. Vidino, "The Muslim Brotherhood's Conquest of Europe," Middle East Forum, 2005, http://www.meforum.org/687/the-muslim-brotherhoods-conquest-of-europe.
43. L. Vidino, "Aims and Methods of Europe's Muslim Brotherhood," Hudson Institute, November 1, 2006, https://www.hudson.org/research/9776-aims-and-methods-of-europe-s-muslim-brotherhood.
44. A. Mansour, "Salafisten machen die bessere Sozialarbeit," *FAZ*, September 28, 2015, http://www.faz.net/aktuell/feuilleton/buecher/islamismus-salafisten-machen-die-bessere-sozialarbeit-13826637.html.
45. L. Nimmervoll, and Ahmad Mansour: "Ein Kind mit Kopftuch ist Missbrauch," *Der Standard*, October 9, 2016, https://derstandard.at/2000045516816/Ahmad-Mansour-Ein-Kind-mit-Kopftuch-ist-Missbrauch.
46. B. Stritzel, "Islamismus-Experte kritisiert Radikal-Imam," Bild, January 4, 2018, http://www.bild.de/politik/inland/islamismus/experte-kritisiert-radikal-imam-54312298.bild.html.

47. V. Colombo, "Gli imam 'global terrorist' dell 'Ucoii che fregheranno Alfano," August 24, 2016, http://www.informazionecorretta.com/main.php?mediaId=115&sez=120&id=62177.
48. V. Colombo, "Il terrorismo islamico colpisce in tutto il mondo," *La Nuova Bussola Quotidiana*, June 27, 2015, http://www.lanuovabq.it/it/il-terrorismo-islamico-colpisce-in-tutto-il-mondo.
49. K. Bauer, "Aiman Mazyek vom Zentralrats der Muslime: Der Islamverteidiger," *Badische Zeitung*, July 17, 2015, http://www.badische-zeitung.de/deutschland-1/aiman-mazyek-vom-zentralrats-der-muslime-der-islamverteidiger--107829449.html.
50. L. Vidino, "For Too Long, London Has Been a Hub for the Muslim Brotherhood," *The Telegraph*, October 19, 2014, http://www.telegraph.co.uk/comment/11171454/Lorenzo-Vidino-For-too-long-London-has-been-a-hub-for-the-Muslim-Brotherhood.html.
51. K. Calamur, "Muslim Brotherhood: A Force Throughout the Muslim World," NPR, August 17, 2013, https://www.npr.org/sections/parallels/2013/08/17/212583097/muslim-brotherhood-a-force-throughout-the-muslim-world.
52. L. Vidino, "The West and the Muslim Brotherhood After the Arab Spring," Foreign Policy Research Institute, March 1, 2013, http://europeandemocracy.eu/2013/03/the-west-and-the-muslim-brotherhood-after-the-arab-spring/.
53. H. Kalb, R. Potz, and B. Schinkele, Religionsrecht, Wien 2002 (Wien: WUV, 2007), 25.
54. F. Hafez, "One Representing the Many, Institutionalized Austrian Islam," in *Debating Islam. Negotiating Religion, Europe, and the Self*, Bielefeld, eds. S. Behloul, S. Leuenberger, and A. Tunger-Zanetti (Bielefeld: Transcript Verlag, 2013), 227–242.
55. F. Hafez, "Muslim Protest Against Austria's Islam Law. An Analysis of Austrian Muslim's Protest Against the 2015 Islam Law," *Journal of Muslim Minority Affairs* 37, no. 3 (2017), 267–283.
56. F. Hafez, "Die MJÖ als Projektionsfläche für Verschwörungen," in *Jung, muslimisch, österreichisch. Einblicke in 20 Jahre Muslimische Jugend Österreich*, eds. Farid Hafez, Reinhard Heinisch, Raoul Kneucker, and Regina Polak (Vienna: New Academic Press & Alhamra, 2016).
57. F. Hafez, "Whose Austria? Muslim Youth Challenge Nativist and Closed Notions of Austrian Identity," *Anthropology of the Middle East* 12, no. 1 (Summer 2017), 38–51.
58. E. Nuller, Radikale kapern Muslimische Jugend. Initiative Muslimbrü-der raus aus der SPÖ. *Hass-Kampagne gegen Islamgesetz* 29 (Oktober 2014), Seite 4.

59. F. Hafez, "Die MJÖ als Projektionsfläche für Verschwörungen," in *Jung, muslimisch, österreichisch*, ed. F. Hafez, et al., p. 315.
60. "Österreich ist eine gute Basis für Muslimbrüder," *Kurier*, November 11, 2014, http://kurier.at/politik/inland/oesterreich-ist-eine-gute-basis-fuer-muslimbrueder/96.304.361.
61. Ibid.
62. MJÖ, "Gegendarstellung der Muslimischen Jugend Österreich," Heute, August 29, 2017, http://www.heute.at/politik/news/story/Multiethnische-Jugend---begehrt-folgende-Gegendarstellung-46754194.
63. Profil, "Richtigstellung: Muslimische Jugend Österreich (MJÖ)," *Profil*, May 9, 2015, https://www.profil.at/oesterreich/richtigstellung-muslimische-jugend-oesterreich-mjoe-5638610.
64. L. Vidino, "The Muslim Brotherhood in Austria," GW Programm on Extremism, August 2017, https://extremism.gwu.edu/sites/extremism.gwu.edu/files/MB%20in%20Austria-%20Print.pdf.
65. "'We Don't Need Them': Austrian FM Wants to End Islamic Kindergartens to Boost Integration," Russia Today, June 22, 2017, https://www.rt.com/news/393550-austria-closure-islamic-kindergartens/.
66. "Studie über Muslimbruderschaft: Beträchtlicher Einfluss," Religion ORF, September 15, 2017, http://religion.orf.at/stories/2866308/.
67. B. Tóth, F. Klenk, J. Redl, and N. Horaczek, "Die Affäre Silberstein," *Falter* 40/17, October 3, 2017, https://www.falter.at/archiv/wp/die-affaere-silberstein.
68. F. Hafez, "Austria's New Programme for Government En Route to a Restrictive Policy on Islam?," *qantara.de*, December 21, 2017, https://en.qantara.de/content/austrias-new-programme-for-government-en-route-to-a-restrictive-policy-on-islam.
69. G. Larsson, "Sweden," in *Yearbook of Muslims in Europe*, ed. J. S. Nielsen, S. Akgönül, A. Alibašić, B. Maréchal, and C. Moe (Leiden and Boston: Brill, 2010), 498–499.
70. Ibid., 500.
71. Ibid., 500.
72. Ibid., 501.
73. "Vi har fått bidrag - Organisationsbidrag, Projektbidrag, EU-bidrag | MUCF," April 13, 2017, https://www.mucf.se/vi-har-fatt-bidrag?org=Sveriges%20Unga%20Muslimer&projekt=&bidragsnamn=&bidragstyp=All&ort=&beviljatar=All.
74. S. Olsson, "Religion in the Public Space: 'Blue-and-Yellow Islam' in Sweden," *Religion, State & Society* 37 no. 3 (2009) (277–289), 282.
75. M. Norell, A. Carlbom, and P. Durrani, *The Muslim Brotherhood in Sweden*, 2017, https://clarionproject.org/wp-content/uploads/2017/06/Muslim-Brotherhood-Sweden-Magnus-Norrell.pdf, 4.

76. M. Norell, A. Carlbom, and P. Durrani, "Muslimska Brödraskapet i SverigeRed," 2017, https://www.msb.se/Upload/Kunskapsbank/Studier/Muslimska_Brodraskapet_i_Sverige_DNR_2107-1287.pdf.
77. M. Norell, "The Muslim Brotherhood in Sweden," *Zeitung*, October 10, 2017, https://clarionproject.org/wp-content/uploads/2017/06/Muslim-Brotherhood-Sweden-Magnus-Norrell.pdf.
78. "Clarion Project," Islamophobia Network, https://islamophobianetwork.com/organization/clarion-project/.
79. T. Jerlerup, "Muslimska Brödraskapet – eller: att anklaga utan bevis!," Ligator Wordpress, February 26, 2017, https://ligator.wordpress.com/2017/02/26/muslimska-brodraskapet-eller-att-anklaga-utan-bevis/.
80. "Undermålig forskning i svensk myndighetsrapport," Religions vetenskaplig omvärldsanalys, March 2, 2017, http://religionsvetenskapligakommentarer.blogspot.co.at/2017/03/debatt-undermalig-forskning-i-svensk.html.
81. Ibid.
82. M. Norell et al., *Muslim Brotherhood in Sweden*, 9–11.
83. Ibid., 17.
84. Ibid., 21.
85. M. Norell, "The Muslim Brotherhood in Sweden," Huffington Post, July 9, 2017, https://www.huffingtonpost.com/magnus-norell/the-muslim-brotherhood-in_1_b_10880432.html.
86. Ibid.
87. Ibid.
88. G. Larsson, S. Sorgenfrei, and G. Larsson, "Sweden," in *Yearbook of Muslims in Europe*, vol. 9, eds. J. S. Nielsen, O. Scharbrodt, and A. Alibašić (Leiden and Boston: Brill), 657–658.
89. MSBs Anneli Bergholm Söder, quoted in Kasurinen, Anton, "Vi vet väldigt lite om Muslimska brödraskapet," SVT, March 3, 2017. https://www.svt.se/nyheter/inrikes/msb-vi-faktagranskar-inte-rapporter.
90. MSB om förstudien Muslimska brödraskapet i Sverige, MSB, March 3, 2017. https://www.msb.se/sv/Om-MSB/Nyheter-och-press/Nyheter/Nyheter-fran-MSB/MSB-om-forstudien-Muslimska-brodraskapet-i-Sverige/.
91. M. Gardell and M. Muftee, "Islamophobia in Sweden," in *European Islamophobia Report 2017*, eds. F. Hafez and E. Bayrakli (Ankara: SETA), 617–646.
92. G. C. Spivak, "In Other Worlds: Essays in Cultural Politics" (London: Routledge, 1988).
93. All online references were accessed on 5th January 2018.

CHAPTER 8

Islamophobia in Al-Qa'ida's and IS' English-Language Magazines

Julian Droogan and Shane Peattie

This chapter presents an analysis of themes related to Islamophobia in *Inspire* and *Dabiq*—two prominent English-language e-zines produced by Al-Qa'ida in the Arabian Peninsula (AQAP) and the self-proclaimed 'Islamic State' (IS). Both organizations have used these e-zines to promote their cause, celebrate their successes and inspire violence by radicalized individuals in the West and beyond. A research methodology derived from Jennifer Attride-Stirling's method of Thematic Network Analysis is used to present a comprehensive account of the themes contained in the first fourteen issues of *Inspire* and the first thirteen issues of *Dabiq*. Through a comparative analysis of themes contained in both magazines, it is shown that while Al-Qa'ida (AQ) and IS do reference Islamophobia in their propaganda, both organizations do so sparingly and in usually only in relation to a constellation of differing related themes. Indeed, *Inspire* and *Dabiq* primarily asserts narratives of Muslim victimhood not by highlighting Islamophobia experienced by Muslims in the West, but by focusing instead

J. Droogan (✉) · S. Peattie
Macquarie University, Sydney, NSW, Australia
e-mail: julian.droogan@mq.edu.au

S. Peattie
e-mail: shane.peattie@mq.edu.au

© The Author(s) 2019
J. L. Esposito and D. Iner (eds.), *Islamophobia and Radicalization*,
https://doi.org/10.1007/978-3-319-95237-6_8

on the mistreatment of Muslims residing outside of the West. However, this research does not preclude experiences of Islamophobia by Muslims in the West from contributing to the ways in which they consume and perhaps become receptive to these extremist materials.

INTRODUCTION

Islamophobia has been associated with processes of cumulative extremism, radicalization and violent extremism across a range of diverse and multicultural Western nations.[1] Anti-Muslim sentiment and resulting experiences of marginalization and siege have negatively affected Islamic communities in Western Europe, North America and Australia (among others), but the exact relationships—if any—between Islamophobia and radicalization toward violent extremism remain unclear. One area of research that has not been fully explored is how Islamophobia and related concepts are used in the propaganda content produced by transnational Salafi-jihadist organizations such as AQ and the so-called and self-proclaimed IS, who both seek to reinforce and promote extremist narratives and calls for violence against perceived enemies.

This chapter presents foundational research on this issue. It conducts a thematic network analysis of two influential online magazines (e-zines) produced and distributed by AQAP and IS—*Inspire* and *Dabiq*. The chapter draws on research conducted by the authors over 2016–2017, which presented the first comprehensive and detailed thematic analysis of these e-zines, including how their thematic landscapes have shifted over time.[2] In this previous research, the authors performed thematic network analyses derived from Jennifer Attride-Stirling's 2001 method of thematic analysis,[3] which resulted in a comprehensive account of the themes contained in the first fourteen issues of *Inspire* and the first thirteen issues of *Dabiq*. The purpose of this chapter is to build on this research by specifically identifying and exploring narrative themes within these publications that relate to Islamophobia and discrimination. This study visualizes Islamophobia in relation to wider themes included within both magazines, and it seeks to determine to how frequently groups like AQ and IS utilize Islamophobia against Muslims living in the West to support their own extremist narratives and to achieve their violent aims.

For the purposes of the thematic content analysis, the theme 'Islamophobia and Discrimination' was defined narrowly as 'anti-Muslim bigotry and discrimination committed against Muslims living in the West'. This was in order to specifically capture the narratives used by

AQ and IS that refer to the negative experiences of Western Muslims. It is acknowledged that this relatively restrictive definition of Islamophobia differs from wider viewpoints in which Islamophobia may be taken to refer to experiences of non-Western Muslims, or to forms of structural and systemic violence in the international system. Indeed, many of the themes coded for could be considered as referring to Islamophobia when defined more broadly. For instance, 'Western malevolence', 'the occupation of Muslim lands', or 'humiliation of Muslims'. This issue is explored further below in the Themes Related to Islamophobia section.

Since 2010, violent Salafi-jihadist groups such as AQ and IS have experimented in the production of multilingual e-zines ostensibly aimed at legitimizing each group's beliefs and actions and encouraging individuals to join their cause—including by engaging in acts of violent extremism at home and abroad. In addition to attracting significant strategic analysis from security analysts and policymakers,[4] these magazines have been interpreted in a variety of ways within the academic literature. This includes through the lens of political myth,[5] behavioralism,[6] Hermeneutics,[7] and in-group, other, crisis and solution constructs.[8] The concept of Islamophobia has not been entirely absent from interpretations and commentary on these e-zines, in particular, IS' *Dabiq*. An infamous and much-quoted 10-page Editorial in *Dabiq* from early 2015,[9] for instance, has been interpreted as proclaiming that conducting dramatic terror attacks in the West will serve to encourage Western governments to isolate and alienate Muslim communities, thereby forcing Muslims to abandon the 'grey zone' they allegedly inhabit between secular Western identities and the extremist interpretation of Islam practiced by IS. As such, and if taken at face value, the article is a clear example of IS attempting to provoke Islamophobia and harsh counterterrorism responses as part of a—largely failed—strategy to mobilize Western Muslims to its cause.[10]

Largely missing from these debates, however, have been any attempts at a detailed understanding of the relationship between the wider narratives, Islamophobia and related concepts. This chapter argues that the specific theme of 'Islamophobia and Discrimination', as it relates to the experiences of Muslims living in Western nations, has a relatively insignificant presence in both *Inspire* and *Dabiq*, and that both magazines primarily assert narratives of Muslim victimhood by focusing on the mistreatment of Muslims residing outside of the West. In addition, although the Western Muslim experience with Islamophobia is not a prevalent theme in either e-zine, this does not mean that related themes (such as 'blasphemy' or 'the occupation of Muslim lands') do not draw on wider perceptions of Western/Muslim confrontation that could well be defined as broadly 'Islamophobic' according to more expansive definitions. It also does not mean that direct experiences of Islamophobia and discrimination by Western Muslims do not contribute to the ways in which they consume and perhaps become receptive to this extremist material. It should also be emphasized that although Islamophobia can be used in a narrative intended to motivate people to political action, Islamophobia is never simply a narrative, but refers to set of real and lived injustices experiences by Muslims living both within and outside the West.

This more nuanced understanding of how Islamophobia and discrimination are used in the narratives of AQ and IS has implications for constructing effective counternarratives to reduce the impact and influence of extremist materials. As Ashourt argues, it is crucial for countering violent extremism and societal resilience building strategies to recognize the role of narratives, and for counternarratives to "address every dimension [of the original narrative] as well as to tailor the message to different audiences."[11] To that end, this research will prove useful to those wishing to identify prominent themes contained in extremist propaganda, which could assist the development of counternarratives that seek to negate the ideological influence of these or similar e-zines among their reader base.

INSPIRE AND *DABIQ*

First published in early 2010, *Inspire* magazine was, at the time, a seminal addition to a growing milieu of online violent jihadist discourse. It was first produced by Samir Khan, an American citizen of Pakistani descent, who later worked on its production with Anwar Al-Awlaki, a popular Yemeni-American jihadist ideologue and AQAP's Chief of External Operations. Due to restrictions imposed by US-led global counterterrorism efforts during this time, AQAP had begun to adopt a strategy of inspiring self-starter terrorists to conduct their own operations with no direct training, funding, or direction from the organization itself. *Inspire* was produced as a central limb of this strategy.

Within the academic literature and mainstream reporting, *Inspire* has often been interpreted as a Western-centric instrument of violent Salafi jihadi discourse.[12] Its Western Muslim target audience, anti-Western themes and calls for individualized terrorism against Western targets are the frequent subject of discussion among media, political commentators, and academic terrorism analysts.[13] Its 'Open Source Jihad' section, in particular, has received significant attention by academic and government researchers due to its 'do-it-yourself' approach to publishing instructional terrorist tactics, as well as its association with a series of terror attacks in the United States and Europe. The killing of both Samir Khan and Anwar Al-Awlaki by United states drone strikes in 2011 led to a diminishing regularity in the e-zine's publication. However, to date there have been 17 issues produced and distributed in online PDF format, the most recent being in August 2017.

Dabiq was first published in mid-2014 by the al-Hayat ('Life') Media Centre, then part of IS' growing media apparatus. Similar to *Inspire*, but without a focus on encouraging self-motivated terrorist attacks in the West, issues of *Dabiq* are typically 40–80 pages long, consisting of articles, transcribed speeches and political, religious and social commentary produced by IS affiliates and supporters.[14] The magazine generally presented the so-called IS as a divinely inspired state-building project, with an emphasis on legitimizing this project in political and religious terms, calling supporters to arms and maligning and denigrating perceived enemies. Indeed, *Dabiq* and *Inspire's* format are broadly similar, with both e-zines publishing sections aimed at justifying a transnational violent Salafi-jihadist narrative and both often using similar titles and subtitles for articles (such as 'From the Ages of History' and 'In the Words of the Enemy').[15]

Between July 2014 and July 2016, IS produced fifteen issues of *Dabiq* and published them online in PDF format. The e-zine lost much of its currency when IS lost control of the previously-held township of *Dabiq* in Syria, which is considered important in some strands of Islamic eschatology. In many ways, the loss of *Dabiq* highlighted IS' loss of forward momentum in terms of territorial conquest. In September 2016, the al-Hayat Media Centre replaced it with a new e-zine publication titled *Rumiyah* ('Rome'). However, since September 2017, *Rumiyah*'s publication also appears to have at least temporarily ceased.

Although clearly influential, neither *Inspire* nor *Dabiq* should not be read as the sole, or even the major, propaganda tool in AQ or IS' communications toolkit. Nor, as tools of propaganda, should they be seen as objective windows into understanding the strategies of these terrorist organizations. Through online channels, both AQ and IS have also distributed rich and extensive catalogues of popular videos, short films, articles, speeches, news reports and translations of violent Salafi-jihadi materials to spread their message and to garner recruits. *Inspire* and *Dabiq*, while popular and implicated in several terrorist plots,[16] are but one part of this larger strategy. While it is dangerous to overemphasize their strategic rather than propaganda value, or their unique stand-alone importance, these e-zines do represent a significant vehicle for the spread of AQ and IS' ideas, including attempts to legitimize their aims and actions and a call to arms. Accordingly, a lucid understanding of their contents in relationship to Islamophobia will prove important to those attempting to counter the influence of violent Salafi-jihadist propaganda.

METHOD AND FOUNDATIONAL RESEARCH

This chapter draws on comprehensive thematic analyses of the first fourteen issues of *Inspire* and the first thirteen issues of *Dabiq*. It seeks to identify the prevalent themes contained within each e-zine, how these themes relate to one another and their relationship to the concept of Islamophobia.[17]

Copies of *Inspire* and *Dabiq* were anonymously obtained from public sources without payment. Within each issue, blocks of text containing identifiable narrative themes were analyzed, including essays, opinion pieces, battlefield reports and interviews. A qualitative analysis method based on Jennifer Attride-Stirling's 2001 thematic network analysis technique was adopted. This method consists of a six-step analytic process designed to facilitate the identification and presentation of themes within textual data. This thematic network analysis ultimately allowed for the presentation and analysis of textual themes as visual thematic networks.

The qualitative analysis software *NVivo 11* was used in all cycles of coding. Two coding frameworks were employed to generate thematic codes. This included a combination of a priori themes sourced from a literature review of academic and professional research conducted on these e-zines and broader Salafi-jihadist ideology, as well as a grounded theory coding framework that identified themes from the magazines themselves. This combination of literature review and the use of grounded theory allowed for the discovery of previously unidentified themes not identified through prior research. A series of 80 discrete themes were identified in *Inspire*, and 82 were identified in *Dabiq*. 'Islamophobia and Discrimination' was identified as a theme in both e-zines.

With these theme lists developed, each issue was then re-coded on a paragraph-by-paragraph basis using the identified themes. This second coding cycle produced two quantitative calculations: the total number of paragraphs containing *any* narrative theme and the total number of paragraphs containing each *specific* theme. By dividing the latter by the former for each theme, a third quantitative measurement was provided— the percentage of an issue's paragraphs containing each individual theme. This third measurement revealed how pervasive or present each theme was within each issue.

These themes were used to construct thematic networks. This process involved grouping the basic themes into 'organizing themes' and 'global themes'. Organizing themes were developed by grouping together basic themes centered on shared issues. Similarly, global themes arose from commonality among organizing themes. For instance, in our analysis of *Inspire*, themes such as 'blasphemy', 'clash of civilizations' and 'lies and hypocrisy' have been grouped under the organizing theme 'the West', while this and the other organizing themes were grouped together under the global theme 'Islam is at war' (Fig. 8.1).

In the resulting thematic maps, arrows linking themes in the network indicate the relationships between 'basic themes', 'organizing themes' and 'global themes'. Grey-scale color-coding was applied to these thematic networks to indicate the pervasiveness of each basic theme. Using color-coding in this way allows the reader to visualize the thematic focus of each issue. White basic themes are present in < 10% of an issue's theme-containing paragraphs and are considered 'minimally pervasive'. Light grey basic themes are present in 10.0–19.9% of theme-containing paragraphs and are considered 'moderately pervasive'. Dark grey basic themes are present in 20.0–29.9% of theme-containing paragraphs and are considered 'highly pervasive'. Finally, black basic themes are present in 30%+ of the issue's theme-containing paragraphs and are considered 'critically pervasive'. Insignificant themes (those appearing in < 2.5% of an issue's theme-containing paragraphs) were removed from the thematic networks produced to reduce the visualization's complexity and to avoid clutter. This is important, as the 'Islamophobia and Discrimination' theme was found to appear in less than 2.5% of the time in all issues across both e-zines.

This method allowed a series of new insights into the nature of these e-zines; in particular, the sophisticated, wide-ranging and dynamic nature of the themes employed. In the case of *Inspire*, it was shown that a

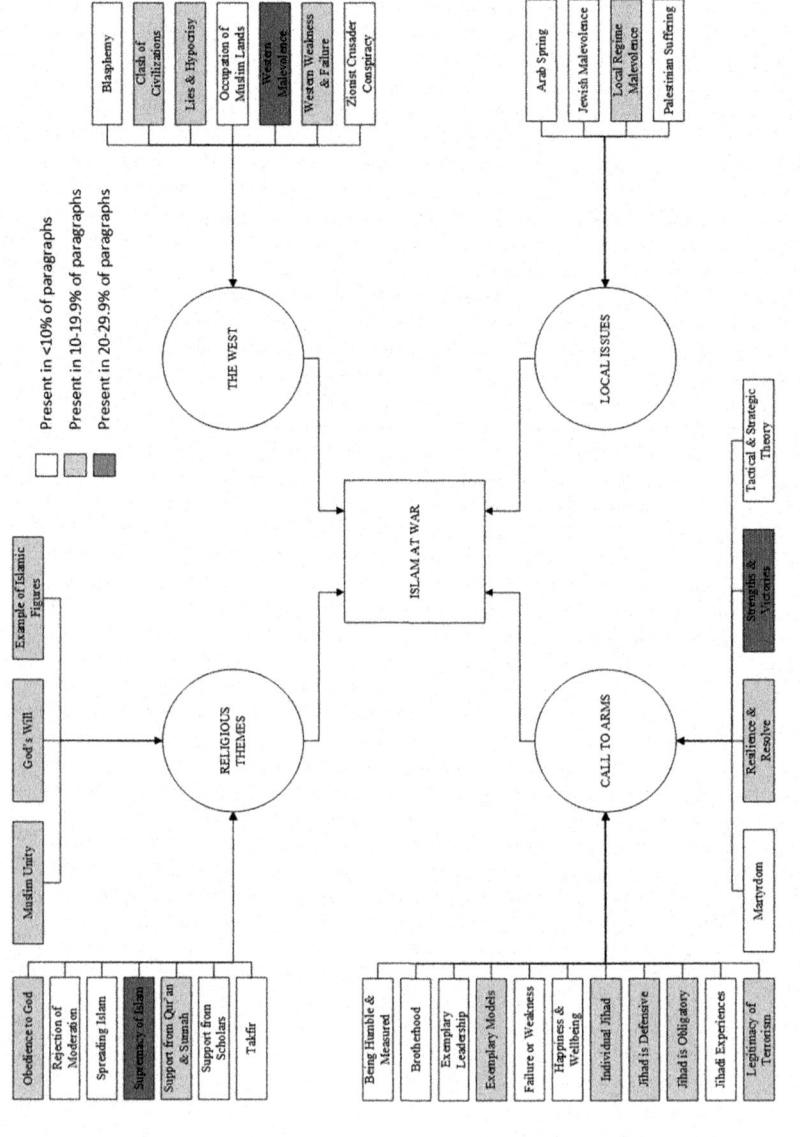

Fig. 8.1 A thematic network generated from *Inspire*'s first fourteen issues

consistent thematic structure was maintained across all fourteen issues, although the specific focus of individual issues was highly dynamic and often responded in an opportunistic way to current affairs.[18] All issues upheld a consistent 'Islam is at War' narrative as their global theme, and this was supported by the same four categories of organizing themes: 'The West', 'Call to Arms', 'Religion' and 'Local Issues'. Although these organizing themes remained constant, they were expressed through a diverse and relatively fluid array of basic themes throughout individual issues. For instance, the magazine's earliest and most recent issues all placed a heavy emphasis on themes related to the West, and a comparatively minimal emphasis on themes related to local issues. *Inspire*'s middle phase, however, saw an increased focus on themes within the 'Religion' and 'Local Issues' organizing themes. This meant that *Inspire* struggled to maintain an anti-Western focus throughout its lifecycle.

This thematic promiscuity largely resulted from responses to a series of real-world events. For instance, the magazine shifted away from 'Anti-Western' to 'Local Issues' themes during the turmoil in the Middle East and North Africa during the early phases of the Arab Spring. However, there was a sudden and significant intensification of the magazine's 'Call to Arms' themes immediately following the killing of Osama Bin Laden in mid-2011.

In the case of *Dabiq*, both consistencies and variations were identified in its narrative structure over time, but with a strong focus on creating group-level identities.[19] As with *Inspire*, the e-zine's basic thematic structure remained remarkably constant. The same global theme 'Islam is at War' was supported by the same four organizing themes across all issues: 'Religion', 'Enemies', 'Call to Arms' and 'Building the Caliphate'. Yet, the remaining 82 basic themes shifted in presence and pervasiveness according to four distinct phases.

The first of these phases focused on themes within the 'Building the Caliphate' organizing theme and emphasized the alleged religious and functional legitimacy of the IS' Caliphate-building project and leadership. The second thematic phase saw a reduction in focus on state-building matters and a shift in attention to anti-Western themes. After a third phase, wherein *Dabiq*'s thematic focus varied significantly on an issue-to-issue basis with no clear trends present, phase four included a strong focus on out-groups and IS' purported enemies. Thematic analysis also showed that *Dabiq* was particularly engaged with group-level identities. *Dabiq* drew on a persistent and stark distinction between Muslims and non-Muslims; it uncompromisingly asserted the superiority of the former over the latter, conveying an accompanying theme of Muslim unity throughout. *Dabiq* also identified an array of out-groups—both Muslim and non-Muslim—whom IS considers its enemies. It aggressively rejected the authority of local regimes, the legitimacy of other violent jihadi groups, the religious authenticity of Shi'a Muslims, the alleged weakness and malevolence of the West and the supposed deviousness of non-Islamist militias in Iraq and Syria (among others). In such a way, the magazine habitually expressed IS' identity and authority not just in its own right, but also through contrast with other groups—particularly al-Qaeda and local militias.

Group-level identity was a crucial element of the magazine's narrative. Themes related to allegiance, IS' strengths and victories, territorial expansion and brotherhood all featured consistently and prominently. These themes sought to create an in-group identity centered on victory and to frame IS' expansion and successes as a group achievement on behalf of Islam itself. *Dabiq* provided its readers with the narrative of a cohesive, powerful group that is not just engaged in conflict, but in a protracted Islamist revolution. In this way, the e-zine offers a narrative of cosmic war wherein Muslims—led by IS—are waging a war against a coalition of organizations and states who are unified through their opposition to Islam. This construction of an enemy also includes Muslim majority states and Muslim groups through the assertion that they are 'heretical' or 'apostate' because of their accommodation of modern and Western institutions, or their rejection of IS-style Salafi-Jihadist principles. IS uses its own highly unorthodox process of *takfir* (excommunication) in order to delegitimize a range of Muslim organizations and states, and to justify violence against them.

Differences and Similarities Between *Inspire* and *Dabiq*

Our previous research found that, at their highest level of thematic interpretation, both *Inspire* and *Dabiq* had the same overarching global theme—'Islam is at War'. Both magazines conveyed a narrative wherein the religion and its followers are engaged in an enduring and existential battle with non-Muslims. This similarity should perhaps be expected given that AQ and IS share the same ideological and organizational roots. However, the e-zines did exhibit notable differences at the more precise level of thematic interpretation provided by organizing themes and basic themes, and these differences almost certainly speak to the groups' diverging strategic objectives at the time of each magazine's publication.

Inspire's attempts to address issues within the Muslim world were primarily focused on the 2010 Arab revolutions (the 'Arab Spring'), authoritarian regimes in the Muslim world and the suffering of Palestinians. Accordingly, we grouped these themes into the broad 'Local Issues' organizing theme discussed previously and shown in Fig. 8.1. *Dabiq*, on the other hand, primarily discussed local issues through themes related to the establishment of 'Islamic' governance, territorial expansion and delivering justice. Discussions of ISIS's strengths and military victories were also largely conveyed through the lens of the group's state-building project, so these themes were grouped into the more precise 'Building the Caliphate' organizing theme as shown in Fig. 8.2.

Inspire and *Dabiq* also differed significantly in the enemies and adversaries they addressed throughout the course of their publication. While *Inspire*'s focus on the West did briefly diminish following the Arab Spring and the deaths of key AQ figures in 2011,[20] its overall thematic network reveals a magazine intently fixated on grievances relating to the West. The magazine repeatedly drew attention to alleged acts of Western malevolence, the occupation of Muslim lands and perceived Western weaknesses and failures. *Dabiq* was considerably more diverse in the enemies it identified, and its focus was much more local. Its thematic network shows that while themes related to the West were certainly present in the magazine, they appeared less frequently than they did in *Inspire* and they were accompanied by an assortment of other themes related to local adversaries in the Middle East and internal conflicts within the broader Salafi-jihadist movement. This included pervasive anti-Shi'a sectarian themes and themes related to the rejection of other jihadists, local tribal groups and other militant groups operating in Syria and Iraq.

Both e-zines contained ubiquitous religious themes and both attempted to motivate readers through persistent calls to action. Within each magazine's thematic network, we grouped these themes into the 'Religious Themes' and 'Call to Arms' organizing themes outlined above. Regarding religious themes, both *Inspire* and *Dabiq* consistently featured themes of a theological nature, including interpretations of religious texts and classical scholarship, appeals to the alleged will of God and assertions of Islam's inherent supremacy over other religions and

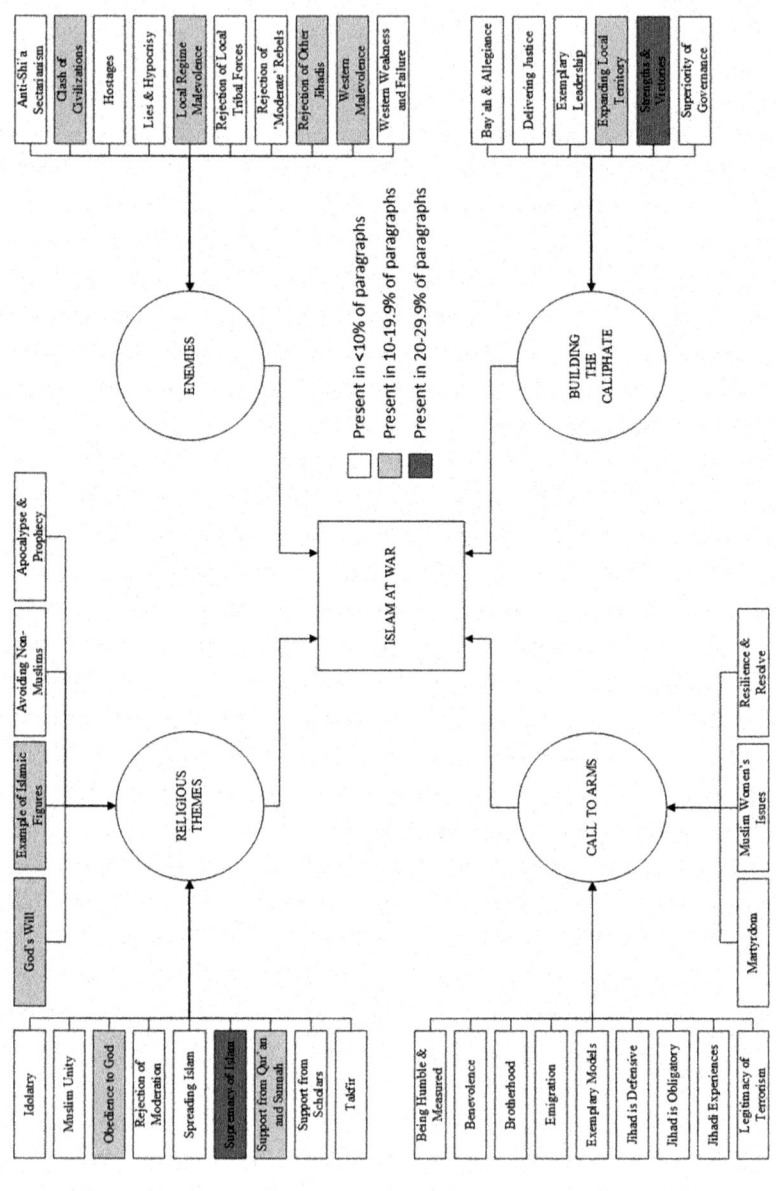

Fig. 8.2 A thematic network generated from the first thirteen issues of *Dabiq*

governance models. The magazines also featured themes that sought to create in-group/out-group divisions along the lines of religious identity, including appeals to Muslim unity and calls for the rejection of non-Muslims and anyone who failed to practice the specific version of Islam advocated by AQ and IS. While both groups featured ubiquitous religious themes in their magazines, we observed some slight differences in how they were presented. Specifically, *Dabiq* included a stronger overall presence of religious themes and it also placed greater emphasis on themes related to idolatry and Millenarian prophecy. Across both magazines, 'Call to Arms' themes sought to provide readers with role models, to legitimize terrorism and to set expectations for how individuals should respond to the range of threats, opportunities and obligations proclaimed by each group. Staying true to its title, *Inspire* had a stronger overall presence of 'Call to Arms' themes and it also placed significant emphasis on the concept of 'individual jihad', which calls for lone actors and small groups to plan, resource and execute their own acts of terrorism without direct support from an organization.[21] *Dabiq* does not feature this 'individual jihad' theme to the same degree. Instead, its thematic network included an 'emigration' theme, which primarily arose from the magazine's repeated calls for readers to emigrate to IS's so-called Caliphate in Syria and Iraq.

With the above analysis considered, it is apparent that *Inspire* and *Dabiq* contain distinct thematic differences despite AQ's and IS' shared ideological and organizational roots. The issues of *Inspire* that we analyzed for this research are best summarized as a propaganda product focused on channeling and promoting grievances and victimhood in order to inspire the reader toward taking violent extremist action. They framed their call to arms as a retributive endeavor and they placed great emphasis on the role of individuals in pursuing this endeavor. The magazine identified the West as AQ's key enemy and it largely neglected to offer any challenge to rival jihadist groups. The issues of *Dabiq* we analyzed were less focused on the grievances and were decidedly aspirational. They framed their call to arms as an opportunity to join an Islamic revolution engaged in the offensive spread of Islam and the establishment of an IS. *Dabiq* did address the role of individuals within this movement, but the magazine's preference was for addressing supporters and enemies at the level of their group identity. At the time of *Dabiq*'s publication, IS was engaged in aggressive competition with AQ for its position at the vanguard of the violent Salafi-jihadist movement and its immediate strategic objectives were also mostly confined to Syria and Iraq.[22] Accordingly, *Dabiq* spent considerably more effort challenging other jihadist groups and local actors than it did the West.

THEMES RELATED TO ISLAMOPHOBIA

When coding *Inspire* and *Dabiq*, we included a specific 'Islamophobia and Discrimination' theme to capture references to bigotry or discrimination directed against Muslims living in the West.[23] This theme was defined as 'anti-Muslim bigotry and discrimination committed against Muslims living in the West: does not include outward aggression against Muslims outside of the West'. All passages in the e-zines that referred to this concept—whether they used the term 'Islamophobia' or not, and they generally did not—were captured through the thematic analysis. This definition is most closely related to that used in the Georgetown University *Bridge Project*, which defines Islamophobia fairly narrowly as "prejudice towards or discrimination against Muslims due to their religious, national, or ethnic identity associated with Islam".[24]

The definition of Islamophobia adopted was further restricted in two significant ways, both of which have implications for the significance of this research. First, the focus was on Muslims living in the West only. Since both *Inspire* and *Dabiq* appear to be Western focused in their target audiences, it was considered valuable to determine just how the editors attempted to appeal to the concerns and experiences of Muslims living as parts of minority communities in Western nations. Forms of structural and systemic violence and discrimination targeted at Muslims in non-Western and Muslim majority states were captured instead through related themes such as 'Western malevolence', 'occupation of Muslim lands', 'local regime malevolence', and 'Palestinian suffering'.

Second, Islamophobia was defined as primarily a *social* phenomenon that relates to issues of prejudice, discrimination and bigotry. In this regard, broader definitions of Islamophobia that place it as systemically embedded in unequal and discriminatory global power structures, or disparities in economic, political, social or cultural relations, were rejected.[25] While broader definitions that embed Islamophobia within global structures of repression and violence may be highly useful in some research, they were considered as not providing sufficient analytical clarity for the purposes of a thematic analysis of AQ and IS materials. Indeed, if defined at its most broad, all themes generally relating to perceived Western aggression, violence, and oppression within the Muslim world—as well as the meta 'Islam is at War' global theme and the implicit clash of civilizations thesis that it rests upon—would be reduced to 'Islamophobia'. Our examination took a different route and coded for each of these issues under separate themes. However, this does not preclude Islamophobia being related to these wider themes, as discussed below.

The 'Islamophobia and discrimination' theme is not represented in either magazine's overall thematic network because both magazines included the theme in less than 2.5% of their paragraphs. Overall, *Inspire* contained the 'Islamophobia and discrimination' theme in only 1.4% of paragraphs and *Dabiq* contained the theme in only 0.1% of its paragraphs. This indicates that neither AQ nor IS placed significant emphasis on Islamophobia, anti-Muslim bigotry, or acts of prejudice or discrimination against Western Muslims in the English-language propaganda magazines examined.

However, while the specific 'Islamophobia and discrimination' theme, as narrowly defined, had a relatively insignificant presence in both magazines, we also coded for themes that were related to the perceived mistreatment of Muslims more generally (which certainly do relate to Islamophobia when defined more broadly). This included a 'blasphemy' theme, a 'humiliation of Muslims' theme, an 'occupation of Muslim lands' theme and a 'Western malevolence' theme—all of which were often co-occurring within the texts. The 'blasphemy' theme—which captured alleged incidents of insult or blasphemy against Islam, the Prophet and the Qur'an—appears in *Inspire*'s thematic network due to the inclusion of articles on the depiction of Muhammad in cartoons and the 2012 '*Innocence of Muslims*' film scandal. In total, *Inspire* featured this theme in 3.3% of its paragraphs and *Dabiq* featured it in 1.2%. The 'occupation of Muslim lands' theme also appears in *Inspire*'s thematic network and the broader 'Western malevolence' theme appears in both magazines' thematic network. These themes captured references to the invasion or occupation of Muslim lands by non-Muslim armies and claims that Western countries behave in a malicious, oppressive, aggressive, colonialist, or generally malevolent manner toward Muslims. Overall, the 'Western malevolence' theme had a significant presence in both magazines and it was one of the three most pervasive themes featured in *Inspire*. This suggests that while Islamophobia as narrowly defined as a form of social discrimination and prejudice against Muslims living in the West is not a concept widely adopted by the editors, there are host of other themes used in these e-zines that are certainly related, particularly if broader definitions of Islamophobia are used. The relative absence of the 'Islamophobia and Discrimination' theme and the strong presence of the much broader 'Western Malevolence' theme in both magazines suggests that *Inspire* and *Dabiq* primarily asserted narratives of Muslim victimhood by focusing not on the Western Muslim experience with Islamophobia and discrimination, but on the West's alleged mistreatment of Muslims residing outside of its own borders. Instead of drawing consistent attention to the perceived mistreatment of Muslims living in the West, both e-zines focused on the perceived injustices committed against the Muslim world, including military activities, acts of humiliation, foreign policies and occupations. These themes go well-beyond prejudice and discrimination and focus on violence, war, occupation, and death.

Do Al-Qaeda and IS Exploit Islamophobia for Propaganda Purposes?

When *Inspire* and *Dabiq*'s themes are considered holistically, and when they are analyzed through a rigorous and dispassionate qualitative research methodology, it is evident that themes specifically related to Islamophobia, anti-Muslim bigotry and discrimination against Muslims living in the West are only minimally present in both magazines. In this sense, the editors of *Inspire* and *Dabiq* do not appear to have pursued a consistent strategy of highlighting actual or perceived examples of Islamophobia against Muslims living in Western countries to fuel radicalization or to justify their actions. Instead, both magazines focused more generally on themes related to alleged Western malevolence and the West's treatment of Muslims living outside its borders (specifically *not* defined as Islamophobia in this research). Thus, in terms of themes used, both e-zines focused on an international political perspective to support their key assertion that 'Islam is at War' rather than a using a domestic frame that highlighted real or perceived Islamophobia occurring within Western states.

Identifying a relative absence of themes relating to the Western Muslim experience with Islamophobia in jihadi discourse represents a useful step toward understanding whether Islamophobia contributes to radicalization. The minimal presence of such themes in *Inspire* and

Dabiq may suggest that jihadists themselves do not view Islamophobia as a highly effective or relevant factor in the radicalization process, or that consumers of propaganda are not necessarily being exposed to significant amounts of content that highlights or addresses their experience with Islamophobia. Alternatively, the insignificant presence of these themes in *Inspire* and *Dabiq* may suggest that contributors to these magazines have a limited understanding of how Islamophobia manifests in Western culture, or the lived experience of Muslims in the West. In addition, the international geopolitical context—particularly conflicts in Iraq, Afghanistan, Palestine, Yemen, Libya, North Africa, the Caucuses and Kashmir—may provide more ample, extreme and provocative imagery and examples of violence and atrocities perpetrated against Muslims that are useful in bolstering the violent Salafi-jihadist narrative that Islam is at war.

Either way, these findings only address the producer side of the producer–consumer relationship that exists in strategic communications. As Ingram has observed, Islamophobia and Islamophobic rhetoric can "intensify perceptions of crisis across Muslim communities and fuel the psychosocial conditions within which extremist propaganda tends to resonate".[26] Themes addressing alleged Western barbarism, hostility and malevolence toward the Muslim world also seek to instill and appeal to a similar sense of crisis. Accordingly, it is conceivable that such themes may resonate with those who have experienced a sense of crisis through Islamophobia, and this may be the case even if the propaganda they are consuming focuses on international issues instead of directly attempting to exploit their experience with Islamophobia.

To improve our understanding of how experiences with Islamophobia may or may not contribute to radicalization, it is suggested that researchers should, therefore, concentrate their efforts not on how the Western Muslim experience with Islamophobia is addressed or exploited in propaganda—our research indicates that it largely is not. Instead, further research should focus on propaganda from the perspective of audiences and consumers. Future research could explore, for instance, how consumers of propaganda themselves deconstruct and internalize AQ and IS messaging, and whether audiences who have experienced Islamophobia directly and in a personal way themselves are empirically more susceptible to accepting crisis claims that are more enduring and pervasive in jihadi discourse.

Notes

1. Adrian Cherney and Kristina Murphy, "Support for Terrorism: The Role of Beliefs in Jihad and Institutional Responses to Terrorism," *Terrorism and Political Violence* (2017), https://doi.org/10.1080/09546553.2 017.1313735; Tamar Mitts, *Terrorism, Islamophobia and Radicalisation* (Unpublished PhD dissertation, Columbia University, New York, 2017); and Matthew Feldman and Mark Littler, *Tell MAMA Reporting 2013/14: Anti-Muslim Overview, Analysis and 'Cumulative Extremism'* (Centre for Fascist, Anti-Fascist and Post-Fascist Studies, 2014), https://www.tellmamauk.org/wp-content/uploads/2014/07/finalreport.pdf, accessed April 26, 2018.
2. Julian Droogan and Shane Peattie, "Reading Jihad: Mapping the Shifting Themes of Inspire Magazine," *Terrorism and Political Violence* (2016), https://doi.org/10.1080/09546553.2016.121152; Julian Droogan and Shane Peattie, "Mapping the Thematic Landscape of *Dabiq* Magazine," *Australian Journal of International Affairs* 71, no. 6 (2017): 591–620.
3. Jennifer Attride-Stirling, "Thematic Networks: An Analytic Tool for Qualitative Research," *Qualitative Research* 1, no. 3 (2001): 385–405.
4. Naureen Chowdhury and Benjamin Sugg, "A Tale of Two Jihads: Comparing the Al-Qaeda and ISIS Narratives," IPI Global Observatory (2015), https://theglobalobservatory.org/2015/02/jihad-al-qaeda-isis-counternarrative, accessed April 26, 2018; Charlie Winter, "The Virtual 'Caliphate': Understanding the Islamic State's Propaganda Strategy," Quilliam (2015), https://www.stratcomcoe.org/charlie-winter-virtual-caliphate-understanding-islamic-states-propaganda-strategy, accessed April 26, 2018.
5. Xander Kirke, "Violence and Political Myth: Radicalising Believers in the Pages of *Inspire* Magazine," *International Political Sociology* 9, no. 4 (2015): 283–298.
6. Anthony F. Lemieux et al., "*Inspire* Magazine: A Critical Analysis of Its Significance and Potential Impact Through the Lens of the Information, Motivation and Behavioural Sills Model," *Terrorism and Political Violence* 19, no. 1 (2014): 354–371.
7. Brandon Colas, "What Does Dabiq Do? ISIS Hermeneutics and Organizational Fractures Within *Dabiq* Magazine," *Studies in Conflict and Terrorism* 40, no. 3 (2016): 173–190.
8. Haroro J. Ingram, "The Strategic Logic of Islamic State Information Operations," *Australian Journal of International Affairs* 69, no. 6 (2015): 729–752; Haroro J. Ingram, "An Analysis of *Inspire* and *Dabiq*: Lessons from AQAP and Islamic State's Propaganda War," *Studies in Conflict and Terrorism* 40, no. 5 (2017): 357–375.
9. Islamic State, "The Extinction of the Grayzone," *Dabiq* 7 (2015): 54–66.

10. Scott Atran, "Mindless Terrorists? The Truth About Isis Is Much Worse," *The Guardian*, November 16, 2015, https://www.theguardian.com/commentisfree/2015/nov/15/terrorists-isis, accessed April 26, 2018.
11. Omar Ashour, "Online De-Radicalization? Countering Violent Extremist Narratives: Message, Messenger and Media Strategy," *Perspectives on Terrorism* 4, no. 6 (2010), http://www.terrorismanalysts.com/pt/index.php/pot/article/view/128/html.
12. Gabriel Weimann, "Lone Wolves in Cyberspace," *Journal of Terrorism Research* 3, no. 2 (2012), https://cvir.st-andrews.ac.uk/articles/10.15664/jtr.405, accessed April 26, 2018; Bill Braniff and Assaf Maghadam, "Towards Global Jihadism: Al-Qaeda's Strategic, Ideological and Structural Adaptations Since 9/11," *Perspectives on Terrorism* 5, no. 2 (2011), http://www.terrorismanalysts.com/pt/index.php/pot/article/view/braniff-towards-global-jihadism/html, accessed April 26, 2018; Benedict Wilkinson and Jack Barclay, "The Language of Jihad: Narratives and Strategies of Al-Qa'ida in the Arabian Peninsula and UK Responses," The Royal United Services Institute for Defence and Security Studies, 2011, https://rusi.org/sites/default/files/201201_whr_language_of_jihad_0.pdf, accessed April 26, 2018.
13. John Curtis Amble, "Combating Terrorism in the New Media Environment," *Studies in Conflict and Terrorism* 35, no. 5 (2012): 343; Department of Homeland Security, "Second Edition of *Inspire* Magazine: Continues to Encourage Attacks in the West," Public Intelligence Website, October 15, 2010, http://info.publicintelligence.net/DHS-Inspire2Warning.pdf, accessed April 26, 2018; and Joint Regional Intelligence Center. "*Inspire* Magazine at a Glance," Investigate Project Website, May 29, 2012, http://www.investigativeproject.org/documents/misc/756.pdf, accessed April 26, 2018.
14. Celine Marie I. Novenario, "Differentiating Al Qaeda and the Islamic State Through Strategies Publicized in Jihadist Magazines," *Studies in Conflict and Terrorism* 39, no. 11 (2016): 953–967.
15. Ingram, "An Analysis of *Inspire* and *Dabiq*: Lessons from AQAP and Islamic State's Propaganda War," *Studies in Conflict and Terrorism*.
16. Julian Droogan and Shane Peattie, "Reading Jihad: Mapping the Shifting Themes of *Inspire* Magazine," *Terrorism and Political Violence*.
17. For detailed results, as well as a full description of the method adopted, see Julian Droogan and Shane Peattie, "Reading Jihad: Mapping the Shifting Themes of *Inspire* Magazine," *Terrorism and Political Violence*.
18. Julian Droogan and Shane Peattie, "Reading Jihad: Mapping the Shifting Themes of *Inspire* Magazine," *Terrorism and Political Violence*.
19. Julian Droogan and Shane Peattie, "Mapping the Thematic Landscape of *Dabiq* Magazine," *Australian Journal of International Affairs*.

20. Julian Droogan and Shane Peattie, "Reading Jihad: Mapping the Shifting Themes of *Inspire* Magazine," *Terrorism and Political Violence*; Julian Droogan and Shane Peattie, "Mapping the Thematic Landscape of *Dabiq* Magazine," *Australian Journal of International Affairs*.
21. Julian Droogan and Shane Peattie, "Reading Jihad: Mapping the Shifting Themes of *Inspire* Magazine," *Terrorism and Political Violence*, 10.
22. Lina Khatib, *The Islamic State's Strategy: Lasting and Expanding* (Washington, DC: Carnegie Endowment for International Peace, 2015).
23. Julian Droogan and Shane Peattie, "Reading Jihad: Mapping the Shifting Themes of *Inspire* Magazine," *Terrorism and Political Violence*, 10.
24. The Bridge Initiative, Georgetown University, http://bridge.georgetown.edu/about, accessed April 18, 2018.
25. See for instance, the broad definition of Islamophobia Adopted by the Islamophobia Research Documentation Project: Centre for Race and Gender, University of California, Berkley, https://www.crg.berkeley.edu/research-projects/islamophobia-research-documentation-project, accessed April 20, 2018.
26. Haroro J. Ingram, "This Is How Islamist Extremists Use Western Anti-Islam Rhetoric to Help Recruit," *The Washington Post*, August 11, 2016, https://www.washingtonpost.com/news/monkey-cage/wp/2016/08/11/how-islamophobic-rhetoric-feeds-extremist-propaganda, accessed April 10, 2018.

PART III

Countering Terrorism & Islamophobia

CHAPTER 9

Deepening Divides? Implementing Britain's Prevent Counterterrorism Program

Paul Thomas

INTRODUCTION

The reciprocal and recursive relationship between radicalization and Islamophobia, and the extent to which state policy interventions exacerbate or ameliorate this relationship, can be examined through analysis of terrorism prevention programs. This chapter, therefore, seeks to provide such insight through analysis of Britain's 'Prevent strategy', launched in the wake of the 7/7 London bombings of July 2005.[1] Here, Britain was a forerunner in such preventative, 'soft' counterterrorism approaches and has attracted much interest.[2] Prevent has been highly controversial throughout its existence,[3] arguably both reflecting and re-enforcing a state and societal Islamophobic focus on British Muslims as an existential threat. The chapter recognizes that 'Islamophobia' remains a highly-contested concept[4] but it argues that Prevent's very establishment as a counterterrorism program initially focused only (and on a very large-scale)[5] on Muslims both reflected and re-enforced a growing Islamophobic trend within British media and political discourse. Here, the chapter does not claim that Islamophobia *causes* radicalization (as this very concept

P. Thomas (✉)
University of Huddersfield, Huddersfield, UK
e-mail: d.p.thomas@hud.ac.uk

© The Author(s) 2019
J. L. Esposito and D. Iner (eds.), *Islamophobia and Radicalization*,
https://doi.org/10.1007/978-3-319-95237-6_9

is highly problematic) but rather that misguided policy measures in the name of counter-radicalization can re-enforce and deepen Islamophobia. The chapter argues that whilst previous allegations of Prevent being a state surveillance scheme[6] and having only malign impacts,[7] on British Muslims were over-stated, Prevent's initial design had a negative impact on state-Muslim relations and trust, so deepening divides between British Muslims and their fellow British citizens and being counter-productive in its own stated counterterrorism terms. Here, Prevent significantly damaged the 'human intelligence' vital to defeat terrorism (see Grossman, this volume), whilst very possibly hardening defensive and antagonistic identifications and mind-sets within some alienated subsections of Muslim communities.[8] Subsequent modifications to Prevent have, for some, deepened this problem[9] but may also be showing the potential to 'de-toxify' Prevent,[10] partly through more progressive 'policy enactment' at the local level.[11]

To develop this case, the chapter firstly provides a brief, factual overview of the development of Prevent. It then briefly develops a theoretical understanding of recent developments in British multiculturalism, within which Prevent's initial, negative impacts can be understood. In doing so, the paper offers a positive analysis of British post-2001 community cohesion[12] strategies. It also discusses the relationship between British multiculturalism, anti-Muslim racism and Islamophobia. It then goes on to analyze Prevent and its problematic impacts in two stages. First, it analyzes the assumptions, nature and content and (often) malign impacts of Prevent in its establishment from 2007 onwards ('Prevent 1'), Second, it discusses the significant, post-2011 changes ('Prevent 2') that are arguably more complex, at least in their ground-level enactment.

The Development of Britain's Prevent Program

Britain's Prevent program has developed through two distinct phases. 'Prevent 1' ran from its inception under the-then Labor government in 2007 until the 2011 Prevent Review[13] initiated by the new Coalition government. 'Prevent 2' has run from 2011 to date. Whilst there have been some aspects on continuity within and between these phases, there have also been significant adjustments during each phase. These adjustments partly reflect unexpected events—Britain did not originally envision a domestic threat and so had to rapidly create Prevent in the wake of 7/7[14]; similarly, the Syria/ISIS crisis provided new challenges.

These adjustments also reflect tensions and different perspectives within national government (between different government departments and between different political parties during the 2010–2015 Coalition government[15]), and between the national state and the local government bodies being asked to implement Prevent.

Prevent 1 was rapidly operationalized through an initial 'pathfinder' year of 2007–2008 and then significantly expanded between the 2008 and 2011 period. This development involved funding to all local authority areas having a certain number of Muslim residents via the Department for Communities and Local Government (DCLG), attempts to develop more polyphonic consultation structures with Muslim communities (particularly with women and young people) both nationally and locally, promotion of more 'moderate' forms of Islamic practice through initiatives such as the 'Radical Middle Way' roadshow and over 300 dedicated Police posts via the security-focused Home Office and its Office for Security and Counter-Terrorism (OSCT). Together, this program represented almost £150 millions of spending on a program purely being about community engagement, rather than crime detection.[16] Local authorities took a variety of approaches, with some distributing all monies to Muslim community organizations, whilst others used it to develop their own programs. A significant priority nationally was developing contact with Muslim young people through youth work[17] and the development of Muslim civil society, such as greater training for staff of Mosque schools.[18]

The rapidly-increasing dominance of the Police in the direction and even delivery of local Prevent work[19] prompted hostile press coverage, accusations of 'spying'[20] and a critical Parliamentary Select Committee Inquiry.[21] The incoming Coalition government first paused the program then launched a revised 'Prevent 2' in June 2011.[22] This removed the DCLG from the program and focused on a significantly smaller number of local authorities, supposedly identified on an intelligence basis, with much-reduced funding. Funding for this work was to be centrally controlled by the OSCT, with this and the continuing Police element of Prevent emphasizing the increasingly securitized nature of the program. Prevent 2 broadened the focus from 'violent extremism' to a rather vague 'extremism' but did also expand to include far-right/neo-Nazi extremism. A new priority was the 'Channel' scheme, whereby young people viewed as 'vulnerable' to radicalization would be referred for individual counseling. Nevertheless, the public profile of the Prevent scheme seemed to be reducing until the twin events of the 2013 Islamist murder of a soldier in London and the Syria crisis led to a re-energizing and re-growth of Prevent[23] and the introduction of the 'Prevent duty' on all education, welfare and health professional institutions and staff through the 2015 Counter-Terrorism and Security Act. This duty was to 'safeguard' people against extremism, supported by large scale, compulsory training. Alongside this, has come a new requirement for schools to promote 'fundamental British values'.[24]

British Multiculturalism, Policy Enactment and Prevent

Prevent can be seen as part of wider British multiculturalist policy approaches through both its initial targeting of Muslims as an essentialized 'community' and its operations via specific ethnic and religious organizations. Britain was one of the Western states to overtly adopt multiculturalist policies involving legal protections and specific funding measures for distinct ethnic and religious groups, although these policies have often been called other things and have experienced distinct stages of operation.[25] Whilst a highly centralized state, Britain's multiculturalist policy experience is one of tension between national objectives and local perspectives, with measures often being significantly mediated at local level. For this reason, the concept of 'policy enactment',[26] how ground-level practitioners understand and mediate such policies, is highly relevant to British multiculturalist experience and this is illustrated by controversies over the direction of policy towards community cohesion[27] following the 2001 riots in northern towns that largely involved young Muslims. Official analysis explicitly criticized the previous multiculturalist approach of programs dedicated to specific ethnic communities and measuring outcomes for each, essentialized group. This approach was seen as having contributed to 'parallel lives',[28] to hardened, separate ethnic identifications[29] and to a resulting 'white backlash'[30] against perceived state favoritism towards (Muslim) minority communities, all seen as central to the 2001 riot triggers. In this climate, multiculturalist policy approaches per se were blamed for creating both Muslim 'ghettos'[31] and a terrorist threat seen as directly stemming from these supposedly separate communities,[32] views implicitly endorsed by Britain's Prime Minister.[33] There was, of course, a long-standing progressive critique of multiculturalist policies operationalized through the 'leaders' of essentialized 'communities' and increasingly focusing on culture, *'taking it away from a focus on structural inequalities'*[34] that encouraged the multi-ethnic anti-racist and equality movements of the 1970s and early 1980s.

The policy response of community cohesion stressed both commonality and support for 'shared values', leading to characterizations of this being a retreat to assimilationism. However, theories of policy enactment stress the need to understand this contingent, ground-level experience. Here, my own research[35] on how community cohesion was practised by youth workers in Oldham (scene of one of the 2001 riots) showed that practice was still acknowledging distinct ethnic/religious identifications and experiences but seeking to augment them with stronger forms of commonality through cross-community work based around 'contact theory'.[36] This approach was inherently (and necessarily) operationalizing policy notions of more complex and fluid identifications in an increasingly diverse society,[37] with other empirical studies showing significant practitioner support for this policy approach and the grounded realities it spoke to.[38] This highlights the contradiction of Prevent but also suggests the need to draw on empirical studies to understand the reality of Prevent's operation.

Beyond dispute is the fact that both the community cohesion and Prevent policy initiatives emerged as public antipathy to British Muslims seemed to be growing. Here, multiculturalist policy approaches may have been double-edged for Muslims, allowing justifiable claim-making as a group[39] but this very profile and advances towards individual and collective equality it enabled provoked antagonism from elements of the majority community. Whilst the events of the 9/11 and 7/7 attacks have clearly fueled such anti-Muslims sentiments, Hussain and Bagguley chart how such sentiments have been growing steadily since the late 1980s:

> Paralleling the developing discourse amongst politicians and the media… overall from the opinion polls it appears that slightly less than one third of the UK population are consistently hostile towards Muslims and Islam.[40]

This would seem to support Abbas's assessment of the higher profile enabled by multiculturalist policy, much of it enacted in response to claim-making by a rapidly-growing Muslim population. Here, events such as the Satanic Verses crisis and the first Gulf War have also played a role. Some have interpreted such sentiments as 'Islamophobia' but this remains a highly-contested concept,[41] with some seeing it as indistinct from, or even undermining acknowledgement of, racism. Others see it as a way of closing down through a racialized homogenization legitimate criticism of (often gendered) cultural practices within Muslim-background communities, where use of 'Islamophobia'.

Nevertheless, Hussain and Bagguley argue that racism and Islamophobia should not be conflated, using empirical evidence drawn from the communities that the 7/7 bombers originated from to argue that the situated and contingent discriminatory behavior subsequently experienced by local Muslims is specifically about their faith identification, not their ethnicity or skin color:

> Whilst Muslims might be identified using racialized criteria, it is notable that verbal insults reported here are specifically inferring the Islamic identity of their targets.[42]

It is certainly true that far-right political activity in both Britain and Europe has increasingly focused on Muslims and the supposed 'Islamification' of Europe.[43] Arguably, the very establishment of the Prevent program has confirmed that British Muslims are now an undifferentiated, 'suspect community' in the way that Britain's Irish community was previously.[44] Whilst this is disputed below, it is clear that the perception of Muslims as a cultural threat has now been re-enforced by a growing securitization of state-Muslim relations. Here, it is argued that Prevent's very establishment suggested that Muslims per se were a national security threat, a public perception subsequently re-enforced by the scale and nature of Prevent's surveillance approach. For Frost,[45] such dominant state and media representations of Muslims as being connected to terrorism inevitably contribute to increased race hate towards Muslims at ground level. As is outlined below, it is beyond dispute that the Police became increasingly dominant within the Prevent program but does this inevitably represent an overt use of disciplinary power by the state or is that too simplistic an assumption about the messy reality of policy enactment at ground level? More relevant here, arguably, to analysis of how Prevent has impacted on Muslim state relations are more complex notions of neoliberal governmentality[46] that normalize a securitized focus on Muslims as a supposedly 'objective' threat.

Prevent 1: Deepening Divides

Despite the shock of 7/7, the new Prevent strategy was not welcomed by many at ground level, including the local authorities in West Yorkshire, home of the 7/7 attackers. Here, the local authorities fully understood the terror threat but saw the establishment of Prevent, explicitly targeted at Muslims only, as counterproductive. Instead, they wanted to use their developing community cohesion work as a non-stigmatizing platform to tackle extremism, of all types, more robustly.[47] This preference was over-ruled, Prevent was imposed from above and, under huge national pressure, local authorities did their job and implemented it. However, their fears that Prevent would stigmatize Muslims, deepen already problematic community divides and side-track community cohesion work were fully realized in time.[48]

These malign effects flowed directly from the initial Muslim-only focus of Prevent and it's large-scale. The program was first developed in all local authority areas with 5% or more of their residents being Muslims, this blanket approach showing the lack of state intelligence about threats. Despite warm words in policy documents about a 'tiny minority' of terrorists, this large-scale approach suggested a different governmental perspective in practice. Indeed, early Prevent guidance to local authorities spoke of the need for '*demonstrable changes in attitudes amongst Muslims*'.[49] The large scale of Prevent activity between 2008 and 2011 clearly suggested to the public that support for extremism amongst Muslims was wide spread and an urgent threat to society.

The scale of this program also meant that the impacts within Muslim communities were significant. Whilst large numbers of young Muslims were engaged in normal but Muslim-only youth activities largely devoid of any anti-extremism educational content,[50] Prevent also attempted more significant 'social engineering' of Muslim communities. At the local level, there was significant state engagement with Muslim faith organizations[51] and efforts to strengthen the governance and transparency of such organizations. At the national level, new representative bodies were established, including 'Advisory Groups' for Muslim youth and women, and explicit attempts to promote more 'moderate' forms of Islamic thought and practice through the 'Radical Middle Way' roadshow. This, alongside significant financial support for new anti-extremism groups like the Quilliam Foundation (who claimed the problem of extremism within Muslim communities was significant) and government breaking off contact with the umbrella representative body, the Muslim Council of Britain, all strengthened the perception that Muslim communities per se had a problem and this urgent government intervention was needed to address it. Sociologist Stuart Hall described this package of interventions as '*the most profound internal penetration of an ethnic community*' under British multiculturalism.[52] The internal impacts of this 'penetration' included significant disagreements within Muslim communities over whether to take this money, complicated by wider, austerity-driven cuts in public spending.[53] Here, some supported the idea of gaining from this 'Muslim money'[54] but others highlighted how such Muslim community development activity was being funded by explicitly anti-terrorism funding.

This very significant funding and intervention package had exactly the negative impacts on perceptions that local authorities feared. The large-scale focus on Muslim communities suggested to many Muslims that they were, indeed a 'suspect community', a feeling exacerbated by Prevent's lack of focus on far-right/racist extremism. This could only harden feelings within Muslim communities of being the 'other' and strengthen internal political voices claiming that Muslim would never be accepted as equal citizens.[55] At the same time, the scale of Prevent funding for Muslims-only provoked 'resource envy' from other communities, an echo of one of the key triggers of the 2001 riots. Other major Faiths were explicitly resentful in their evidence to a Parliamentary Inquiry[56] whilst local evidence shows that white resentment of supposed funding favoritism towards Muslims continues.[57]

From the start, many saw Prevent as little more than a program of state spying on Muslims, given the very significant Police role within the program. Specific allegations of overt pressure on youth workers to reveal information[58] (Kundnani 2009), part of the 'chilling effect'[59] experienced by many ground-level Muslim professionals, led to the Parliamentary Inquiry. Whilst the Inquiry and government itself rejected this characterization of Prevent as a disciplinary regime of surveillance, Sir David Omand, the spymaster who devized Prevent, didn't offer such re-assurances when giving evidence to the All-Party Parliamentary Group on Homeland Security in 2010, saying that:

> you can't divide government in two, into those people that go around spying on the population, and there are another lot of people going round to

the population and they just don't talk to each other. It just simply doesn't work like that.[60]

Omand was even blunter in an interview given to the Financial Times weeks before that, when he suggested that it would be naïve of the state to not use any intelligence from community-based Prevent activities, in the face of a very serious terrorist threat.[61] The stark allegation of Prevent as a spying scheme is challenged, though, by some of the ground-level data about the experience of implementing Prevent 1. Here, there is acknowledgment that it enabled stronger relationships between the local state and Muslim communities and specifically enabled an increased role for Muslim faith organizations. More broadly, the evidence of significant Muslim involvement in and agency around local Prevent design and governance[62] in the face of the acknowledged criticisms highlighted here argues for an analysis of Prevent implementation as 'contested practice',[63] rather than simply being an exercizing of state disciplinary power.

Nevertheless, the supposedly multi-agency local Prevent arrangements were quickly 'captured' by the Police, through both their cultural power and organizational strength,[64] with clear evidence of Police controlling local Prevent funding decisions and even directly delivering the program to community groups. More broadly, a similar process both nationally and locally saw Prevent side-line community cohesion. The net result of both Prevent itself and its impact on the local authorities asked to implement Prevent and community cohesion at the same time was a growing securitiszation of the state's relationship with Muslim communities whilst the cohesion policies that offered Muslims a broader, cross-community conception of citizenship were progressively undermined.

Underpinning this malign Prevent development were contested ideological assumptions about both the nature of any terrorist threat and of the dispositions of Muslims themselves. Birt[65] characterized the ideological tensions here as being between 'means-based' and 'values-based' perspectives, with these characterizations relating both to the nature/scale of the threat and therefore how policy should respond to it. The means-based approach saw causes of moves towards extremism as multiple and individual. This suggested a pragmatic engagement with a range of organizations that might be able to intercede and positively influence alienated individuals. The values-based approach, in contrast, sees the threat of terrorism as directly connected to beliefs and practices held more broadly within Muslim communities. This is expressed most starkly by neoconservative thinkers such as Conservative politician Michael Gove,[66] who see Western values under explicit threat from a totalitarian, ideological 'Islamism', so conflating conservative cultural practices within Muslim communities, various forms of political Islamism and specific acts of terrorism as one monolithic 'Islamism'. This perspective argues that widespread state intervention in and change within Muslim communities is essential to defeat Islamist terrorism. Central to such perspectives is a belief in the highly contested concept of 'radicalization'[67] and the 'conveyer belt' from Islamic organizations and practices towards terrorism.

It can be argued that some of the-then Labor government's approach to Prevent 1 was 'means-based' in that they allowed some initial local discretion over funding allocation and worked with a range of organizations. However, it is impossible to dispute that the 'values-based' perspective dominated through Prevent's very establishment in clear contradiction to community cohesion, its explicit attempts to socially engineer British Muslim life and organization and its progressive securitization of community relations. The chapter argues that this all reflected wider media and political Islamophobic discourse but also confirmed and deepened it by operationalizing a program, the very existence of which seemed to confirm that Muslims were a tangible threat to wider society.

Prevent 2: Securitizing Divides

This step change was introduced by the 2011 Prevent Review but it has actually been specific events (the 2013 Woolwich murder, the developing Syria crisis and the so-called 'Trojan Horse' affair) that have together provided the opportunity for the ideological drive towards surveillance to be accelerated. The 2011 Review was delayed by ideological fights over the values and means-based approaches within the governing Coalition. The eventual triumph of those argue for 'values-based' approaches saw the DCLG cut out of Prevent, the local authority program greatly reduced and such local work rigidly controlled by the OSCT. This significantly more centralized and security-dominated version of Prevent means that it is now almost impossible for local or national Muslim community groups, previously 'responsibilized'[68] by Prevent 1, to demonstrate leadership within, or even exercise influence over, Prevent activity. This clearly undermined any positive interpretation of Prevent 1's impact on Muslims at ground level.

A key justification for this shift was that Prevent 1 had damaged community cohesion work, as identified by the House of Commons Inquiry. However, the Coalition government promptly terminated Labor's 'twin track' approach of equal funding for local Prevent and cohesion work by ending all national funding, monitoring or even interest in community cohesion work. Now any cohesion, or 'Integration', as they termed it, activity was purely a local matter.[69] After having sidelined and securitized community cohesion perspectives and activities in Prevent 1, Prevent 2 officially killed off community cohesion. Ironically, 'Integration' returned to the fore in a recent speech by PM Cameron, but the assimilationist focus here was entirely on what Muslims should and must do to integrate. This conflated cultural practices or limited English use with 'extremism', and returned to the post-2001 trope that ethnic segregation had been 'chosen' by Muslims.[70]

Arguably the most significant development within Prevent 2 was the broadening of the strategy's focus from 'violent extremism' to an ill-defined 'extremism'. This represented the triumph of the 'values based' approach championed by politicians such as Michael Gove. This perspective overtly posited that extremist perspectives motivating would-be terrorists were shared by significant sections of broader Muslim communities and that terrorists made a 'conveyer belt' journey through legal but extremist Muslim political and religious groups, being influenced by these extremist ideologies as they moved towards actual violence. For Britain's Prime Minister:

> You don't have to support violence to subscribe to certain intolerant ideas which create a climate in which extremists can flourish.[71]

This understanding is central to Prevent 2's guiding but highly contested concept of 'radicalization', a post-2001 concept that seems to only be applied to Muslims. The immediate result was the removal of funding from a number of Muslim organizations seen as legal but 'extremist' in their supposed hostility to 'fundamental British values'.[72] Nevertheless, this new version of Prevent had a relatively low profile until a series of events in 2013 and 2014 enabled Prevent to be greatly expanded and foregrounded. The 2013 murder of soldier Lee Rigby was a genuine shock and Britain was also taken by surprise by the numbers of young

Muslims attempting to reach Syria, although whether such individuals could be described as 'radicalized' is highly contentious. The ideological, arguably Islamophobic lens, being applied by government can best be illustrated, though, by their opportunistic use of the so-called 'Trojan Horse' affair concerning state schools in Birmingham.[73] Here, a so-called 'extremist' take-over of Muslim-dominated state school was used to justify the operationalization of Prevent 2's ideology within the education sector. What was, in reality, community elements attempting to utilize conservative cultural practices in support of improving Muslim educational attainment was deliberately portrayed as part of a wider and threatening Muslim extremism. Gove commissioned a report from the ex-Counter-Terrorism Police chief and immediately instructed all schools nationally to teach 'fundamental British values', a term first coined by the 2011 Prevent Review. Schools were pressured to do so through inspection and have subsequently had a legal duty to implement Prevent imposed on them.[74]

This legal duty applies to all public bodies and is directly leading to a very significant and rapid securitization of British education and welfare services generally and of their interface with Muslim citizens in particular. Prevent training has been subsequently rolled out nationally to front-line practitioners on a very large scale. It is clear here that, whilst Muslim communities were 'responsibilized' for terrorism prevention in the 'Prevent 1' phase, it is now professional practitioners, such as teachers, lecturers and health staff who have been responsibilized by 'Prevent 2'. It is suggested here, though, that this should still not be seen as centrally-directed surveillance in a simplistic, top-down sense. Rather, Prevent 2 can be understood as neo-liberal governmentality, a policy approach by which front-line practitioners are 'responsibilized' for spotting radicalization. For McKee[75]:

> Governmentality does not restrict its analysis to the institutions of political power of the state. Rather, it defines the 'art of governing' more broadly as the 'conduct of conduct'.

For some critics, what this has led to is a situation where individual professionals (whose professional training is increasingly technocratic and has little focus on equality and social justice perspectives) enact approaches that stigmatize and mark Muslim young people as dangerous 'others'. It is in schools and colleges where the most controversy has resulted from this significant policy acceleration. National media concern has focused on a number of troubling individual cases, all involving Muslim pupils, of apparent mis-referral to Channel on a questionable, arguably Islamophobic basis. The scale of Channel has increased significantly since 2013, with over 6000 referrals nationally. More than half of these have been under 18's—the large majority of them Muslims.

What has been less clear, though, is the extent to which the malign cases highlighted represent the ground-level reality of Prevent duty implementation. Recent empirical research on the duty's implementation in English schools and colleges[76] found, unexpectedly, little overt opposition to the duty. Here, the 'safeguarding' paradigm of Prevent is largely accepted by professionals, with its focus on individual vulnerability to extremist influence seen as realistic. This focus on individual vulnerability is shifting the professional debate away from Muslims as a group, although the policy connection of Prevent with 'safeguarding' is significantly contentious.[77] Professionals surveyed by Busher et al.[78] were aware of the risk that the duty and its political/media discourse could well stigmatize Muslim students nationally but were adamant that this was not happening in *their* educational institutions, because of concrete policy and anti-racist educational measures they were taking to avoid it. Such evidence may be starting to alter British Muslim perceptions that Prevent is only aimed at them as one undifferentiated, 'suspect' community. This also seems to suggest, once again, that local processes of policy enactment are significantly altering the ground-level experience of Prevent. There is also evidence of local authorities enacting 'Prevent 2' in ways that are gaining support from local Muslim communities.[79]

Conclusion

This chapter has used Britain's Prevent strategy to illustrate how such counterterrorism policies can both illustrate and impact on the relationship between radicalization and Islamophobia. In particular, it has argued that, through its original design, Prevent initially exacerbated this malign relationship and so deepened already problematic divides between Muslims and the majority community. Whist Islamophobia remains a contested concept, the evidence for specifically anti-Muslim fears and prejudices growing in Britain and Europe before the 7/7, or even the 9/11, attacks is strong. Prevent's very establishment, in flat contradiction to the post-2001 policy reworking of multiculturalism as 'community cohesion', fueled these fears and so deepened divides by suggesting that extremism was a widespread problem within Muslim communities, as evidenced by such a large-scale intervention program.

However, the importance of 'policy enactment' in understanding the reality of British multiculturalist policy operation both enables support for this more positive understanding of what community cohesion can and does represent but also suggests caution about trenchant criticisms of Prevent. Here, there was some grounded evidence of 'Prevent 1'[80] bringing broader community development benefits and even enabling Muslim involvement in its governance. This suggests that, rather than simply being a disciplinary exercise of state surveillance of Muslim communities, Prevent 1 involved 'contested practice' at ground level. This claim initially seemed impossible to sustain under the 'Prevent 2' phase. The 2011 Prevent Review represented the triumph of the 'values-based' perspective that sees the terrorist threat as intimately connected to broader 'extremism' within Muslim communities and its foregrounding of the 'conveyer belt' conception of radicalization. The Woolwich murder, Syria crisis and the 'Trojan Horse' affair provided the opportunity for this perspective to be operationalized on a very large-scale in Prevent 2, with the 'responsibilization' of front-line professional practitioners through the 2015 'Prevent duty'. The resulting individual examples of malign, arguably Islamophobic, impacts on young Muslims were entirely predictable and seemed to lend greater weight to the previous claim that British Muslim were the new 'suspect community'. However, emerging research on the implementation of the Prevent duty suggests the continued importance of policy enactment in understanding the grounded, complex reality of Prevent in Britain. Here, both professional practitioners and local authorities are making conscious efforts to avoid the stigmatization of British Muslims, as they take responsibility for implementing preventative counterterrorism measures at ground level. Beyond dispute is the continued need both for more empirical research and more informed public debate on the complex relationship between counterterrorism policies, radicalization and Islamophobia in British society.

Notes

1. Department for Communities and Local Government (DCLG), *Preventing Violent Extremism: Winning Hearts and Minds* (London: DCLG, 2007); P. Thomas, *Responding to the Threat of Violent Extremism—Failing to Prevent* (London: Bloomsbury Academic, 2012).
2. P. Neumann, *Preventing Violent Radicalisation in America* (Washington, DC: National Security Preparedness Group, 2011); F. Ragazzi, *Towards 'Policed Multiculturalism'? Counter-Radicalisation in France, the Netherlands and the United Kingdom* (Paris: Sciences Po, 2014).
3. House of Commons Communities and Local Government Committee, *Preventing Violent Extremism: Sixth Report of Session 2009–10* (London: The Stationary Office, 2010); Open Society Foundation Justice Initiative (OSFJI), *Eroding Trust: The UK's Prevent Counter-Extremism Strategy in Health and Education* (New York: OSFJI, 2016).
4. Y. Hussain and P. Bagguley, "Securitised Citizens: Islamophobia, Racism and the 7/7 London Bombings," *The Sociological Review* 60 (2012): 715–734.
5. P. Thomas, "Failed and Friendless—The Government's Preventing Violent Extremism Agenda," *British Journal of Politics and International Relations* 12, no. 3 (2010): 442–458.
6. A. Kundnani, *Spooked: How Not to Prevent Violent Extremism* (London: Institute of Race Relations, 2009).
7. T. O'Toole, N. Meer, D. DeHanas, S. Jones, and T. Modood, "Governing Through Prevent? Regulation and Contested Practice in State-Muslim Engagement," *Sociology* 50, no. 1 (2016): 160–177.
8. P. Thomas and P. Sanderson, "Unwilling Citizens? Muslim Young People and National Identity," *Sociology* 45, no. 6 (2011): 1028–1044.
9. OSFJI (2016).
10. J. Busher, T. Choudhury, P. Thomas, and G. Harris, *What the Prevent Duty Means for Schools and Colleges in England: An Analysis of Educationalist's Experiences* (Huddersfield: University of Huddersfield, 2017).
11. P. Thomas, "Changing Experiences of Responsibilisation and Contestation Within Counter-Terrorism Policies: The British Prevent Experience," *Policy and Politics* 45, no. 3 (2017): 305–322.
12. T. Cantle, *Community Cohesion—A Report of the Independent Review Team* (London: Home Office, 2001).
13. Her Majesty's Government (HMG), *Prevent Strategy* (London: The Stationary Office, 2011).
14. S. Hewitt, *The British War on Terror: Terrorism and Counter-Terrorism on the Home Front Since 9/11* (London: Continuum, 2008).

15. P. Thomas, "Divorced But Still Co-Habiting? Britain's Prevent/ Community Cohesion Tensions," *British Politics* 9, no. 4 (2014): 472–493.
16. Thomas (2012).
17. V. Lowndes and L. Thorp, *Preventing Violent Extremism—Why Local Context Matters*, in Eatwell and Goodwin, 2010, pp. 123–141.
18. C. Husband and Y. Alam, *Social Cohesion and Counter-Terrorism: A Policy Contradiction?* (Bristol: Policy Press: 2011).
19. S. Knight, "Preventing Violent Extremism in Britain," *Financial Times Magazine*, February 26, 2010.
20. Kundnani (2009).
21. House of Commons (2010).
22. HMG (2011).
23. Her Majesty's Government (HMG), *Tackling Extremism in the UK: Report from the Prime Minister's Task Force on Tackling Radicalisation and Extremism* (London: HM Government, 2013).
24. Busher et al. (2017).
25. J. Solomos, *Race and Racism in Britain*, 3rd ed. (Basingstoke: Palgrave).
26. A. Braun, M. Maguire, and S. Ball, "Policy Enactments in the UK Secondary School: Examining Policy, Practice and School Positioning," *Journal of Education Policy* 25, no. 4 (2010): 547–560.
27. P. Thomas, *Youth, Multiculturalism and Community Cohesion* (Basingstoke: Palgrave Macmillan, 2011).
28. Cantle (2001).
29. Thomas and Sanderson (2011).
30. R. Hewitt, *White Backlash: The Politics of Multiculturalism* (Cambridge: Cambridge University Press, 2005).
31. R. Leiken, "Europe's Angry Muslims," *Foreign Affairs* 84, no. 4 (2005): 120–135.
32. G. Prins and R. Salisbury, "Risk, Threat and Security: The Case of the UK," *RUSI Journal* 153, no. 1 (2008): 6–11.
33. D. Cameron, "*Extremism Speech*" 20th July, Birmingham, 2015.
34. T. Abbas, "The Symbiotic Relationship Between Islamophobia and Radicalisation," *Critical Studies in Terrorism* 5, no. 3 (2012): 351.
35. Thomas (2011).
36. M. Hewstone, N. Tausch, J. Hughes, and E. Cairns, "Prejudice, Intergroup Contact and Identity: Do Neighbourhoods Matter?" in *Identity, Ethnic Diversity and Community Cohesion*, ed. M. Wetherell, M. Lafleche, and R. Berkley, 2007.
37. D. McGhee, *Security, Citizenship and Human Rights: Shared Values in Uncertain Times* (Basingstoke: Palgrave Macmillan, 2010).

38. H. Jones, *Negotiating Cohesion, Inequality and Change: Uncomfortable Positions in Local Government* (Bristol: Policy Press, 2013).
39. N. Meer and T. Modood, "The 'Multicultural State We're in: Muslims, "Multiculture' and the 'Civic Re-Balancing of British Multiculturalism," *Political Studies* 57, no. 3 (2009): 473–497.
40. Hussain and Bagguley (2012: 716).
41. Ibid.
42. Ibid., 730.
43. Abbas (2012).
44. M. Hickman, S. Silvestri, L. Thomas, and H. Nickels, *'Suspect Communities': The Impact of Counter-Terrorism on Irish Communities and Muslim Communities in Britain 1974–2007*, Paper at the British Sociological Association Annual Conference, Glasgow, 7th April, 2010.
45. D. Frost, "Islamophobia: Examining Causal Links Between the State and 'Race Hate' from 'Below'," *International Journal of Sociology and Social Policy* 28, no. 12 (2008): 546–563.
46. K. McKee, "Post-Foucauldian Governmentality: What Does It Offer Critical Social Policy Analysis?," *Critical Social Policy* 29, no. 3 (2009): 465–486.
47. Thomas (2012).
48. Thomas (2014).
49. DCLG, *Pathfinder Fund Guidance Note for Local Authorities* (London: DCLG, 2007), 7.
50. P. Thomas, "Youth, Terrorism and Education: Britain's Prevent Programme," *International Journal of Life-Long Education*, Special Issue, *Youth, Social Crisis and Learning* 35, no. 2 (2016): 171–187; Lowndes and Thorp (2010).
51. G. Iacopini, L. Stock, and K. Junge, *Evaluation of Tower Hamlets Prevent Projects* (London: Taivstock Institute, 2011).
52. BBC Radio 4, *Thinking Allowed*, Broadcast 16th March, 2011.
53. Ragazzi (2014).
54. Lowndes and Thorp (2010).
55. Abbas (2012).
56. House of Commons (2010).
57. P. Thomas, S. Miah, and M. Purcell, *The Kirklees Prevent Young People's Engagement Team—Learning from the First Year* (Huddersfield: University of Huddersfield, 2017).
58. Kundnani (2009).
59. Husband and Alam (2011).
60. All-Party Parliamentary Group on Homeland Security (APPGHS), *Keeping Britain Safe: An Assessment of UK Homeland Security Strategy* (London: The Henry Jackson Society, 2011), 107.

61. Knight (2010).
62. T. O'Toole, D. DeHanas, T. Modood, N. Meer, and S. Jones, *Taking Part: Muslim Participation in Contemporary Governance* (Bristol: University of Bristol, 2013).
63. O'Toole et al. (2016).
64. J. Bahadur Lamb, "Preventing Violent Extremism: A Policing Case Study of the West Midlands," *Policing* 7, no. 1 (2012): 88–95.
65. Y. Birt, "Promoting Virulent Envy—Reconsidering the UK's Terrorist Prevention Strategy," *Royal United Services Institute (RUSI) Journal* 154, no. 4 (2009): 52–58.
66. M. Gove, *Celsius 7/7* (London: Weidenfeld and Nicolson, 2006).
67. A. Kundnani, "Radicalisation: The Journey of a Concept," *Race and Class* 54, no. 2 (2012): 3–25.
68. Thomas (2017).
69. DCLG, *Creating the Conditions for Integration* (London: DCLG, 2012).
70. Cameron (2015).
71. Ibid.
72. HMG (2011).
73. S. Miah, *Muslims, Schooling and Security: Trojan Horse, Prevent and Racial Politics* (Basingstoke: Palgrave Pivot, 2017).
74. HMG, *Prevent Duty Guidance for England and Wales* (London: HM Government, 2015).
75. McKee (2009: 486).
76. Busher et al. (2017).
77. V. Coppock and McGovern, "Dangerous Minds? De-Constructing Counter-Terrorism Discourse, Radicalisation and the 'Psychological Vulnerability' of Muslim Children and Young People in Britain," *Children and Society* 28 (2014): 242–256.
78. Busher et al. (2017).
79. Thomas (2017).
80. Ibid.

CHAPTER 10

How Counterterrorism Radicalizes: Exploring the Nexus Between Counterterrorism and Radicalization

Haroro J. Ingram

This paper explores the nexus between counterterrorism and radicalization. It argues that misguided counterterrorism and counter violent extremism strategies may drive radicalization of not only the form of extremism being targeted by these measures (e.g. militant Islamists), but inadvertently help to fuel other forms of extremism (e.g. right-wing extremists). Radicalization that is driven by counterterrorism efforts are described here as "iatrogenic radicalization" (the term "iatrogenic", adj. relating to illness caused by medical treatment, being adopted from medical literature). With reference to Australian examples, this study analyzes three ways in which counterterrorism strategies targeting militant Islamists may inadvertently drive radicalization. The first relates to the often myopic and disproportionate focus of counterterrorism efforts on Muslim communities supported by the example of unprecedented counterterrorism laws and heavily policed antiterror raids.

H. J. Ingram (✉)
Australian National University, Canberra, ACT, Australia
e-mail: haroro.ingram@anu.edu.au

H. J. Ingram
International Centre for Counter-Terrorism, The Hague, The Netherlands

© The Author(s) 2019
J. L. Esposito and D. Iner (eds.), *Islamophobia and Radicalization*,
https://doi.org/10.1007/978-3-319-95237-6_10

The second concerns misguided counter violent extremism initiatives that fuel militant Islamist narratives of a "government-approved Islam" being championed in Muslim communities by compromised "moderates" and enforced by the state's counterterrorism apparatus. Anwar al-Awlaki's "Battle of Hearts and Minds" is analyzed to examine how such counter violent extremism (CVE) approaches are leveraged in violent extremist propaganda. The third relates to how counterterrorism strategic communications may inadvertently reinforce (rather than counter) violent extremist propaganda. This study cites the example of Man Haron Monis, an individual who appears to be more akin to a disturbed lone shooter than a terrorist, and the missed opportunities to both proactively and reactively confront Islamic State propaganda praising the Sydney Lindt Café attack. The overarching message of this research is positive: by understanding the *potential* for both "hard" and "soft" counterterrorism efforts to drive radicalization, strategic-policy decision-makers are better placed to ensure that their efforts not only "do no harm" to communities but "do no favors" for their violent extremist adversaries.

INTRODUCTION

With reference to Australian case studies, this chapter explores how counterterrorism measures may inadvertently drive radicalization: a phenomenon described here as "iatrogenic radicalization". It argues that counterterrorism measures enacted by liberal democracies tend to have a higher iatrogenic radicalization potential when characterized by three traits: (i) a disproportionate and myopic targeting of a single community, (ii) implement ideology-centric "soft" counterterrorism initiatives, and/or (iii) disseminate strategic communications messaging that reinforces rather than counters militant narratives. Such counterterrorism measures tend to increase perceptions of a crisis in target communities which extremist elements then leverage to drive the radicalization of vulnerable constituencies. This paper concludes by arguing that, unlike other drivers of radicalization which are notoriously difficult to control, counterterrorism agencies can diminish the impact of iatrogenic drivers of radicalization via greater scrutiny of operational and strategic-policy decision-making.

Western governments have spent extraordinary amounts of blood and treasure countering the threat of Islamist militancy since 2001. Yet, the national security assessments of many western governments suggest that the threat posed by Islamist militancy—both domestically and internationally—has continued to increase. In Australia, the number of

Australians that have reportedly traveled overseas to join violent extremist groups exceeded those of many other western nations on a per capita basis during the rise of so-called Islamic State circa. 2014–2015[1] while Islamist-inspired homegrown terrorists reportedly remain the primary domestic security threat.[2] Rather than ask how these trends have occurred *despite* counterterrorism efforts, the purpose of this study is to explore how counterterrorism measures may have acted as drivers of radicalization: a phenomenon described here as iatrogenic radicalization.

Adopted from medical literature, the term "iatrogenesis" refers to the "inadvertent and preventable induction of disease or complications by the medical treatment or procedures of a physician or surgeon".[3] Thus "iatrogenic radicalization" refers to the inadvertent and preventable "blowback" effects that counterterrorism and CVE efforts may have on the radicalization of individuals and groups toward support of or engagement in acts of politically motivated violence. Rather than a distinct form of radicalization, iatrogenic radicalization is framed here as a unique set of drivers linked to counterterrorism efforts that may *contribute* to individual and collective radicalization more broadly. While individuals and groups may radicalize as a consequence of a complex litany of factors, this study focuses specifically on developing a conceptual framework of iatrogenic radicalization which it then applies to explore the dynamics of the phenomenon with reference to Australian case studies.

This paper offers two key assertions to the field. First, it argues that the iatrogenic radicalization potential of counterterrorism efforts increases, especially in liberal democratic societies, if the measure (i) disproportionately and myopically targets a single community, (ii) adopts an ideology-centric approach to so-called "soft" counterterrorism initiatives, and/or (iii) deploys strategic communications messaging that reinforces rather than counters militant narratives. However, this potential is unlikely to be realized, i.e. the actions act as a driver of radicalization, without the influence of radicalizing actors in the form of, for example, violent extremist charismatic figures or propaganda messaging. Drawing on primary sources including Anwar Al-Awlaki's *Battle of Hearts and Minds*, Al-Qaeda in the Arabian Peninsula's *Inspire* and Islamic State's *Dabiq* and *Rumiyah* magazines, this study argues that iatrogenic radicalization must be understood within the broader context of how militant groups either forewarn of or respond to counterterrorism measures that have a high iatrogenic radicalization potential, i.e. counterterrorism measures characterized by the three aforementioned traits.

Thus iatrogenic radicalization tends to emerge when the experience or perceptions of counterterrorism efforts by the "target" community are effectively leveraged by radical actors to shape and polarize perceptions in order to maximize the crisis-generating "blowback" effects for vulnerable members of that population. This study both offers the field a conceptual framework for understanding the iatrogenic radicalization phenomenon and applies it to case studies.

Second, unlike many other drivers of the radicalization process which are notoriously difficult to identify let alone counter, government agencies have comparatively greater control over the catalysts of iatrogenic radicalization. After all, the iatrogenic radicalization potential of counterterrorism measures can be significantly reduced through the methodical scrutiny of operational, strategic, and policy decisions. By acknowledging and understanding the fundamental dynamics of iatrogenic radicalization, architects of counterterrorism initiatives can devise approaches which not only reduce the iatrogenic radicalization potential of "hard" and "soft" countermeasures but, in so doing, significantly undermine the veracity of violent extremist claims that would otherwise be considered pertinent by vulnerable constituents. Consequently, reducing the iatrogenic radicalization potential of counterterrorism efforts may have compounding benefits when it comes to confronting the threat of terrorism.

IATROGENIC RADICALIZATION: A CONCEPTUAL FRAMEWORK

This study offers the field a framework for understanding iatrogenic radicalization based on a multidisciplinary conceptualization of the radicalization process. For the purposes of this paper, "radicalization" is understood as the process by which an individual or collective increasingly adheres to a selectively literalist interpretation of an ideology, a response that is triggered and catalyzed by perceptions of crisis which, in its latter stages, *may* lead to the legitimation and use of violence against perceived enemies as the solution to that crises.[4] This understanding of radicalization is built on three conceptual pillars that represent points of broad consensus in the scholarly field.

First, radicalization is framed here as a process of escalating phases, each of which is characterized by unique factors and signatures, that *can* lead to individuals or groups engaging in violence against perceived enemies.[5] The phases of the radicalization process are representative of cognitive changes, shifting ideological beliefs and changing political attitudes that are ultimately driven by a complex interplay of psychological and social (i.e. psychosocial) forces.

Second, the field broadly recognizes that feelings of alienation and marginalization are important drivers of the radicalization process because they tend to generate a need in individuals to alleviate these anxieties via an explanatory narrative (e.g. an ideology) and belonging to a group of like-minded people with a sense of purpose.[6] Building on this scholarly legacy, this study argues that "perceptions of crisis"—characterized by uncertainty, the breakdown of tradition and the Other—constitutes a crucial "pushing force" during the radicalization process. A corollary to these "push" factors is the role of a "solution" construct—characterized by certainty, the reinforcement of tradition and membership to an in-group identity—which acts as an important "pulling force" during radicalization. It is this mutually reinforcing dynamic between "push" (i.e. perceptions of crisis) and "pull" (i.e. solution) factors that fuel the multifaceted transitions that characterize the radicalization process. It is a dynamic that can be simply summarized as follows: the more extreme the perceptions of crisis, the more likely extreme solutions will be deemed not just legitimate but necessary. Violent extremist propaganda typically attempts to harness these core dynamics of radicalization via messaging that frames Others (i.e. out-group identities) as responsible for "perceptions of crisis" and commitment to the in-group identity and its narrative (e.g. an ideology promising certainty and the reinforcement of tradition) as the mechanism for solving the crisis (i.e. the solution construct).[7]

Third, politically motivated violence (e.g. terrorism) is understood to be a strategic choice that reflects not only a rationalized decision between violent and nonviolent forms of action but the cumulative product of the radicalization process itself.[8] Radicalized individuals and groups thus tend to engage in violence as a consequence of delegitimizing authority institutions due to their *perceived* complicity or ineptitude in dealing with the crisis *and/or* a perceived need to defend in-group identity members from crisis-generating Others.

Iatrogenic Radicalization

Figure 10.1 graphically represents the fundamental dynamics of the iatrogenic radicalization phenomenon.[9] The first dynamic concerns the

Fig. 10.1 Iatrogenic drivers of radicalization

role counterterrorism measures play as catalysts of perceptions of a crisis in "target communities". As the preceding radicalization framework suggests, growing perceptions of crisis increase the *potential* for elements within that community to radicalize. The second relates to the influence of militant actors—either via direct contact with members of the community (e.g. extremist leaders or broader extremist networks) or through the dissemination of violent extremist propaganda—that leverages the iatrogenic radicalization potential of counterterrorism measures to increase perceptions of crisis and offer a solution to the perceived malaise. These broad dynamics of iatrogenic radicalization reflect the mutually reinforcing dynamic of perceptions of crisis acting as "push forces" and solution constructs as "pull forces" during radicalization. The prominence of iatrogenic drivers of radicalization in a given milieu may increase the likelihood of members of the counterterrorism apparatus being legitimized as targets of terrorist violence. This further underscores the importance of understanding these dynamics as a means to protect law enforcement and national security personnel from such attacks.

Iatrogenic radicalization occurs with the *fusion* of perception of crisis-generating counterterrorism measures *and* the influence of radical actors who leverage those perceptions of crisis to offer solutions to that sense of crisis. Rather than a unique form of radicalization, it is a dynamic that may contribute to the overall radicalization phenomenon of individuals and groups. This study proposes that the iatrogenic radicalization potential of counterterrorism efforts, particularly in liberal democracies, increases if the measure:

   i. disproportionately and myopically targets a single community,
  ii. adopts an ideology-centric approach to so-called "soft" counterterrorism initiatives; and/or,
 iii. deploys strategic communications messaging that reinforces rather than counters militant narratives.

The three key drivers of iatrogenic radicalization will now be explored in greater depth.

Myopic and Disproportionate: Catalysts of Crisis?

This study proposes that the iatrogenic radicalization potential of counterterrorism measures is likely to increase if it myopically and disproportionately targets a single community. A useful means to explore these traits is with reference to the suite of antiterror legislation that has been introduced in Australia since 2001.[10] While the necessity of post-2001 changes to Australia's terrorism laws may remain a point of contention, there is universal agreement that the legislation was and remains unprecedented in both its legal scope and delegation of sweeping and loosely defined powers to authorities.[11] For example, the broad scope and flexibility within Australia's terrorism laws are epitomized by "Section 101.4 Possessing things connected with terrorist acts":

1. A person commits an offence if:
   (a) the person possesses a thing; and
   (b) the thing is connected with preparation for, the engagement of a person in, or assistance in a terrorist act; and
   (c) the person mentioned in paragraph (a) knows of the connection described in paragraph (b).
   Penalty: Imprisonment for 15 years.

2. A person commits an offence if:
   (a) the person possesses a thing; and
   (b) the thing is connected with preparation for, the engagement of a person in, or assistance in a terrorist act; and
   (c) the person mentioned in paragraph (a) is reckless as to the existence of the connection described in paragraph (b).
   Penalty: Imprisonment for 10 years.
3. A person commits an offence under subsection (1) or (2) even if:
   (a) a terrorist act does not occur; or
   (b) the thing is not connected with preparation for, the engagement of a person in, or assistance in a specific terrorist act; or
   (c) the thing is connected with preparation for, the engagement of a person in, or assistance in more than one terrorist act.[12]

Individuals can face severe penalties for possessing essentially any "thing" that can be linked to a terrorist act even if the act not only does not occur but the "thing" is "...not connected with preparation for, the engagement of a person in, or assistance in a specific terrorist act..."[13] The extraordinary scope within this one section is mirrored throughout Part 5.3 of the *Criminal Code Act 1995*.

In addition to its scope and definitional breadth, the legislation sets new legal precedencies in a number of ways but perhaps the most remarkable concerns inchoate liability. The criminal codes of western nations have often included inchoate offences which allow law enforcement agencies to charge individuals for attempting to engage in or conspire to engage in an offence before the act itself is committed as a prevention mechanism. However, as McGarrity, Lynch and Williams argue, Australia's terrorism laws have created "pre-inchoate" liability, i.e. the criminalization of actions that would typically be considered formative to a criminal act, therefore rendering, "...individuals liable to very serious penalties despite the lack of a clear criminal intent".[14] The broader legal implications are that individuals can face severe penalties for actions that would not even attract charges if committed outside of a counterterrorism investigation (e.g. armed robbery).

Australia's terrorism laws undoubtedly challenge fundamental rights and liberties that should be protected in a democracy. As Williams argues, "The result in Australia is a body of anti-terror laws that undermines democratic freedoms to a greater extent than the laws of other comparable nations, including nations facing a more severe terrorist threat".[15] Williams argues that the impact of the legislation is magnified because, "…Australia has copied anti-terror laws from other nations, including the UK, without also copying the corresponding safeguards".[16]

Of course, Australia's terrorism laws were not designed for any single community and could be used against a plethora of individuals and groups, especially given the sweeping powers it affords Australian authorities. However, it is Muslims that have been and remain disproportionately impacted by this legislation.[17] The vast majority of those charged with terrorism offences in Australia have been Muslims and this reflects the largely myopic focus of law enforcement and intelligence agencies on Muslim communities.[18] This trend is mirrored in the Australian government's list of proscribed terrorist organizations with the vast majority of listed groups being Islamists.[19] It is also worthwhile considering how these terrorism laws have been implemented. The resources devoted to, for example, antiterror raids have often far exceeded those of other serious crimes, particularly accounting for results. For instance, on September 18, 2014 over 800 law enforcement officers were deployed across New South Wales as part of Operation Appleby resulting in sixteen arrests.[20] Ten arrestees were released later that day and three others the following day.[21] In total, two men were charged with terrorism-related offences. Given the extraordinary deployment of resources, an operational decision that has been typical of antiterror raids, this may seem disproportionate given the number of resulting arrests and is a trend that has typically not been replicated in operations targeting other violent crimes (e.g. outlaw motorcycle gangs). With the political rhetoric and media coverage around terrorism issues as further contributing factors, perceptions of crisis in the broader Muslim community have risen and this, ultimately, is unlikely to lead to a more stable security environment. For example, the public disclosure surrounding Operation Pendennis was found to have increased the sense of alienation among Muslim communities and exacerbated, if inadvertently, negative attitudes toward Muslim Australians.[22]

During this period, the aforementioned factors were highlighted in a public denouncement of proposed antiterrorism laws by a group of Muslim leaders in 2014.[23] At the heart of their statement was a sense that counterterrorism efforts—legislation, raids and political rhetoric—were myopically and disproportionately focused on the Muslim population:

> These laws clearly target Muslims and they do so unjustly. Whilst the language of the law is neutral, it is no secret that in practice these laws specifically target Muslims.[24]

The statement goes onto state:

> The primary basis of these laws is a trumped up "threat" from "radicalized" Muslims returning from Iraq or Syria. There is no solid evidence to substantiate this threat. Rather, racist caricatures of Muslims as backwards, prone to violence and inherently problematic are being exploited. It is instructive that similar issues about Australian troops travelling abroad to fight or Jews travelling to train or fight with the Israeli Defence Force are simply never raised.[25]

That a sense of crisis exists in the broader Muslim population as a consequence of counterterrorism efforts has been explored in several studies.[26] However, it is important to now consider how militant Islamist groups have attempted to leverage these perceptions of crisis to drive the radicalization of supporters.

AQAP's *Inspire* and Islamic State's *Dabiq* and *Rumiyah* are English language magazines that specifically target Muslims living in the west.[27] Consequently, the content of these magazines provide important insights into how militant Islamist groups attempt to leverage perceptions of crisis in Muslim communities that are rooted in counterterrorism efforts. An overarching theme in much of this messaging is that the myopic focus on Muslim communities using disproportionate measures is a manifestation of an ongoing War on Islam:

> Has the time not come O Ahlus-Sunnah for you to know that you alone are the targets? This war is only against you and against your religion. Has the time not come for you to return to your religion and your jihad and thereby bring back your glory, honor, rights, and leadership? Has the time not come for you to know that there is no might nor honor nor safety nor rights for you except in the shade of the Khilafah?[28]

Militant Islamist propaganda regularly compels western Muslims to see themselves as Western governments supposedly see and treat them: as Muslims. This excerpt from *Inspire* is designed to encourage western Muslims to recognize this reality and use it to empower them toward action:

...your belongingness to Islam is enough to classify you as an enemy. As a matter of fact, they look at us as Muslim youth regardless of our appearance and education. They do not consider our citizenship and the childhood we spent in their neighborhoods [sic].... Our enemies treat us as Muslims only, nothing more.... We must abide by our religion and stand on our ummah's side, one treatment one blame.[29]

Ultimately, violent extremist propaganda targeting Western Muslims does not shy away from identity's central role as a lens through which to understand the world and what needs to be done to solve Muslim crises: "*You have to decide what your identity is. This will help determine your future course of action. Do you de[fi]ne yourself according to your culture or your religion? What really takes more precedence in your heart?*"[30] It goes onto assert,

Finding out where your loyalty lies is the most important struggle in your identity search. The ones who [fi]nd clashes between what their heart tells them and what Islam commands, often fall into an identity crisis and end up justifying their actions or thoughts with [fl]imsy excuses while not realizing that Allah is closer to them than their jugular vein. This is the disease of the so-called 'moderates' who condemn their own mujahidin brothers because they see the fiqh of jihad in the same way America and her allies see it.[31]

Muslim concerns that sweeping antiterrorism legislation and the powers it delegates to authorities is being disproportionately applied to Muslim populations is understandable given the post-2001 history of Australian counterterrorism efforts.[32] The perception that Australia's counterterrorism efforts are myopically and disproportionately targeting Muslims is contributing, to varying degrees, to perceptions of crisis that tend to act as "pushing" forces during radicalization. What is certain is that militant actors are attempting to leverage these perceptions of crisis to increase the lure of their appeals.

The counterargument that Muslims are the subject of counterterrorism efforts because this is where the threat emanates assumes that law enforcement and security agencies are broadly covering all potential security threats with an equal level of scrutiny. That nineteen of twenty proscribed terrorist organizations are Islamist when there are countless violent politically motivated groups motivated by a plethora of ideologies globally suggests the focus has been largely singular. The other possible counterargument that other politically motivated security threats have not resulted in deaths in Australia carries less weight when the fact that an anti-abortionist attacked a Melbourne abortion clinic killing a security guard on July 16, 2001[33] while it was not until September 2014 that there were casualties as a result of "homegrown" Islamist-inspired terrorism.[34] As Australian right-wing extremists emerge on anti-Islam platforms with links to international extremists become more prominent,[35] questions must rightly be asked if Australia's counterterrorism legislation will be applied with equal vigor to these groups or whether their "right to be a bigot"[36] is protected in a way that it is not for Muslims. An even more telling test will be whether the same application of resources and similar evidentiary standards will be applied to cases involving extreme right actors.

Ideology-Centric "Soft" Counterterrorism Approaches: CVE Feeding the Fire?

In many western nations, the first wave of post-2001 counterterrorism measures tended to focus predominantly on enhancing "hard" counterterrorism capabilities through changes to terrorism legislation and increasing resources to law enforcement and security agencies. The next wave of counterterrorism measures were characterized by so-called "soft" counterterrorism strategies—i.e. CVE programs—that typically sought to address the sociocultural factors that were believed to create a conducive environment for radicalization. More often than not, it was Muslim communities that were the primary, if not the sole, target of strategies that tended to have two core aims: (i) to enhance community engagement between government agencies and the community, and (ii) to counter extremist ideologies particularly through counter-radicalization and deradicalization initiatives that tend to fall under the broad umbrella of counter violent extremism.[37] The latter has become a particularly prominent component of CVE efforts with the United Kingdom's PREVENT strategy being one of the most influential. Australia has implemented its own counter-radicalization and deradicalization programs, most notably in Victoria, that have similarly focused on countering extremist ideology.[38] The conceptualization of iatrogenic radicalization outlined in this study suggests that such efforts have the potential to be not just misguided but counterproductive.

The high iatrogenic radicalization potential of ideology-centric counter violent extremism efforts is rooted in two interconnected issues. Firstly, democratic governments dictating—whether directly or indirectly—what is and is not legitimate ideological belief for adherents to a religion is inherently problematic given freedoms of speech, religion and association. Moreover, within the broader context of post-2001 terrorism laws, it takes little for a perception to emerge that government-sanctioned parameters of legitimate religious belief are being enforced by the state apparatus. To overcome this perception, the architects of such counter violent extremism programs have often sought to co-opt "moderate" community figures, especially *imams*, as representatives and champions of "moderate" interpretations of Islam. Such an approach risks de-legitimizing those moderate voices that are most crucial to blunting the appeal of extremist elements due to a perception that those "moderates" are essentially government lackeys. Moreover, those who espouse "moderate" views and are not associated with the government initiatives may be similarly "tainted" for championing the government-sanctioned Islam. The narratives of militant Islamist groups frequently leverage these perceptions in their appeals to vulnerable constituents.

A central theme of militant Islamist propaganda targeting western Muslims is that the "hard" war against Islam (e.g. military interventions in Muslim lands or antiterrorism raids in the west) are merely the crudest manifestations of a deeper effort to fundamentally change Islam itself. As the senior AQ figure Abu Yahya Al-Libi declared:

> O Ummah of Islam: Know that there is a cooperative partnership which is undertaken by the shayatin from among mankind as well as jinn; it has its men, its faculties, its resources, its institutions, its expenses, its plans and programs. It is based and founded on making every effort to mislead people from their religion, to suggest doubt to them with regard to their self-evident 'aqidah, and to support every individual who fabricates lies against it as they wish.[39]

The implicit message underpinning counter violent extremism programs is typically that the fundamental battle for the "hearts and minds" of Muslims is between "moderate" and "extremist" interpretations of Islamic sources. The focus of militant Islamist narratives is often to highlight that the core concepts which these programs are attempting to remove or diminish are in fact the mechanisms that are vital to addressing Muslim crises:

> ...Obama can say things like, 'the terrorists want shari'ah law,' 'they want a global caliphate,' 'they don't practice the true Islam; they are not Muslims,' and so on, and that would by default put him at war with Islam because he wants a type of Islam that Allah didn't choose for us to follow. He wants an Islam empty of jihad, shari'ah, wala' wal bara, khilafah, and such; in fact, its not only him but the entire American administration from top to bottom. Therefore, they are at war with Islam.[40]

Anwar al-Awlaki enjoyed a charismatic appeal in some Muslim Diasporas with powerful messages, spoken in colloquial English, and a credibility inherent to being a child of the west.[41] In al-Awlaki's "Battle for Hearts and Minds",[42] he methodically explores how "soft" counterterrorism efforts are designed to fundamentally change Islam to a set of beliefs that are more palatable to the West. In short, "soft" counterterrorism measures represent an even more malicious attempt to destroy Islam and lead Muslims astray than military actions. It is a theme al-Awlaki often drew upon:

> We are living in a time when the West has publicly stated that it will use Muslim against Muslim in the battle field and will use scholar against scholar in the battle for hearts and minds of the Muslim ummah. As one CIA official stated: 'If you found out that Mullah Omar is on one street corner doing this, you set up Mullah Bradley on the other street corner to counter it.'[43]

The scholars linked to government-led initiatives are often given derogatory titles in these narratives, such as "government scholars" or the "sultan's scholars", and western Muslims are warned to, "...beware of those who speak Islam but do not practice it such as the government scholars who give *fatwa* according to the wills of their governments".[44]

The condemnation of "moderate" Muslims was a regular topic in Islamic State's English language magazines that warned of how "moderates" "...*have had their religion diluted and, not surprisingly, are always amongst the first to speak out in any case where the mujahidin display their harshness towards the crusaders, attempting to disguise their criticism towards the mujahidin as concern for the image of Islam*".[45] *Dabiq* also warns its readers to be cautious of smooth talking Imams regularly referring to the following *hadith* to underscore the inherent legitimacy of their claim:

> Abu Dharr (radiyallahu 'anh) narrated that while he was walking with the Prophet (sallallahu 'alayhi wa sallam), the Prophet said three times, 'Indeed, there is something I fear for my Ummah more than the Dajjal.' Abu Dharr asked him, 'What is this that you fear for your Ummah more than the Dajjal?' He responded, 'The misleading imams' [Sahih: Reported by Imam Ahmad on the authority of Abu Dharr].[46]

By leveraging feelings of crisis rooted in perceived government interference in what is deemed legitimate (even legal) Islamic belief, militant groups provide their audiences with equally stark solutions. Put simply, no "true" Muslim can practice Islam while living in the west:

> Even if one were to spend all his hours at a masjid in prayer, dhikr, and study of the religion, while living amongst Muslims who reside amid kuffar and abandon jihad, then such a person would only be establishing the strongest proof against himself and his sin.[47]

In this bipolar and uncompromising world, western Muslims are supposedly faced with a simple choice according to this propaganda messaging:

> The Muslims in the West will quickly find themselves between one of two choice, they either apostatize and adopt the kufri religion propagated by Bush, Obama, Blair, Cameron, Sarkozy, and Hollande in the name of Islam so as to live amongst the kuffar without hardship, or they perform Hijrah to the Islamic State and thereby escape persecution from the crusader governments and citizens.[48]

STRATEGIC COMMUNICATIONS REINFORCE RATHER THAN COUNTER MILITANT NARRATIVES: CONFIRMING THE BIAS?

The third factor that this study proposes increases the iatrogenic radicalization potential of counterterrorism measures is when government strategic communications—encapsulating a variety of messaging efforts from law enforcement statements to political rhetoric—reinforce rather than counters militant narratives. Of course, the iatrogenic radicalization potential of messaging that inadvertently strengthens militant claims can only be realized if they are effectively leveraged by militant narratives. This study contends that there are two ways these dynamics tend to manifest.

The first concerns the perceived disparity between what western governments say, particularly via its political rhetoric, and what western governments actually do in practice. While it may seem ironic that deeply conservative militant Islamist groups would highlight the gap between the proclamations of western governments that they are the representatives and protectors of democratic rights and liberties and their actual politico-military actions, it is a potent narrative strategy:

> We will not talk through the falsity of the portrayal of the nature of the morals of America, the country found on the violation of others' rights: It killed and annihilated the America's native peoples, the Indians. But we are certain that the sweet dream America propagated vanished into a terrifying nightmare: Abu Ghraib, black sites, Guantanamo and the US soldiers' crimes in Afghanistan and Iraq are too clear to need clarification.[49]

The second relates to how *possible* acts of politically motivated violence are reported by government agencies and the media. A pertinent example is the December 2014 Lindt cafe siege in Sydney which resulted in the deaths of Man Haron Monis and two innocent civilians.[50] While government statements were initially cautious about labeling Monis a terrorist, media reporting quickly labeled the siege a terrorist incident. This is certainly how Monis wished his actions to be portrayed given his messages to the media and his choice of attire. Islamic State skilfully used the Sydney siege and Monis as an example to its audience of,

> …a Muslim who resolved to join the mujahidin of the Islamic State in their war against the crusader coalition. He did not do so by undertaking the journey to the lands of the Khilafah and fighting side-by-side with his brothers but rather, by acting alone and striking the kuffar where it would hurt them most – in their own lands and on the very streets that they presumptively walk in safely.[51]

Dabiq's authors even responded to media reporting that highlighted Monis's criminal past by declaring:

...any allegations levelled against a person concerning their past are irrelevant as long as they hope for Allah's mercy and sincerely repent from any previous misguidance. This is so with one who embraces Islam and thereby has his past history of shirk and transgression completely erased – as was even the case with many Sahabah. So how much more so in the case of one who followed up his repentance by fighting and being killed in the path of Allah....[52]

Dabiq referred to Monis in several articles and his appearance in Islamic State messaging has been used to justify the assessment that Monis was a "home-grown", Islamic State affiliated terrorist.[53]

However, as the coronial inquest revealed,[54] Monis' life story was that of a deeply disturbed individual with a history of desperately seeking power and attention. Monis had previously described himself as a former Iranian intelligence officer, had a long history of bizarre political activism, had established a business as a spiritual healer and clairvoyant that appeared to be a front for sexually abusing women, and had been rejected as a member of the Rebels outlaw motorcycle gang.[55] Despite presenting himself as an Islamic State aligned Sunni Islamist, Monis had previously presented as a Shia cleric—indeed an Ayatollah—but also rejected religion during a period of more secular leanings.[56] Even during the Sydney siege, it became clear that Monis had little grasp of his own Islamic State allegiances reflected in the fact that he brought the wrong flag and requested authorities bring him the correct one.[57]

This raises an important question: what if these facts about Monis' life, which seem to paint a far more comprehensive picture than the image he wished to portray of an Islamic State aligned militant, were used to portray Monis? What if, instead of Monis being portrayed as a "terrorist", he was portrayed as a deranged shooter? Moreover, what if instead of *Dabiq's* articles being used as evidence of Monis' terrorist motivations, it was framed in counterterrorism strategic communications as evidence of Islamic State's desperation to portray even the acts of a deranged shooter as part of its warped caliphate? All of these questions can be summarized in the contention that strategic communications in a counterterrorism context need to be calibrated toward refuting, not giving veracity to, violent extremist claims whether it is those of militant Islamists or the extreme right. The example of Monis provides a pertinent example of how a more nuanced approach to strategic communications could be used to support counterterrorism strategic objectives and undermine the veracity of militant Islamist claims.[58]

Conclusion: Counterterrorism Implications

By acknowledging and understanding the fundamental dynamics of iatrogenic radicalization, architects of counterterrorism initiatives can devise approaches which not only reduce the "iatrogenic radicalization potential" of "hard" and "soft" countermeasures but, in doing so, significantly undermine the veracity of violent extremist claims that would otherwise be considered pertinent by vulnerable constituents. While this study has focused specifically on the iatrogenic effects of counterterrorism measures on Muslim communities, counterterrorism strategies that have a high iatrogenic radicalization potential tend to make the entire national security environment more volatile; a trend evident in the simultaneous surge of radical right-wing groups in many western nations emerging on anti-Islam platforms. Consequently, reducing the iatrogenic radicalization potential of counterterrorism efforts may have compounding benefits when it comes to confronting the threat of violent extremism in its various manifestations.

For instance, with the rise of right-wing extremists espousing anti-Muslim sentiments and often excusing (if not condoning) violence, using terrorism legislation to charge and prosecute such groups with similar enthusiasm would demonstrate both an equal application of terrorism laws and counter the perception that such laws are disproportionately applied to Muslims. By avoiding counter-proselytizing efforts and co-opting "moderate" Muslim champions, western governments would go a long way toward giving Muslim communities the space they need to confront extremism. Synchronizing more nuanced counterterrorism practice with an overarching strategic communications campaign would also be vital. Targeted messaging must be used to *proactively* shape how counterterrorism efforts are perceived by the whole community, while appropriately *responding* with counternarratives that refute (not reinforce) extremist messaging (whether from Islamist, right-wing or other extremists). Done effectively, this combination of strategic-policy shifts could have a "force multiplying" effect on counterterrorism efforts while having a "force nullifying" effect on violent extremist strategies.

Liberal democracies are faced with complex challenges when dealing with national security issues that require the careful balancing of security enforcement with the protection of rights, liberties and the rule of law. These challenges are perhaps particularly exacerbated in the counterterrorism sphere. As Maley argues,

> The protection of national security is an important responsibility of the state, but it requires a measured, balanced and mature approach, based on partnerships with the community, in which agencies of the state can be effectively educated as to the complexities of the faith communities with which they may be called to interact.[59]

Faced with increasingly volatile national security environments, law enforcement and intelligence agencies must also take into account the often inadvertent second and third order effects of their operational, strategic and policy decisions. This requires greater and more nuanced consideration being given to how extremist elements may attempt to leverage counterterrorism efforts to drive radicalization in vulnerable communities. Taking into account the potential "blowback" effects of counterterrorism decisions is *not* pandering to the whims of terrorist adversaries. What should be clear from this study is that having little regard for the counterproductive impact of counterterrorism efforts and inadvertently fuelling the conditions within which radicalization flourishes is doing exactly what our shared adversaries want. "Do no harm" is an oft-cited mantra for counterterrorism practitioners. Perhaps of equal, if not greater importance, would be "do no favors" for violent extremists of all types.

Notes

1. For more see J. Bishop, "Global Counterterrorism Forum, Palace Hotel, New York," September 27, 2015 (Transcript), http://foreignminister.gov.au/transcripts/Pages/2015/jb_tr_150927.aspx?w=tb1CaGpkPX%2FlS0K%2Bg9ZKEg%3D%3D.
2. For more see T. Abbott, "Review of Australia's Counterterrorism Machinery for a Safer Australia," Media Release, February 23, 2015, https://www.pm.gov.au/media/2015-02-23/review-australias-counterterrorism-machinery-safer-australia-0.
3. For example, the drug thalidomide was prescribed to ease the symptoms of morning sickness but it was found to cause severe birth defects.
4. For a more detailed description of the radicalization framework that informs this study see H. Ingram, *The Charismatic Leadership Phenomenon in Radical and Militant Islamism* (Oxford: Routledge), 63–74.

5. For example, see E. Sprinzak, "The Process of Delegitimation: Towards a Linkage Theory of Political Terrorism," *Terrorism and Political Violence* 3, no. 1 (1991): 50–69; M. Crenshaw, "The Logic of Terrorism: Terrorist Behaviour as a Product of Strategic Choice," in *Origins of Terrorism*, ed. W. Reich (Washington, DC: Woodrow Wilson Center Press, 1998); and R. Pape, *Dying to Win* (Melbourne: Scribe Publications, 2005).
6. For example, see J. Rabbie, "A Behavioural Interaction Model," *Terrorism and Political Violence* 3, no. 4 (1991): 134–163; C. Kinnvall, "Globalization and Religious Nationalism," *Political Psychology* 25, no. 5 (2004): 741–767; M. Ruthven, *Fundamentalism: The Search for Meaning* (Oxford: Oxford University Press, 2004); and C. McCauley and S. Moskalenko, "Mechanisms of Political Radicalization: Pathways Toward Terrorism," *Terrorism and Political Violence* 20, no. 3 (2008): 415–433.
7. This has been explored extensively by the author. For example, see H. Ingram, "The Strategic Logic of Islamic State Information Operations," *Australian Journal of International Affairs* 69, no. 6 (2015): 729–752; H. Ingram, "An Analysis of *Inspire* and *Dabiq*: Lessons from AQAP and Islamic State's Propaganda War," *Studies in Conflict and Terrorism* 40, no. 5 (2017): 357–375; and H. Ingram, "Deciphering the Siren Call of Militant Islamist Propaganda," *International Centre for Counterterrorism* 7, no. 9 (2016). Also see, J. Berger, "Countering Islamic State Messaging Through 'Linkage-Based' Analysis," *International Centre for Counterterrorism* 8, no. 2 (2017); K. Ingram, "IS's Appeal to Western Women: Policy Implications," *International Centre for Counterterrorism* 8, no. 4 (2017).
8. For more see M. Juergensmeyer, "Terror Mandated by God," *Terrorism and Political Violence* 9, no. 2 (1997): 16–23; A. Silke, "The Psychology of Suicidal Terrorism," in *Terrorists, Victims and Society*, ed. A Silke (West Sussex: Wiley, 2003); E. Sprinzak, "The Process of Delegitimation: Towards a Linkage Theory of Political Terrorism," *Terrorism and Political Violence* 3, no. 1 (1991): 50–68.
9. The terms was adopted from medical literature because it captures the complex, often inadvertent, but nonetheless negative repercussions of well-meaning interventions.
10. For more on Australia's terrorism legislation see Part 5.3, *Criminal Code Act 1995*.
11. G. Williams, "A Decade of Australian Anti-Terror Laws," *Melbourne University Law Review* 35 (2011): 1136–1176; A. Lynch, N. McGarrity, and G. Williams, *Inside Australia's Anti-Terrorism Laws and Trials* (Sydney: NewSouth Publishing, 2015).
12. Section 101.4, *Criminal Code Act 1995*, 146–147.
13. Ibid., 147.

14. A. Lynch, N. McGarrity, and G. Williams, *Inside Australia's Anti-Terrorism Laws and Trials* (Sydney: NewSouth Publishing, 2015), 33.
15. G. Williams, "A Decade of Australian Anti-Terror Laws," *Melbourne University Law Review* 35 (2011): 1171.
16. Ibid.
17. For more see W. Maley, "Australian Approaches to Dealing with Muslim Militancy," in *Muslims in Australia: The Dynamics of Exclusion and Inclusion*, ed. S. Yasmeen (Melbourne: Melbourne University Press, 2010), 270–290.
18. For example, see "Terrorism Court Cases," *Parliament of Australia*, http://www.aph.gov.au/About_Parliament/Parliamentary_Departments/Parliamentary_Library/Browse_by_Topic/TerrorismLaw/Courtcases.
19. See "Listed Terrorist Organisations," *Australian National Security*, http://www.nationalsecurity.gov.au/Listedterroristorganisations/Pages/default.aspx.
20. "Anti-Terror Operation in Sydney and Brisbane 'Thwarted' Beheading Plot," *ABC News*, September 18, 2014, http://www.abc.net.au/news/2014-09-18/anti-terror-police-mount-large-scale-raids-in-sydney-brisbane/5752002.
21. "Media Release: Clarification of Operation Appleby Numbers," *Australian Federal Police*, September 20, 2014, http://www.afp.gov.au/media-centre/news/afp/2014/september/media-release-clarification-of-operation-appleby-numbers.
22. "Effectiveness and Implications: Impact on Arab and Muslim Australians," *Parliament of Australia*, pp. 30–33, http://www.aph.gov.au/parliamentary_business/committees/house_of_representatives_committees?url=pjcis/securityleg/report/chapter3.pdf.
23. "Australian Muslims Denounce Proposed 'Anti-Terror' Laws," *ABC*, August 21, 2014, http://www.abc.net.au/religion/articles/2014/08/21/4071617.htm.
24. Ibid.
25. Ibid.
26. For a study on the impact of counterterrorism efforts on Muslims in Australia see "Effectiveness and Implications: Impact on Arab and Muslim Australians," *Parliament of Australia*, http://www.aph.gov.au/parliamentary_business/committees/house_of_representatives_committees?url=pjcis/securityleg/report/chapter3.pdf; For a study on the perspectives of British Muslims on counterterrorism measures see G. Mythen, S. Walklate, and F. Khan, "I'm a Muslim, But I'm not a Terrorist: Victimisation, Risky Identities and the Performance of Safety," *British Journal of Criminology* 49 (2009): 736–754.

27. The author has engaged in content analyses of these magazines, see H. Ingram, "An Analysis of *Dabiq*," *Australian Journal of Political Science* 51, no. 3 (2016): 458–477; H. Ingram, "An Analysis of *Inspire* and *Dabiq*: Lessons from AQAP and Islamic State's Propaganda War," *Studies in Conflict and Terrorism* 40, no. 5 (2017): 357–375; and H. Ingram, "Islamic State's English-Language Magazines, 2014–2017," *International Centre for Counter-Terrorism* 8, no. 15 (2018).
28. Anonymous, "And Allah Is the Best of Plotters," *Dabiq*, no. 9 (2015): 56.
29. Jonas the Rebel, "Dear American Muslim," *Inspire* (Al-Malahem Media, Spring 1434 [2013]), 17.
30. Samir Khan, "The Egyptian," *Inspire*, no. 5 (2011): 45.
31. Ibid.
32. "Effectiveness and Implications," *Parliament of Australia*; Mythen, Walklate, and Khan. 2009. "I'm a Muslim, But I'm not a Terrorist".
33. P. Anderson, "Deluded Pro-Life Crusader Peter James Knight Kills Guard, But Wanted More Dead After He Brought His Gun and Hatred to an Abortion Clinic in Melbourne," *Herald Sun*, March 11, 2014, http://www.heraldsun.com.au/news/law-order/deluded-pro-life-crusader-peter-james-knight-kills-guard-but-wanted-more-dead-after-he-brought-his-gun-and-hatred-to-an-abortion-clinic-in-Melbourne/story-fni0ffnk-1226850504649.
34. The disruption of terrorism plots (e.g. Operation Pendennis and Operation Neath) has often occurred at the very early stages of a suspected terrorist act making it difficult to accurately assess intent.
35. "Police on Alert as Reclaim Australia Rally Descends on Melton," *News.com.au*, November 22, 2015, http://www.news.com.au/national/crime/police-on-alert-as-reclaim-australia-rally-descends-on-melton/news-story/7dec4ffedddf0fcc85d74b06985086da; S. Anderson, "Reclaim Australia: Government Accused of Failing to Condemn Violence from Anti-Islam Extremists," *ABC News*, November 23, 2015, http://www.abc.net.au/news/2015-11-23/government-accused-of-failing-to-address-anti-islam-violence/6967278; and C. El-Khoury, "Anti-Muslim Extremists: How Far Will They Go?" *ABC News*, 2015, http://www.abc.net.au/news/2015-11-24/el-khoury-anti-muslim-extremists-how-far-will-they-go/6968034.
36. E. Griffiths, "George Brandis Defends 'Right to Be a Bigot' Amid Government Plan to Amend Racial Discrimination Act," *ABC News*, March 24, 2014, http://www.abc.net.au/news/2014-03-24/brandis-defends-right-to-be-a-bigot/5341552.
37. For an analysis of global counterterrorism programs see P. Neurmann, "Prisons and Terrorism: Radicalization and De-Radicalization in 15 Countries," *The International Centre for the Study or Radicalization and*

Political Violence (2010); A. Schmid, "Radicalization, De-Radicalization, Counter-Radicalization: A Conceptual Discussion and Literature Review," *International Centre for Counterterrorism—The Hague* (2013).
38. S. Neighbour, "Battle of Ideas to Curb Terror," *The Australian*, November 2, 2010, http://www.theaustralian.com.au/news/inquirer/battle-of-ideas-to-curb-terror/story-e6frg6z6-1225946335133.
39. Abu Yahya Al-Libi, "The Middle Path and the Enemy's Plot," *Inspire*, no. 5 (2011): 13.
40. Brothers et al., Qaeda in the Arabian Peninsula, "Inspire Responses: Responding to Inquiries," *Inspire*, no. 5 (2011): 10.
41. For analysis of Anwar al-Awlaki's charismatic appeal see H. Ingram, *The Charismatic Leadership Phenomenon in Radical and Militant Islamism*.
42. Anwar al-Awlaki, "Battle of the Hearts and Minds," Dar Al Murabiteen Publications, 2008.
43. Anwar al-Awlaki, "The New Mardin Declaration: An Attempt at Justifying the New World Order," *Inspire*, no. 2 (2010): 39.
44. Al-Malahem, "Interview with Shaykh Abu Sufyan," *Inspire*, no. 2 (2010): 44.
45. Anonymous, "The Burning of the Murtadd Pilot," *Dabiq*, no. 7 (2015): 6.
46. Anonymous, "Irja': The Most Dangerous bid'ah," *Dabiq*, no. 8 (2015): 50.
47. Anonymous, "Hijrah from Hypocrisy to Sincerity," *Dabiq*, no. 3 (2014): 32.
48. Anonymous, "The Extinction of the Grayzone," *Dabiq*, no. 7 (2015): 62.
49. Abu Abdillah Almoravid, "Shattered: A Story About Change," *Inspire*, no. 12 (2014): 53.
50. "Sydney Siege: Two Hostages and Gunman Dead After Heavily Armed Police Storm Lindt Café in Martin Place," *ABC News*, December 16, 2014, http://www.abc.net.au/news/2014-12-16/sydney-siege-gunman-two-hostages-dead/5969162; "The Siege of Martin Place: Terrorism in Australia," *The Economist*, December 15, 2014.
51. Anonymous, "Foreword," *Dabiq*, no. 6 (2014): 3.
52. Ibid.
53. J. Kidd, "Sydney Siege Inquest: Man Haron Monis a 'Radicalized Terrorist', Expert Tells Inquiry," *ABC News*, August 25, 2015, http://www.abc.net.au/news/2015-08-25/sydney-siege-inquest-hears-monis-a-radicalized-terrorist/6723172.
54. For more information on the interactions of Monis with the Government and further biographical history, see "Martin Place Siege: Joint Commonwealth—New South Wales Review," *Department of the Prime Minister and Cabinet*, January 2015, pp. 4–18, http://www.dpmc.gov.au/sites/default/files/publications/170215_Martin_Place_Siege_Review_1.pdf.
55. For more see B. Ryan, "Sydney Siege Inquest: Hostage Taker Man Haron Monis Tried to Join Rebels Bikie Gang, Rejected as 'Weird'," *ABC News*,

May 26, 2015, http://www.abc.net.au/news/2015-05-25/sydney-siege-inquest-man-monis-lindt-cafe-martin-place/6493752; R. Kerbaj, "Call to Probe Mystery Shia Cleric," *The Australian*, January 28, 2008, http://www.theaustralian.com.au/national-affairs/defence/call-to-probe-mystery-shia-cleric/story-e6frg8yx-1111115413357; and M. Safi, "Who Was Man Haron Monis? Plenty of Intrigue But No Clear Answers from the Sydney Siege Inquest," *The Guardian*, June 5, 2015, http://www.theguardian.com/australia-news/2015/jun/05/who-was-man-haron-monis-plenty-of-intrigue-but-no-clear-answers-from-the-sydney-siege-inquest.

56. For a brief outline of Monis' religious affiliations see "Martin Place Siege: Joint Commonwealth—New South Wales Review," *Department of the Prime Minister and Cabinet*, January 2015, p. 15, https://www.dpmc.gov.au/sites/default/files/publications/170215_Martin_Place_Siege_Review_1.pdf.
57. "Sydney Siege: Gunman 'Demands Islamic State Flag," *The Telegraph*, December 15, 2014, http://www.telegraph.co.uk/news/worldnews/australiaandthepacific/australia/11293809/Sydney-siege-gunman-demands-Islamic-State-flag.html.
58. For more see H. Ingram, "A 'Linkage-Based' Approach to Combating Militant Islamist Propaganda," *International Centre for Counter-Terrorism* 7, no. 6 (2016).
59. W. Maley, "Australian Approaches to Dealing with Muslim Militancy," in *Muslims in Australia: The Dynamics of Exclusion and Inclusion*, ed. S. Yasmeen (Melbourne: Melbourne University Press, 2010), 286.

CHAPTER 11

When the 'Right Thing to Do' Feels So Wrong: Australian Muslim Perspectives on 'Intimates' Reporting to Authorities About Violent Extremism

Michele Grossman

'Intimates'—especially close friends and family—are often among the first to see changes or early warning signs that someone close to them may be heading toward, or already engaged in, violent extremist activity, including plans to travel overseas and participate in violent conflict.[1] The role of family and friends in sharing information with authorities is critical to early intervention that can prevent greater harms from occurring, both for the person radicalizing to violence and for communities at large. Yet, community reporting can be experienced as a 'harm' when it is linked to concerns about stigmatization, discrimination, shame and backlash from both intra- and inter-community and government players.

Despite the importance of early reporting by intimates of those radicalizing to violence, virtually no evidence-based research has been conducted in Australia or elsewhere until now that solicits community

M. Grossman (✉)
Alfred Deakin Institute for Citizenship and Globalisation, Deakin University, Burwood, VIC, Australia
e-mail: michele.grossman@deakin.edu.au

© The Author(s) 2019
J. L. Esposito and D. Iner (eds.), *Islamophobia and Radicalization*, https://doi.org/10.1007/978-3-319-95237-6_11

views on what reporting means for community members, or explicitly addresses experiences, perceptions and concerns from Australian Muslim communities experiencing increased scrutiny and pressure around countering violent-extremism reporting imperatives.

Based on recently completed research with Australian Muslims and government stakeholders on community reporting thresholds for violent extremism, key study findings suggest that Australian Muslim community members see reporting to authorities as a last resort. There are significant psychosocial, cultural and structural barriers to sharing concerns related to individual and community sentiment. These involve perceived impact of reporting on social networks and relationships; flawed or confusing reporting processes and channels; lack of trust in government; lack of confidence in protective rather than punitive reporting outcomes for those at risk; lack of support for those who report as well as those reported on, and general anxiety about the personal, social, religious and legal impacts and consequences of reporting. A new approach to community education and awareness about reporting is needed, combined with new mechanisms to improve the integrity, support structures and transparency of the reporting process from community perspectives.

INTRODUCTION

Operation Pendennis, in 2005, and Operation Neath, in 2009, are two of Australia's best-known antiterrorism operations. In both these cases, the initial tip-offs to law enforcement that resulted in lengthy and large-scale police surveillance, arrests and trials came from within local Australian Muslim communities, through contact made by people close to alleged terrorist actors who had become concerned over the prospect of imminent or planned domestic acts of terrorism in Australia.[2]

Information tips from families and other community insiders in Australia and elsewhere relating to potential terrorist threats have led to heightened awareness of the ways in which communities serve as a frontline of defense against threats to national security and community safety, as well as playing a key role in helping influence vulnerable young people in particular away from violent extremist beliefs and settings.[3] Those closest to people involved in supporting or planning terrorist actions are often among the first to notice changes in behavior, attitude or orientation that may provide early signs that someone is considering violent action that will harm others—and they can sometimes be the first ones to provide support and intervention.[4]

At some level, the key role of what we term 'intimates', such as family, friends and community insiders, in the terrorism reporting landscape may seem counterintuitive: either because people think detecting terrorist threats is primarily about the tools and tactics of law enforcement and security agencies, or else because it seems unlikely that those close to someone who may pose a risk of violent harm will take the difficult step of coming forward to share what they know. This is particularly so when there are heightened perceptions of risk and vulnerability about sharing sensitive information with authorities, including perceptions of psychological risks, social risks, and legal and safety risks, or being unsure of where or to whom to turn.[5]

Yet how well do we understand what the experience of coming forward must be like for intimates, especially when they are in particularly close relationships with those they report: parents, siblings, spouses, lovers, children and friends? How do intimates navigate the psychological territory of reporting, which can involve significant feelings of guilt, betrayal and self-doubt? Or the institutional context of reporting, in which people may fear that they will be placing themselves, their families or their community at increased risk of stigma or intrusion by law enforcement or intelligence agencies? Or the social contexts of reporting, in which the very people to whom they would ordinarily turn to for support (such as other family members) may be seen as risky because of fears or concerns about their response? Or the aftermath of reporting, in which the person coming forward may feel isolated and unsettled, even traumatized, by the reporting process and its consequences?

The Australian university-led research study on *Community Reporting*,[6] supported by an Australian Government research grant, was an effort to engage with these issues and questions through community-engaged research with Australian Muslims, who for a variety of reasons are most frequently in the spotlight of public consciousness when it comes to issues around preventing or intervening in violent extremism. In so doing, the study was perforce compelled to engage with a central paradox involved in thinking about community reporting. This paradox is that the very action of seeking to prevent one form of harm—in this case, a terrorist attack—can risk creating other perceived harms for people who report on someone close, as well as for the person about whom they are reporting. A similar phenomenon occurs in the dynamics of bystander reporting, where guilt and fear of reprisals can inhibit people from intervening or sharing what they know or have seen.[7]

This is especially the case when, as for some people within Australian Muslim communities, one of the perceived harms created through sharing information with authorities is the intensifying of Islamophobic reactions that can inadvertently strengthen the persistent discursive association between Islam as religion and terrorism as ideology.[8]

At the time of the initial Australian study, there was virtually no open-source literature devoted to the issue of thresholds or concerns around community reporting related to terrorism. Subsequently, new work that replicates and expands the original Australian study has been conducted in the UK,[9] and US scholars have explored the role of young people as 'associate gate-keepers' in relation to bringing forward concerns about friends to authorities when they are worried that someone may be radicalizing to violence.[10] Previous research suggests that many Muslim community members in Western diaspora settings generally distrust both the intentions of police and the motives of government. In the UK, for instance, the literature reveals that Muslims there believed that counterterrorism initiatives such as the Prevent strategy became 'spying programs' devoted primarily to gathering intelligence on innocent bystanders,[11] and similar views were expressed in relation to the widespread NYPD surveillance program that broke in the media in 2013.[12] These results were mirrored in Australia by a 2013 study on community perspectives on radicalization and extremism.[13] Such distrust may be due in part to the fact that some members of immigrant populations may have a fear of law enforcement resulting from their own negative experiences and persecution in their homelands.[14] Significantly, however, this does not obviate the conclusion that a sense of persecution can also arise from diaspora Muslims' experiences with the police in their adopted lands.

In the current study on community reporting, Australian Muslims often made the point that they would not report their loved ones to the police for fear of criminalizing them. Their goals are to prevent tragedies from occurring and to rehabilitate would-be offenders, not see young Muslim men and women caught up in the criminal justice system. Further, many Muslims feel that the authorities are intent on locking young people up rather than addressing what draws them to violent extremist ideologies in the first place.[15] Joblessness, lack of education, disenfranchisement and identity struggles are all issues that must be tackled. Punitive measures designed to punish people do not address the root causes of radicalization and, if anything, are seen to make matters worse. Security-based repression measures can be counterproductive because they can increase the sense of victimization felt by Muslims more generally.[16]

Community members are also reluctant to share information with the police because they do not know what will happen to the information, or to the individual about whom the report was made, once they have shared their concerns with the appropriate authorities. Unwillingness to make a report can also stem from the fact that those sharing information with authorities will effectively lose control of the issue once they have made the report. It will be taken out of their hands and, furthermore, most Australian Muslim community members in the study were aware that they would not receive any feedback or follow-up on the case, even though they would have genuinely liked to be kept informed. Many Australian Muslims were unaware that in the event of sharing their concerns with the local police, those police agencies are likely to find that information on the individual/s in question will be withheld by other law enforcement agencies. In the United States, for instance, Wasserman maintains that both communities and police may sometimes be reluctant to share information with federal law enforcement agencies because they perceive that those agencies are unwilling to share information with them.[17]

Finally, Australian Muslim community members might not share information with the authorities out of ignorance of the appropriate steps to take or the proper individuals or agencies to contact. Not knowing who to approach or where to go can be a major stumbling block for community members with information on suspicious activity. If the person making the report does not already have an established relationship with a law enforcement officer or a trusted community intermediary, they are likely to feel overwhelmed by the thought of sharing sensitive information with someone they do not know. This brings us back to the importance of building and maintaining strong and trusting relationships between Australian Muslim community members and law enforcement officers and agencies, as well as between law enforcement and community or civil society organizations.

The *Community Reporting Thresholds* study has thus broken new ground in seeking to identify community knowledge and concerns around reporting experiences and processes; to propose new understandings and approaches to community reporting based on these insights, and to develop new platforms for community education and awareness based on the project's findings.

The Reporting Context in Australia: Previous Community Information Campaigns

Our focus on 'intimates' reporting that draws on community perspectives also marks a distinct departure from previous Australian government community reporting campaigns that have focused strongly on *general* community reporting. For example, in the United States, the 'If you see something, say something' campaign was launched in July 2010 to raise public awareness of indicators of terrorism and terrorism-related crime and to emphasize the importance of reporting suspicious activity to the proper law enforcement authorities. During the same period, the International Association of Chiefs of Police (IACP) received funding through the Dept. of Homeland Security's Federal Emergency Management Agency (FEMA) to develop strategies to improve the public's awareness and reporting of suspicious activity. IACP conducted primary research to better understand the motivations and barriers that affect community members' awareness and willingness to report suspicious activity.[18]

Based on the insights gathered from IACP's research, the following range of strategies to improve the public's reporting of suspicious activity was identified in a publicly available FEMA Resource Guide on community reporting[19]:

- Emphasize that community safety is a shared responsibility
- Engage the community in planning and promoting local campaigns
- Inform the public about the indicators of terrorism planning
- Address the community's privacy, civil rights and civil liberties concerns
- Leverage technology to promote anonymous methods of reporting
- Adopt simple and accessible methods to promote suspicious activity reporting
- Respond quickly to reports and follow-up, and
- Improve efforts by seeking feedback and tracking successes and challenges

Recognizing that law enforcement agencies depend on partnerships with local communities, the Building Communities of Trust (BCOT) initiative was also developed.[20] It includes recommendations such as training law enforcement officers in cultural sensitivity so that they can distinguish behavior that is constitutionally protected from criminal or terrorist activity; encouraging law enforcement to embrace community policing by emphasizing partnerships and problem solving; and encouraging communities to view information-sharing with law enforcement authorities as key to crime prevention and counterterrorism.[21] The program's objective is to bring about a better understanding by communities of how law enforcement is using the information to protect neighborhoods and citizens, while at the same time educating law enforcement on the priorities and needs of residents.[22]

In October 2014, the FBI launched a campaign asking the public for help in identifying foreign fighter terrorists, setting up an online form for submitting potential tips. As part of this initiative, the FBI took the unprecedented step of posting a video on its website of a masked fighter in Syria who speaks with a North American accent and urges Westerners to join Islamic State. The FBI posting includes a link to a newly established tip line promising anonymity to those who provide information about Americans joining al-Qaeda offshoots in Syria.[23] The FBI video was prompted in part by concerns officials had about the prospect of radicalized Westerners returning from Syria to carry out attacks in their homeland.

Both previous and current community reporting campaigns in Australia have been focused strongly on the National Security Hotline (NSH), the central mechanism for receiving, collating and distributing information provided by the public on national security information and concerns. The NSH was set up shortly after the 9/11 attacks in the United States, and reports information received to agencies including Australian Federal Police (AFP), Australian Security and Intelligence Organisation (ASIO) and State or Territory policing jurisdictions as relevant. Australian Commonwealth government public information campaigns designed to encourage people to report suspicions or information to the NSH have targeted general community reporting through (at various points) television, radio, print and, more recently, digital advertising. These campaigns began with the 'Let's look out for Australia' campaign (2002–2003), followed by 'Every piece of information helps' (2004–2006), 'Every detail helps' (2007–2016) and the current campaign (2017–present), 'If it doesn't add up, speak up'.[24]

The first of these campaigns, 'Let's Look Out for Australia' (known informally as the 'Be Alert but Not Alarmed' campaign), launched in 2002 with a $15 million investment and received wide publicity and comment. This campaign attempted a softer, more domesticated approach to previous efforts, which had emphasized the militarized and conflict dimensions of terrorism overseas. The 'blitz' style campaign, translated into 28 languages, saw the distribution of 'Be Alert but Not Alarmed' information kits, including fridge magnets, to Australian households across the country. In retrospect, this campaign was largely seen as a misfire, pilloried both in Australia and internationally for perceived excesses of cost and misguided messaging.[25]

Each of these campaigns, while slightly different in content, is linked by a common focus on the importance of casual observation in every day settings, on intuition or gut instinct for members of the general public that something is 'not right', and on small details being as important as more blatant or obvious signs that someone may be involved at various stages of planning a terrorist attack. Each campaign has been careful to ensure that listeners and readers are aware that their anonymity will be guaranteed if they choose.

However, these campaigns have had relatively little resonance or purchase with Australian Muslim communities. They have successively focused on broad community imperatives around safety and security; targeted cognitive rather than emotional responses to the threat of terrorism, and have not engaged with the fears, anxieties or doubts that people who actually know something or someone relevant, but who may feel conflicted about sharing it, can experience.

Moreover, the campaigns have drawn on aspects of *'us' and 'them'* discourse (particularly in the 'Every detail helps' campaign that ran from 2007–2016), which has arguably alienated many in Australian Muslim communities who have felt targeted and stigmatized by such approaches, not least because they run directly counter to the complex spaces of *'we'* that intimates who consider coming forward to authorities must navigate.

Community Reporting Thresholds: *Study Design*

The *Community Reporting Thresholds* study was designed as a qualitative research study, with data collection conducted between July and November 2014. Research participants across three cohorts (community members, community leaders and government stakeholders) were engaged in individual, in-depth face to face ($n=27$) and telephone-based ($n=4$) interviews of approximately 1.5 hours each.

A total of 33 participants contributed to the study (slightly in excess of the 24–30 participants anticipated in the research design). Of these, 16 participants were Australian Muslim community members (including community leaders) and 17 were Australian State and Commonwealth government stakeholders. The gender distribution of male to female participants was approximately two-thirds male ($n=22$) to one-third female ($n=10$) across the combined cohorts.

Community-based participants were sampled purposively and through snowball techniques in Melbourne, Sydney, Brisbane and Canberra, while government stakeholders were drawn from Victoria, New South Wales and Queensland policing jurisdictions; AFP; ASIO; Department of Immigration and Border Protection; Attorney-General's Department; federal and state-based government social service providers, and the NSH.

The recruitment of participants on a sensitive and confronting topic for Australian Muslim community members presented some challenges, but the project was able to slightly exceed its community and government target sample populations for the study as a whole. However, sampling in Sydney was further limited by community-based participant withdrawals from the project in October 2014 after potential participants there indicated initial willingness to contribute. These potential participants cited their unhappiness with the public climate surrounding the introduction of new counterterrorism legislation by the federal government in late 2014, which among other things increased the ability of security agencies to access private information about Australians both at home and abroad,[26] as the reason for declining involvement in this project. Accordingly, we were able to include fewer participants from Sydney than planned.

The research methodology and questions sought to understand and assess the experience and views of those who have shared, or considered sharing, concerns about others with authorities in relation to suspected involvement in violent overseas conflict. We also sought views from government stakeholders involved in developing and implementing reporting mechanisms and channels that enable information brought forward by community members to be analyzed and operationalized. Project participants were asked interview questions that covered the following topics and themes:

- The reasons Australian Muslim community members and leaders might feel motivated to share concerns about those suspected of involvement in violent overseas conflict with authorities
- What they would want to know or find out more about before deciding to share their concerns
- What factors might encourage or discourage people to share their concerns
- Expectations, if any, about the kind of support people might need or want at various stages of the reporting process, including after they make a report
- Expectations, if any, about the outcomes of the process
- Concerns and fears, if any, about the process and its impacts (personal, family, community)
- Views on what authorities who listen to community members' concerns during reporting need to know from a community point of view when dealing with members of the public on these issues
- Strategies for improving existing approaches to community reporting
- Strategies for strengthening public awareness and knowledge about the process coming forward with information to authorities

Government stakeholders were asked a series of semi-structured interview questions to guide their thinking and responses on these issues. Because of the sensitive nature of the research topic, a slightly different strategy was used for community-based participants who, in addition to semi-structured interview questions, were given a choice of two detailed scenarios to 'think through' in responding to the questions posed by the research team. Using a hypothetical yet realistic scenario around which participants could respond without fear of disclosing sensitive, personal or confidential information that might place them or others at personal or legal risk was a successful strategy, generating trust and confidence in the research process as well as very rich data. At the end of each interview, community participants were given the opportunity to speak, if they so wished, about actual events or scenarios in which they may have been involved or had knowledge of. It was made clear that this was in no way a requirement of the research, but rather an opportunity to be taken up at their discretion. A small number of participants took up this opportunity, while the majority chose to stay exclusively with the scenario throughout the interview.

After reading through both scenarios and having any questions answered by the research interviewers, all community participants chose to work with Scenario 1, which dealt with a young man, 'Jay', who had converted to Islam and become increasingly radicalized to the point of planning to go overseas and fight. The scenario was based on some aspects of a scenario included in the Australian Multicultural Foundation's 2013 TRIM-based community education resource,[27] but also introduced new elements appropriate to the current project's focus. The scenario was slightly revised following an initial pilot interview and was thereafter commended as highly realistic by project participants. 'Jay's' scenario is reproduced below.

Scenario 2 focused on a young woman, 'Catherine', who played a support role for a radicalized group planning to travel overseas for training to effectively conduct violent extremist activity at home in Australia. No participant selected scenario 2, perhaps reflecting the preoccupation of community and government stakeholders in 2014 on issues relating to largely male foreign fighters attempting to join Islamic State.

In both scenarios, the key focus was on the decision-making process undergone by the research participant as they put themselves in the position of being a relative of 'Jay's' or a close friend of 'Catherine's', faced with choices about whether or not to report their concerns.

Community Reporting Thresholds: *Selected Key Findings from Community Participants*

Our findings address various dimensions of the current national security reporting context from community and government stakeholder standpoints, including the *psycho-social landscape*, the *information landscape*, the *communication landscape*, the *trust landscape* and the *education and outreach landscape*. In the limited space available here, I cover selected salient themes emerging from our community interview sample. These findings help us reorient the way in which we think about the reporting experience, and how we might create new climates and discourses around the sharing of information that can reduce potential stigmatization, create greater transparency, acknowledge real fears and concerns, and offer supportive and constructive intervention both for those at risk of violent action *and* for those who make the decision to come forward.

Unsurprisingly, virtually all our community-based participants said reporting to authorities was a **last resort** for them. Before taking this step, people said they would use a range of other intra-community strategies before choosing to report, such as seeking counsel and support from community and religious leaders, doing background research on the person's activities and associates, challenging the person's interpretation of Islam, involving family or friends as counterinfluences, removing people from negative influence settings, or confronting them directly to bring home the consequences of their choices and actions. People spoke of how important it was that such strategies were activated at an early stage of concern within the community, family or peer circle.

There was a strong focus in this part of the data on the importance of understanding and engaging with a person's *emotional state*, rather than concentrating only on the ideological or cognitive dimensions of a person's movement toward violent action. In reflecting on the emotional landscape for a person beginning to consider involvement in foreign conflict, for example, participants cited internal conflict, anger, confusion, social isolation and lack of belonging, sense of helplessness at events unfolding overseas, and heightened desire to assist other Muslims struggling for justice as being most likely to characterize the emotional mindset of someone on the road to supporting or becoming involved in foreign conflict. As participants noted,

> When you are looking for answers in life, your response can be skewed by emotions, by someone looking for your weaknesses and feeding off them. (Male community participant, Sydney)
>
> A young man can have all sorts of things going on mentally, lots and lots of things. One of those could be that he's not in a relationship; another could be that he's not satisfied in his career, he wants to have a purpose, and maybe fighting overseas gives him a purpose and a focus. (Female community participant, Brisbane)

When participants contemplated sharing information with others about someone close to them radicalizing to violence, they were most likely to turn to *trusted community leaders*. However, people also offered compelling reasons for why they would choose to share information with authorities instead of community leaders, and chief among these was the *preventive impulse*, hoping for swift diversion or disruption by authorities to prevent violent action from occurring and to provide support for the person at risk.

But regardless of where people thought they would turn to share what they knew, the most persistent theme was that reporting is deeply *personal*. People come forward overwhelmingly out of care, worry and concern, often combined with a sense of helplessness to prevent multilevel harms from occurring. The central motive for those who report out of *care and concern* for individual, family and community wellbeing bears little relationship, in other words, to abstract convictions about 'doing the right thing'. One participant's narrative sums up these issues with great poignancy:

> If he's booked his ticket, I'd call the [government] department in charge of preventing someone boarding a flight, and I'd try to flag this person because I genuinely don't want them to go and want them to be stopped and get the right counselling and treatment here rather than see them progressing with that plan [to fight overseas]. ... I know one distant relative who did engage in fighting in Syria, his parents and family called [a government agency] and begged them to stop their son from traveling, but [the agency] said there was nothing they could do. His parents were devastated. ... How do you stop things from happening before they get to the point where the consequences can't be recovered? This distant cousin was Australian-born, got into the wrong group, wrong time – left his wife and children behind and a mother who is just a shadow of herself; skin and bone. (Female community participant, Melbourne)

In fact, a number of people spoke about the central tension they imagined between thinking cognitively that they were 'doing the right thing', yet feeling emotionally that reporting was 'the wrong thing', generating not relief or satisfaction but guilt, anxiety and doubt: '*I would feel I'd deceived someone. Confused, anxious, worried, fearful for both sides of the dilemma*' (male community participant, Brisbane). These contradictory pulls are compounded by the profound *loneliness of the reporting experience*. Reporting can be isolating and intimidating. It can involve highly conflictual emotions, loyalties and fears including sense of betrayal, sense of responsibility, duty, shame and remorse, and this can especially be the case when it becomes difficult or impossible to share the decision-making process with others to whom you would normally turn for support.

We may think of reporting as a discrete moment in time, an 'event' or 'moment' with a 'before' and an 'after'. However, our participants suggested that reporting is better understood as a highly *complex process*, rather than as a single act in time. It involves volatile stages of decision-making, comparison, reflection and judgment that we need to better understand in order to support people effectively at different stages. This is particularly so in the aftermath of reporting, when the trauma of one's choices may hit home the hardest—yet, this is also the point at which participants suggested they are most likely to be left to their own devices.

Lying at the heart of reporting's aftermath are key issues about *loss of power and control*. Prior to reporting, people are able to maintain control—both imaginatively and materially—of what they know and what they do with that knowledge. Yet, once information is shared with others who have the power to act independently, both the sense and the reality of losing control over the consequences and outcomes of this can become acute.

This loss of control can create another layer of vulnerability for those coming forward, and this is further intensified if there is a wide gap between expectations of how what one shares will be used and how it, in fact, goes on to be used. The biggest disjunction to emerge in our study revolved around the lack of alignment between *anticipated reporting expectations versus actual reporting outcomes*. While participants stressed their expectation that authorities would use information to help those heading toward or engaged in violent extremism and prevent them from continuing down this path, they also referred to a number of instances in which they felt that information had been used to prosecute or punish rather than prevent, divert or rehabilitate. This emerged particularly in relation to foreign travel to participate in overseas conflicts, and some people spoke with great passion about unmet expectations that authorities would use information provided to stop family members and friends from traveling.

The views of government stakeholders on this issue were not uniform, and this goes to the complexities navigated by different actors in the reporting context. There are morally and ethically difficult choices made by agencies about their responsibilities to prevent the greatest harm to the greatest number of people, and this can mean that individual wellbeing may become secondary to broader imperatives to prevent wide-scale harm. This suggests in turn that much about the current reporting landscape and its knotty moral and ethical dilemmas remains opaque rather than transparent and accessible, including the operational and tactical limits on post-report information-sharing between authorities and communities. While a surprisingly high number of people said they *accepted* or *understood* these limitations, as one participant said pithily, law enforcement and government agencies need to become more '*transparent about the lack of transparency*' inherent in the reporting process. This was seen as a proxy for how well the process did or didn't demonstrate respect and dignity for those who come forward. Another participant noted,

> Respect for those who share information is critical. Even if authorities have a job to do and confidentiality is important, it is about how to say that with some respect. Being honest is also about respect. Keeping someone in the loop means follow-up, having someone call to say how are you doing, this is how you can source help. (Male community participant)

Ultimately, reporting came down for many community members to issues of trust. No matter how it is rationalized, reporting involves on some level betraying the trust of someone close, even when the reporter is centrally motivated by care, concern, a desire protect a loved one, or a wish to prevent even greater harms to others. Under these circumstances, the question of how much one trusts those to whom information is disclosed becomes critical:

> If [my reporting to authorities] just ends in an arrest, I'd feel very guilty. So it really depends on the response. ... Are they just going to arrest and tear the house apart, or are they going to help rehabilitate the individual? It's very confronting to think about these things. It's confronting to make the call and how they respond on the other end is critical. I'd hate it to end up in an arrest and I'd be reluctant to call if I knew it would end up in an arrest. But If I thought my call was going to end up helping and preventing something and putting things in place to prevent Jay form acting, then good. (Female community participant, Melbourne)

Our findings also indicate that reporting can sometimes, though not very often, be opportunistic: people who have lived with knowledge or fears for a while may sometimes decide, seemingly suddenly, to share what they know with the nearest authority figure to hand. More often, however, reporting is the outcome of careful, even agonized deliberation and choices about whom to speak to, when and how. In this sense, reporting is also fundamentally about relationships of trust and credibility, particularly in climates where coming forward lacks legitimacy or creates risks in the eyes of family, peer or community circles.

This helps makes better sense of an otherwise counterintuitive finding to emerge from the research, which is the preference by a majority of participants for **face-to-face rather than remote or anonymous reporting**, say by telephone or online. Face-to-face reporting to community leaders was preferred by almost all participants because these often involved preexisting relationships with some degree of social and cultural intimacy. When reporting to authorities was considered, face to face reporting was seen as a process that allowed people to use interaction cues such as body language, tone, inflection and facial expression to decide how far they were willing to go and how trustworthy the authority figure was. This highlights the imagined or actual experience of the reporting process as an *interpersonal negotiation* built around the dynamics of trust, rather than a simple transaction or exchange of information with others who are themselves anonymous at the other end of a phone line—though this *was* an attractive option for some. The dynamics of **accountability** in reporting emerged as one of the most fascinating insights in the study as a whole: not only that of the authorities to whom people considered reporting, but also for those reporting themselves: '*If I do it it would have to be face to take responsibility and own the decision I've made to report*' (Female community participant, Brisbane).

Where people fear or believe they will be treated with suspicion, contempt, ignorance or discrimination because of what or who they know, the choice to come forward may be discarded or else deferred until it is too late to prevent the harms and consequences they most dread. Our participants suggested that the **fear or experience of Islamophobia** can be a central inhibitor in this context, because it negates the trust that is such a paramount feature of the ability to share difficult and sensitive information with others. Many government stakeholders understood and shared this view, but they were also clear about the need for better engagement and training for front-line responders, especially local law enforcement, to mitigate this. Without addressing the broader climate of trust and engagement in which reporting takes place, and the need for greater support and empathy for its complexities, the thresholds for community reporting within Australian Muslim communities are likely to remain high, and coming forward to authorities at early stages will continue to be seen as a last resort or indeed as an option likely to create difficult, even impossible reckonings between competing sets of harms.

In sum, our data suggest that there can be significant psycho-social and structural barriers to reporting. These barriers relate to individual and community sentiment; impact on social networks and relationships; unclear reporting processes and channels; lack of trust and confidence in reporting outcomes; lack of support following reporting, and, most prominently, fear and anxiety about the personal, social and legal impacts and consequences of reporting.

Special care and consideration need to be given to how people in positions of trust and authority handle the concerns people may articulate about close or intimate others in their lives—and this applies to community leaders and resources as much as to government and law enforcement agencies. Empathy, respect, trust, sensitivity and integrity are vital characteristics of the reporting encounter, and these need to be evinced from the very first moments of the process and followed through until its conclusion.

The act of coming forward is likely to be one of the most difficult, painful and confronting decisions ever taken by those who do so. Understanding the relationship between the broader social and discursive climate in which such difficult and painful choices are made, and ameliorating the ways in which people may feel stigmatized or victimized, rather than validated and supported, when they do is the necessary precondition for beginning to understand this little-considered dimension of the challenges presented by radicalization to violent action. Although there is not space here to detail our recommendations, moving toward a harms-prevention, public health paradigm in thinking about how we handle dimensions of the reporting process would shift significantly the way in which we now engage with those who share what they know out of care and concern, even when doing so creates anxiety, doubt and conflict for those reporting. Australia is now piloting a new outreach service based on public health messaging that encourages family and community members to seek informed, non-judgmental and empathetic advice about how they can support and intervene with people close to them who are at risk of, or have already, radicalized to violence. Such measures hold promise for repositioning the dialogue between government and communities on the early detection and prevention of terrorism, and for creating much-needed relations of trust and understanding by everyone involved in the reporting process.

Notes

1. M. J. Williams, J. G. Horgan, and W. P. Evans, "The Critical Role of Friends in Networks for Countering Violent Extremism: Toward a Theory of Vicarious Help-Seeking," *Behavioural Sciences of Terrorism and Political Aggression* 8, no. 1 (2015): 1–21.
2. See K. Kissane, "Tip-Off Led to Intense 16-Month Investigation," *The Sydney Morning Herald*, September 17, 2008, http://www.smh.com.au/national/tipoff-led-to-intense-16month-investigation-20080916-4hxp.html; J. Miller, "Terrorism Comes to Sydney," *News Weekly*, August 22, 2009, http://newsweekly.com.au/article.php?id=3734; and A. Caldwell, "Terror Cells in Sydney and Melbourne Connected," *ABC News PM with Mark Colvin*, September 20, 2011, http://www.abc.net.au/pm/content/2011/s3321962.htm.
3. Attorney-General's Department, *Preventing Violent Extremism and Radicalisation in Australia* (Canberra: Attorney-General's Department, 2015), http://www.livingsafetogether.gov.au.
4. Attorney-General's Department, *Preventing Violent Extremism*, op. cit.; J. Silvester, "Melbourne Teen Arrested Over Alleged Mother's Day Massacre," *The Age*, May 10, 2015, http://www.theage.com.au/victoria/melbourne-teen-arrested-over-alleged-mothers-day-massacre-20150509-ggxuv0.html.
5. See D. Katz, "Family, Friends of Radicalized Persons Wary of Reporting: Experts," *CIGI*, March 18, 2015, https://www.cigionline.org/articles/family-friends-of-radicalized-persons-wary-of-reporting-experts; M. Grossman, *Community Reporting Thresholds: Sharing Information with Authorities Concerning Violent Extremist Activity and Involvement in Foreign Conflict* (Canberra: Australia-New Zealand Counter-Terrorism Committee, 2015).
6. M. Grossman, *Community Reporting Thresholds*, op. cit.
7. J. Wenik, "Forcing the Bystander to Get Involved: A Case for a Statute Requiring Witnesses to Report Crime," *The Yale Law Journal* 94, no. 7 (1985): 1787–1806.
8. R. Jackson, "Constructing Enemies: 'Islamic Terrorism' in Political and Academic Discourse," *Government and Opposition* 42, no. 3 (2007): 394–426; H. Tahiri and M. Grossman, *Community and Radicalisation: An Examination of Perceptions, Ideas, Beliefs and Solutions Throughout Australia* (Melbourne and Canberra: Victoria Police and Australia-New Zealand Counter-Terrorism Committee, 2013).
9. P. Thomas, M. Grossman, S. Miah, and K. Christmann, *Community Reporting Thresholds: Sharing Information with Authorities Concerning Violent Extremist Activity and Involvement in Foreign Conflict—A UK*

Replication Study (Lancaster: Centre for Research and Evidence on Security Threats, 2017).
10. M. J. Williams, J. G. Horgan, and W. P. Evans, "The Critical Role of Friends in Networks for Countering Violent Extremism: Toward a Theory of Vicarious Help-Seeking," *Behavioural Sciences of Terrorism and Political Aggression* 8, no. 1 (2015): 1–21.
11. P. Thomas et al., *Community Reporting Thresholds*, op. cit.; B. Spalek, L. Z. McDonald, and S. El Awa, *Preventing Religio-Political Extremism Amongst Muslim Youth: A Study Exploring Police-Community Partnership* (Birmingham: Institute of Applied Social Studies, University of Birmingham, 2011).
12. D. Shamas and N. Arastu, *Mapping Muslims: NYPD Spying and Its Impact on Muslim Americans* (New York: School of Law CLEAR Project, City University of New York, 2013).
13. H. Tahiri and M. Grossman, *Community and Radicalisation: An Examination of Perceptions, Ideas, Beliefs and Solutions Throughout Australia* (Melbourne and Canberra: Victoria Police and Australia-New Zealand Counter-Terrorism Committee); see especially Chapter 8 on Operations Pendennis and Neath.
14. R. Wasserman, *Guidance for Building Communities of Trust* (Washington, DC: U.S. Department of Justice, 2010), 14.
15. V. Kim, "Family Focused Outreach Programs Aim to Help People 'Quit' Radical Islam," *The Fix*, October 7, 2014.
16. M. Grossman, "Tough Is Not Enough: Ten Smarter Ways to Counter Violent Extremism," *The Conversation*, October 23, 2014, http://theconversation.com/tough-is-not-enough-ten-smarter-ways-to-counter-violent-extremism-32,690.
17. R. Wasserman, *Guidance for Building Communities*, 16.
18. The ICAP research informing the FEMA Resource Guide (see Note 19 below) on community reporting was not publicly released.
19. Federal Emergency Management Agency, *A Resource Guide to Improve Your Community's Awareness and Reporting of Suspicious Activity—For Law Enforcement and Community Partners*, FEMA P-904 (Washington, DC: U.S. Department of Homeland Security, 2012).
20. J. P. Bjelopera, *Terrorism Information Sharing and the Nationwide Suspicious Activity Report Initiative: Background and Issues for Congress*. CRS Report for Congress (Washington, DC: Congressional Research Service, 2011), 11.
21. Ibid.
22. R. Wasserman, *Guidance for Building Communities*, 8.
23. A. Goldman and G. Miller, "American Suicide Bomber's Travels in U.S., Middle East Went Unmonitored," *The Washington Post*, October 11, 2014.

24. See https://www.nationalsecurity.gov.au/media-and-publications/national-security-campaign/pages/default.aspx#Campaign.
25. S. Lowe, "Terrorism Kit So Dumb It's a Winner," *Sydney Morning Herald*, April 10, 2003.
26. See Naomi Woodley, "Senate Passes New Counter-Terrorism Laws Giving Stronger Powers to Intelligence Agency ASIO," *ABC News*, September 26, 2014, http://www.abc.net.au/news/2014-09-25/new-counter-terrorism-laws-pass-the-senate/5770256.
27. TRIM stands for The Radicalisation Indicators Model. See The Australian Multicultural Foundation, "Community Awareness Training Manual: Building Resilience in the Community," http://amf.net.au/entry/community-awareness-training-manual-building-resilience-in-the-community.

PART IV

Responses

CHAPTER 12

Men on a Mission: Engaging with Islamophobia and Radicalization in Australia 1863–1957

Katy Nebhan

> From sunny far Afghanistan,
> A country great in deed,
> Whose sons are Britain's bulwark
> 'twix India and Russia's greed,
> There came an Afghan gentleman –
> Straight, upward as a stick,
> To clothe and feed Australia's poor,
> Relieve and cure the sick.
> Anonymous[1]

In 1914 Francis James Shaw from Coburg in Victoria registered and was granted speedy copyright approval for The White Australia Game. The aim of the game, that came with 'dark' and light-colored chips, was to get all colored men out of the country and white men in.[2] The game is rare in that it is one of the few artifacts that remain with such blatantly racist and discriminatory sentiments. The historic significance of the game lies in its reflection of the prevailing view, in the early twentieth century, of Australia's ethnic purity as expressed by William Morris

K. Nebhan (✉)
Charles Sturt University, Sydney, NSW, Australia
e-mail: knebhan@csu.edu.au

© The Author(s) 2019
J. L. Esposito and D. Iner (eds.), *Islamophobia and Radicalization*,
https://doi.org/10.1007/978-3-319-95237-6_12

Hughes, future Prime Minister of Australia: 'Our chief plank is, of course, a White Australia. There's no compromise about that. The industrious colored brother has to go – and remain away!'[3] It is also evidence of how ethnic purity was 'internalized' by most sectors of the Australian community. The response of the 'colored' man was irrelevant and the laws, literature and policies of the day gave xenophobia, Islamophobia, racism and accusations of radicalization an open platform. Despite these extreme sentiments, radicalization was far from the path chosen by the Australian Muslim settlers who are the subject of this chapter. There was no place for them within the national narrative and Islamophobia, which obscured their 'voice', was legitimized by contemporary definitions of the national character and the myth of the Australian type.

In his analysis of how 'myths' were invented to define certain public expressions of the national Australian character, Donald Horne referred to Georges Sorel who, in his book *Reflections on Violence*, helped give the word 'myth' the 'secular meaning of a transcendent social force'.[4] Horne was particularly interested in the 'explanatory' power of myths and following on from this, their power of transformation. The ability to transform has been critical to Australia's 'white' national history, which has long struggled with its European origins and the desire to project a distinctive identity. From the outset, and despite the changing attempts to define Australia, there have always been decisive points of exclusion.[5] Most notable are the two enduring national myths, the pioneer legend and the 'Australian' legend which were, as argued by Ann Curthoys, both 'silent on race and ethnicity'.[6]

This chapter begins with a poem written anonymously about a man who became one of the most legendary of the Afghan cameleer drivers of the late nineteenth century, Mahomet Allum. This 'Afghan gentleman' became legendary not because he fit into any of Australia's racially-exclusive historical narratives. Nor was his apparent fame a by-product of any recognition of his work, or that of his peers, in the national historical archive where the mainstream understanding of both historians and society at large pointed to the fact that Australian history was, for a long time, predominantly white and masculine. Such a 'man' was peripheral to what Linzi Murrie has referred to as the 'brotherhood of all men' that also excluded women, the indigenous and non-European males.[7] As argued in the previous chapters, the centuries old Islamophobic mindset perpetuated by various Western discourses was preoccupied with stereotypical images ranging from the exotic and mysterious to the violent and radical Muslim other. Even within revisionist studies, including those of Stevens, Schinasi and Rajkowski, the Afghan cameleers occupy a place outside of serious academic history and like the indigenous people, their representations are:

> very much like European exoticism and 'orientalism', ranging from sympathetic to hostile, sometimes achieving considerable understanding, more often a white-centred form of appropriation and ignorance.[8]

These Orientalist and Islamophobic discourses often eclipsed the efforts made by Muslim immigrants to integrate into their new homelands. The Afghan cameleers occupied an ambiguous position in both the narratives of the explorers whom they accompanied as camel drivers, as well as those latter adventurers who found a story to tell through their exposure to the lives of these so-called 'colorful' and 'exotic' men. Even within those studies that actively sought to engage with their lives and experiences, most notably the works of Christine Stevens and Pamela Rajkowski, the Afghans' voices were often secondary to the stories and images that the authors thought worthy of inclusion in what was essentially, *their* narrative of this group of 'foreigners'.[9] As such, the voices of the Afghan cameleers were often heard as muffled whispers upon a stage whose characters were loud and strong in their pursuit of the heroic and the legendary, and sometimes quiet but persistent in their search for self and at times, the 'other'. This chapter will reflect on one Australian Muslim 'type' that emerged in response to these inherently Orientalist and Islamophobic discourses as well as Australia's own struggle with identity. Although this type may be perceived as a 'reluctant Muslim', 'he' actively sought to 'own' Australia's national myths and legends, appropriate them as well as manipulate them, in order to claim them as 'his own'. In doing so, this type of Australian Muslim attempted to counter centuries-old stereotypes and Islamophobia through civic and activist roles.

Toward the end of the nineteenth century, some sense of an Australian identity began to develop. At its core was a belief in the existence of an Australian 'type' that was given physical and racial characteristics, as well as a moral, social and psychological identity. This development mirrored the Western liberal, national and racial ideologies of the time that were very much preoccupied with 'categorization', particularly in the field of science. By virtue of their color and race, as well as their 'moral superiority', Australia's colonizers were able to justify their imperial expansion and exploitation of the indigenous inhabitants. The emergence of a national 'type' was thus a response to the sociopolitical trends of contemporary Western culture as well as a desire to capture the distinctive essence of this new nation. The Australian 'type' was by no means a static construct, and as documented by Richard White in *Inventing Australia*, it produced a number of iconic figures that were identifiably 'Australian' including the muscular sunburnt bushman, the 'Coming Man' whose self-assurance and physical competence would renew the British race, the resilient Digger who stood fast at Gallipoli and of course the Bondi lifesaver.[10] What was common to all these was firstly, an underlying sexism:

> The emphasis was on masculinity, and on masculine friendships and teamwork, or 'mateship' in Australia. All the clichés – man of action, white man, manliness, the common man, war as a test of manhood – were not sexist for nothing. Women were excluded from the image of 'The Coming Man', and so were generally excluded from the image of the Australian 'type' as well.[11]

Whilst women, who had their own constructed 'types', were often portrayed as a 'negation of the type', colored men were the very antithesis of the Australian type. In the initial period, the pioneers' battle was against the harsh Australian land and the indigenous occupants who were seen by some as 'remnants of the ancient heathen nations'.[12] Some years later the Chinese, or 'yellow peril', who began migrating in the mid-nineteenth century were the main threat. However, there was hostility towards Irish Catholics and all non-British migrants who would dilute the British character of the nation.[13] This hostility was expressed in one of the first Acts of the new parliament in 1901 with the passing of the Immigration Restriction Act, also known as the White Australia Policy. At the time of its passing, a small dispersed Muslim population made up of cameleers from Afghanistan, Pakistan, Kashmir, Egypt, Persia and Turkey had already been living in Australia for some forty years. The racism, social and political exclusion and blatant Islamophobia they had suffered was now officially sanctioned by the nation they had helped explore.

From the outset, these men stood in the shadows of the camels they came to handle as well as the narrative of Australia's exploration of which they were part. Inspired by Dr. David Livingston's crossing of Africa—the first Europeans to do so, and an accomplishment for which he was elevated to 'Fellow' by the Royal Geographical Society in Britain—the Victorian Exploration Committee wanted to reveal the wonders of the Australian continent by arranging for its crossing. In 1858 George Landells was commissioned to purchase camels and recruit native drivers for this purpose. Within twelve months he had bought twenty-four camels and hired three men, Belooch Khan, Botan and their headman Dost Mahomet. All three men were Pathans from the Peshawar district of Afghanistan who had served in the British army as sepoys.

Following Landells' resignation from his position as second in command, what became known as the Burke and Wills expedition prepared to leave on August 20, 1860. The local press took the opportunity to comment on the foreignness of the 'beast' and their unpredictability, describing one incident as follows:

> One of the most laughable was the breaking loose of a cantankerous camel, and the startling and upsetting in the 'scatter' of a popular limb of the law. The gentleman referred to is of large mould... his going-down and uprising were greeted with shouts of laughter in which the erring camel went helter-skelter through the crowd, and was not secured until he showed to admiration how speedily can go 'the ship of the desert'.[14]

This somewhat exoticized focus on the camel dominated most of the studies of those early explorations of Australia in which the animal was used and the handlers actively excluded. However, neither the camels nor their foreign handlers were included in the 'legendary flavor' that surrounded Burke and Wills throughout the following years, and although, as Colwell points out, Burke had made 'disastrous mistakes and hasty decisions, as a man in the field faced with the physical task of conquering a barren wilderness, his display of courage and dogged endurance grips the imagination'.[15]

This 'imagination' was critical to the traditional Australian narratives that brought together the numerous stories of exploration of which Colwell's is an example. Although the cameleers and the 'lumbering evil-smelling camels' initially provided a sense of opposition, exoticism and tension in these epic narratives, their 'picturesque' representations were later demystified by notable artists William Strutt, Ludwig Becker, Sir John Longstaff and Nicholas Chevalier to compliment the artistic and cultural standards of the day.[16] Aside from the complex relationships between English artistic traditions and Australian exploration narratives, one may read these delicate displays of 'imperial intercourse', as Said would refer to them, as part of the 'structure of attitude and reference' of imperial historiography.[17] This structure espoused, even in the post-imperialist discourses that were somewhat influenced by the exploration narratives, the idea of 'imperial possessions' whose 'existence always counts, though their names and identities do not, they are profitable without fully being there'.[18] Australia's earliest Muslim settlers certainly fit into this category. References to them as Afghan *cameleers* conveniently places them on a subjective stage where they exist for their 'use' rather than for themselves. Even when individual names are used, the mainstream historical narrative has tended to connect their identities to ideas, concepts and the experiences from which the national narratives drew support.

At the time in which they were working as camel drivers and hawkers, these ideas and concepts initially drew on the desire for imperial expansion and conquest of the land. The early Muslim settlers were 'marked' aberrations that stood in the way of white progress. Not long after in the 'new commonwealth', blatantly racist discourses of patriotism were to have a significant impact on their experiences and lives in Australia as well as their place within the narratives that documented this period. The racism and exclusion were blatant and unapologetic, as the following statement suggests,

> The yellow, the brown, and the copper coloured are to be forbidden to land anywhere… The patriotic side to this remarkable attitude is that which springs from the love of the Old Land. We possess a boundless confidence in its people, whether at home or transplanted to this strange soil, and in their capacity to solve all difficulties if only they can be kept from admixture with other races… The ultimate result is a national determination to make no truce with coloured immigration, to have no traffic with the unclean thing, and to put it down in all its shapes without much regard to cost… As the successful among them invariably return to their native lands a stoppage of reinforcements means the extinction in one generation of this alien element in our midst.[19]

Many of the Muslim cameleers did not return to their homelands, at least not permanently, and the legacy they came to leave in Australia was for a long time lost as their stories faded within the dominant national historiography and its inherently racist agenda. Whilst their sacrifices during expeditions and their essential contribution to the economic development of the interior was overlooked, their experience of prejudice increased. These men were, in many ways, transitory migrants. They were brought as camel handlers that would help carry forth the white man as he 'discovered' land that he believed was terra nullius ('no one's land'). When Captain James Cook declared it such in 1770, he and the colonists effectively removed more than 750,000 Aboriginal people who inhabited the Island nation at the time, from the stage of legitimate existence.[20] The 'act' of exploration was strictly confined to white men and those who assisted backstage did not feature in the credits so to speak. These acts of exclusion had major ramifications for Australia's early Muslim settlers as they sought a sense of place in the country that was now their home.[21]

When their employment as camel handlers ended, many of these cameleers continued to work and lived in 'Ghan' towns that developed near freight depots, railheads and isolated ports, providing outback cartage. Living at first in all-male communities, popular fear and prejudice distanced them from available women whilst immigration laws prevented them from bringing brides or any family members from their homelands. The extent of their suffering has been described candidly by Stevens:

> Afghan history in Australia is one of alienation and prejudice. Victims of racial and religious intolerance and often economic exploitation, the Afghans were excluded from society beyond their Ghantown boundaries… Feared, despised, alienated, they locked themselves behind their religion and their Ghantown communities… They were heroes. They were villains. Yet their contribution to the opening up and accessibility of the great mass of inland Australia was enormous and vital. Without these men and their transport animals, the progress and expansion of European settlement into the heart of the Australian continent would not have been possible on the same scale for a further fifty years or so. The very backbone of Australia's economy, the traditional spheres of pastoralism and mining, owe an immense historical debt to the camels and cameleers.[22]

Given this unacknowledged success, it is not surprising that they suffered from prejudice born from the jealousy of pastoralists and the Teamsters Union who attempted to resist the almost total transfer of transport to the Afghan camel strings who were experienced cameleers. On a number of occasions, they resorted to skirmishes and fist fights, no doubt exacerbated by the irrational fear of the local populations who were concerned that 'these aliens will have all the benefit of coming into districts that have been pioneered by Europeans at great risk and cost to themselves and families'.[23] Anyone who associated with them was exposed to the same prejudice and loathing. David Gunn, who worked for a successful Afghan cameleer for a period of time, was refused service by a local:

> 'It wouldn't matter if he paid their wages in gold for the things,' growled the smith. 'I'm not going to offend the whole of my reg'lar customers for any heathen alive. I'd as soon work for a Chinaman, an' that's about the lowest thing a white man can do, so now you have it'.[24]

Contemporary media, namely newspapers, were just as contemptuous of these early Muslim settlers. They printed headings like 'The Afghan Camel Invasion', claiming that these men were even 'more dreaded and detested than the ubiquitous Chinaman' and that 'in the eye of the industrial white man there is no redeeming feature about the Afghan'.[25] Whilst according to Andrew Markus, these early Muslim settlers were clearly part of a broader anti-Asian movement that saw these men as monopolizing certain areas of the labor market that included more than just the carrying trade, their religious peculiarities and their unwillingness to 'bow to the dictates of the Europeans' points to underlying Islamophobic sentiments.[26] Aside from everyday prejudice and frequent brawls on the streets of Bourke for instance and on the roads over who should have right of way, in some of the more extreme cases, these men were murdered. In 1894 a miner named J. Knowles from Coolgardie shot dead two 'Afghans' for washing their feet in a waterhole and along with the many miners who supported him and despite his arrest, the editor of the *Coolgardie Miner* wrote that 'force of circumstances has made Knowles for the time being the representative of the whole white race in Western Australia'.[27]

What the locals thought of this group of men who came to be known as the 'Afghan cameleers', particularly 'white' people whose prejudice ran deep, often defined the ways in which these men chose to represent their place in Australia's history. Of particular significance is the book *History of Islamism in Australia from 1863–1932*, compiled by Mohamed Hasan Musakhan in 1905 then edited and reprinted following a donation made by Mahomet Allum in 1932. As one of the few complete documents left by Australia's early Muslim settlers, this book has not been given its due place in their history, as both a narrative of their presence in Australia as *they* saw it, but also as a document that covered many of the areas left out of references to them as merely 'cameleers' in official narratives. Almost one hundred pages in length, the book begins with a quote from St. Peter, 1:12—'Remembrance' and the words 'THE MOSQUES, CAMELMEN AND ISLAM' followed by the dedication, 'To put you always in remembrance of the things done and work and services rendered by CAMEL-MEN to establish ISLAM IN AUSTRALIA: 1863-1932'.[28]

This dedication, printed in bold on the title page of the book, suggests that Musakhan sought to present an 'official' history of this group of men in Australia from 1863–1932, and alludes to the fact that 'remembrance' of these men and their achievements, up to that point in time at least, was overlooked in the national narrative. The place they had occupied which began with an Orientalist vision where they were seen to be 'picturesque, plodding quietly by with their parchment-brown faces, full beards and turbans of colored silk' had long gone by the time this book was compiled.[29] These men appeared only in public records that reeked of Islamophobic stereotyping and fearmongering. Whether they were accused of being 'traitorously disposed' or treated with suspicion because 'the Afghan drinks no grog, consumes no luxuries', they were made to feel unwelcome and treated as social outcasts.[30] Given this context, the existence of this book and the boldness of its dedication may come across as quite unusual, if not unimaginable. That these Muslims were capable of expressing any coherent narrative of both their achievements and those aspects of their 'history' that they saw as worthy of recording at this point in times raises a number of issues regarding the realities in which they found themselves, and the choices they made in reworking them to suit their own version of their place and history in Australia.

Mohamed Hasan Musakhan was not a typical cameleer and his mission to document the establishment of Islam in Australia rests with what marked him as being different to many of his peers: his education. Musakhan was born in Karachi in 1863 and was educated in British schools. He won the Mansfield Scholarship in 1883 and the Sir Frank Soutar Scholarship in 1887 and matriculated from St Xavier's College,

Bombay, in the same year. He spoke five 'Oriental languages' as he refers to them and served as Headmaster at the Anglo-Vernacular and Technical School in Kandiaro, India between 1891–1892.[31] He was the nephew of the early source of camels, Morad Khan, and upon his arrival in Australia in 1896, he worked as a secretary for the well-known cameleer Sultan Raz Mohammed. From 1904 he owned a news agency in Perth and stood out as being an active spokesman against the injustices suffered by Muslims in Perth and across Australia. Unlike many of his peers who were ridiculed for their seeming illiteracy and who were largely confused by foreign authority and a bureaucratic system of law, Musakhan's familiarity with British customs gave him an active 'voice'.

It was a voice that he used diplomatically when confronting the racism, religious intolerance and mainstream radicalism, particularly by unionists. There is a stark difference between the activist Musakhan and the writer of the book. Anti-Afghan feeling had been escalating for years before the legislation of the 'White Australia' Policy allowed full-scale outbursts of racial and Islamophobic hatred to surface. Amongst the most vocal was the militant socialist R. S. Ross, the editor of the *Barrier Truth* newspaper, who described the Afghans as a 'savage people' of tribes and clans 'who played no small part in Asiatic history' and whilst they were an athletic, proud, sober and hardy race, he points out:

> Nothing is finer than the Afghan's physique or worse than his morale and SYPHILITIC DISEASES in repulsive form are common among them... Our new Commonwealth must be a white and decently paid one. If camel be a necessity, his Afghan driver is not... Economically the Afghan is a foe of white toiler and the white man of business.[32]

Musakhan saw himself as an advocate of his community and did not shy away from responding to the degrading claims. He pointed out in a letter to the editor titled 'A Defence of the Afghans', that 'your race must suffer considerably from loathsome diseases that you mention. If Afghans in some few cases suffer they have to thank your people for it'.[33] It would appear that whilst most of the hatred stemmed from the perceived economic threats that the cameleers posed, the majority of the verbal and published backlash targeted their race and religion. The frustration their ignorance caused these early Muslim settlers is evident in another letter written to the editor of the *Barrier Minor*, titled 'Further Defence of the Afghans', in which Musakhan states:

The fact that 130 local men having complained against the Afghans was only the outcome of bitter feelings against the Asiatics throughout Australia. Most of the Colonials without having personally ever seen or known the faults of any Afghan or other Asiatics would readily sign any petition against them without ever troubling to find the truth... Any charge, however unfounded, if laid against any Asiatic race, is taken for a fact and gospel truth, as Europeans (particularly the English-speaking races) with a few exceptions, seem to have a natural antagonism against dark colour. The whole world is convinced that it is a question of colour and nothing else between the Asiatics and the Colonials.[34]

What Musakhan and his peers sought was both understanding and the opportunity to belong. In his *History of Islamism in Australia 1863–1932*, Musakhan distanced his community from the prejudices that plagued them. Whilst the book begins with a brief outline concerning the need to establish a Mosque in Perth in 1905, he distances their lack of success from any 'Asiatic' prejudice and instead aligns the Muslim community with the Judeo-Christian ones when he states, 'as far back as 1895, efforts were made by them to obtain the grant of a piece of ground in the city of Perth (as other communities had attained for their respective Churches and Synagogues) from the Government of Western Australia'.[35] He refers to the 'Mohammedan community' resident in Western Australia and whilst he makes no attempt to hide to emblematic divisions that marked the Muslim community, particularly along ethnic lines, the name chosen for the mosque, 'The Mohammedan Mosque Incorporated', is both inclusive of these differences and identifiable to a Western audience.

Perhaps his Western education afforded him the luxury of successfully appropriating elements of the mythologies that held together the Australian historiographic narrative and the place of his community within it. A significant proportion of the book is dedicated to listing the various contributions made by Muslims towards the building of the Mosque which are meticulously divided along ethnic as well as regional lines. These included Syeds, Durranie, Mohmand, Tareen and Pishorie Afghans as well as Punjabi and Bengali Indians. Given that the 'Afghans' were not a homogenous group, even when only one contribution was made by a member of a particular region, as was the case with Kushki Yar, a Shinwari Afghan, the regional distinction was still included as were donations made by non-Muslims including 'Hindoo and Sikh Indians'.[36]

The contributions came from those living in Perth, North Fremantle, York, Port Headlands as well as the collections made on the 'goldfields'. What is particularly interesting about this careful division of ethno-regional ethnicities is the way in which it is couched within a discourse that stresses a unified 'Islamic' and 'Australian' community. Throughout the reports included by Musakhan there are references to the way the Perth Mosque will give an opportunity to 'all those who live at convenient distances from the Mosque to attend prayers and other religious functions'.[37] More importantly, the building of the Mosque is put forward as a venture that ideally includes the entire Australian community, not the Muslim one alone:

> We also respectfully appeal for assistance to all the friends and well-wishers of our community and the public at large for extending their patronage and support to us for carrying out the project to a successful issue. The completion of this work will be a monument of good citizenship and of thankfulness to the Almighty God, who provides for our daily bread, irrespective of colour, creed, or race, and who we all believe is the Lord of the East and the West.[38]

Although towards the end of this statement Musakhan alludes to the underlying racism and Islamophobia towards his community, he focuses on the positive responses of the 'public' to whom he refers. Writing about the call to prayers that could be heard in the neighborhood once the Mosque was partially completed, Musakhan states that the 'unusual cry at first did, naturally, create a surprise and curiosity in the minds of our neighbors and passers-by, but they are now getting quite accustomed to same'.[39] In choosing to present the experiences of his community in this positive, almost inclusivist way, Musakhan chose to appropriate rather than subvert elements of the established and racist national narrative. On the one hand, his simplification of their experiences was a means of concealing the inadequacies and contradictions of 'white' society and its commitment to a racially-exclusive national myth. Regardless of their 'truth', or lack-of, Horne points to this tendency for 'myth' to simplify, stating that whilst one can dispute the rights and wrongs of the Australian faith in 'national development' for instance, 'who can dispute its transcending force throughout the history of modern Australia?'[40] Whilst Musakhan publicly questioned the existing prejudices and Islamophobia that played a central role in the myth of national development in his numerous letters to newspaper editors, in his 'official' history of Islam in Australia, he chose to imagine otherwise:

> We cannot help appreciating the blessings of protection, religious toleration, and peace which we enjoy, as we do here, under the benign flag of the British nation. We are proud of the privilege we have, and sincerely thank God for the blessings of such privilege... of living under a just and humane Government.[41]

These words were part of a lengthy introduction that outlined, in meticulous detail, the 'Land Purchase and Building Fund' for the Perth Mosque. Partly influenced by his British Indian roots and his loyalty to the British Crown, Musakhan's imagined 'acceptance' of his community was, perhaps deliberately, misplaced within the context of Australian racism and radical exclusion of non-whites. If the British government recognized many of its Muslim immigrants as British 'subjects' and treated them accordingly, this was not the case in Australia. Although Australians around the time of Federation had, as Helen Irving suggests, an 'uncomfortable feeling' that it was not quite 'British' to display and act upon prejudices that were based on color, they nevertheless failed to follow in the footsteps of the British, instead upholding their passionate imaginings of a white nation.[42] The role of Australia as preserver of white bloodlines and the last, best hope of the white race and 'higher civilisation', entailed the burden of maintaining and protecting Australian racial purity.[43] Despite the resistance, radicalism and prejudices they faced and the financial setbacks they suffered as a result, these Muslims chose not to allow these impediments to deter them from aspiring to create a sense of place and identity in Australia. In projecting and pushing for a place of peaceful coexistence, Musakhan was actively rejecting the radicalism and alienation forced upon his community by many of his white contemporaries.

If these first Muslims were brought to Australia to assist in the pioneering ventures outback, their efforts to establish 'Islam in Australia', despite consistent exposure to sanctioned radical Islamophobia, and to *be* pioneers added another set of tracks to their work along the new frontier. These men were pioneering migrants in their own right and were intent on working towards their own vision for the 'new' nation and their place within it. This 'other side' to their pioneering efforts and the shift in their focus to a specifically Australian context formed an underlying thread in many of the letters included in the second section of Musakhan's book and provided a basis for positive relations between these Muslims and their contemporaries. In a statement made on May 11, 1927 to mark the Royal Visit to Perth, Musakhan boldly referred to the building of Australia as being closely associated with the work of the cameleers who were, in this 'New Epoch For Australia', active members of 'the Australian people'.[44] What is particularly interesting about their efforts to create a place for themselves and Islam in Australia is the way they chose to represent both as being 'a part', as opposed to apart, of the local national discourse. When the Duchess of York and Cornwall visited in 1901, she was gifted a riding camel from the 'humble' camel men. Much had changed for this group of Muslims by the time this statement was made in 1927. The construction of railways across the outback, the slow spread of motorized transport and the Camel Destruction Act of 1925 saw the end of cameleering and many of the older cameleers who had been working for over two or three decades were retiring. In his statement Musakhan described how the 'surviving remnants of the camel men in Australia' were 'deeply moved' and that they 'humbly join the Australian people in the expression of their duty and loyalty to the Crown'.[45] Musakhan chose to focus on acts of good citizenship through such expressions of loyalty and duty, rather than the violence that sometimes erupted due to territorial fights as trucks began to carry supplies across routes traditionally used by the cameleers.[46]

Perhaps his reference to these men as 'surviving remnants' suggests that they had moved away from seeing themselves as merely cameleers and British loyalists to more integrated members of the Australian community and a loyal group amongst the 'Australian people'. Whilst there was an underlying sense of insecurity in the book as these Muslims attempted to balance out their expressions of loyalty and sense of being Australian, with what can be described as unrelenting radicalism and Islamophobia at a time when the White Australia Policy was at its most influential, their desire to be part of their local community was unwavering.

This was certainly the case with Mahomet Allum to whom the final section of *Islamism in Australia* is dedicated. Allum's place in this history is a clear illustration of the ambiguous place in which many Muslims found themselves as they straddled aspects of their own culture with elements of the new developing Australian ones. Like Musakhan, Allum was mindful of the need to accommodate a certain degree of western culture to fit into his homeland. Dressed in a smart suit and a contrasting turban, Allum was like many of his countrymen who were often described as adhering to 'typical' Australian dress codes. Perhaps one of the most well-known of the early Muslims who migrated to Australia, what distinguished Allum was his worldly confidence as a man who 'widely traveled in England, America and Australia' and his widespread appeal as the following suggests:

> Endowed with a personality that inspires confidence and affectionate regard... His knowledge of herbs, the heritage of an ancient race, handed from father to son, represents the accumulated wisdom of the ages, and is now applied in a strange land for the benefit of those who, while differing in creed and colour, he regards with an all-embracing love as brother man and sister woman. This noble work he performs without fee or reward, His benevolence, which is but little known apart from those who have reason to render grateful thanks, is extensive.[47]

In working towards a place in the emerging framework of the national mythology, Mahomet Allum features as a central figure in the setup of a strong masculinist discourse in *Islamism in Australia*. He represented everything that was thought to embody the ideal Australian/Muslim male. In the 48 letters from a collection of 'thousands of testimonials' that praise his work in Australia, he is seen as generous, honest and hard-working man with a good sense of humor.[48] What set Allum apart from his fellow Muslim contemporaries was his enterprising spirit. He looked outside the traditional workplace and it was his work as an herbalist that drew him into mainstream society and initiated many of the 'alliances' that helped him foster long-lasting and satisfying relationships with his fellow Muslims and the general Australian public. Allum was 'socially curious' and one of the most interesting letters that highlights his social aptitude was written by Reverend T. P. Willason of the Port Adelaide Methodist Mission who spoke of the sense of commonality between Allum's faith and his own stating that:

> Although we both worship "The Nameless One of a Thousand Names" in a different way, you in the sacred stillness of the Mosque, and I in the Church with its music and song, yet we are brothers in the truest sense. First, as God's creatures, he is our Father and our Creator. Secondly, as lovers of humanity without concern as to their colour, creed or country. Thirdly, we are both dedicated to the sacred work of helping our brother men, in serving whom, we serve God best.[49]

Allum went to great lengths to understand the laws of his new homeland and the customs of those around him. He frequented churches as well as the law courts. This process of socialization was by no means a simple one for Allum who, in the language of the social sciences, stood as an 'external' or 'social Other', and his interactions with those outside his own Muslim community were fraught with a sense of having to continually negotiate several identities simultaneously.[50] Whilst Allum may have stood as the curious 'other', he was drawn to the strong sense of mateship in the outback and although 'Asiatics' were by no means included as active members in this exclusive 'white' male domain, he insisted on situating himself within Australia's pioneering tradition and actively imagining himself into its popular discourses. In a letter he wrote to the press in 1957, Allum stated:

> My strong physique, coupled with being a powerful swimmer, enabled me to get through to stations which would have been without food, had I not got supplies through... The hospitality and respect accorded to me everywhere I travelled is still a happy memory... Finer specimens of Australian manhood could not have been found anywhere, and I am proud to remember them as friends.[51]

Allum liked to imagine that he was one of these 'fine specimens' and was not afraid to express his opinion of those who thought otherwise and to whom he referred to as 'short-sighted, pumpkin-headed politicians'.[52] If we take Todorov's idea of 'social distance' as constituting the physical and psychological distance that 'self' maintains from the 'other', then Allum's efforts were focused on the space it created.[53] Allum used publicity, both good and bad, to focus attention on the innate goodness of the Australia public and his belief that it was politicians and the ignorant few who stood in the way of social acceptance of everyone. The countless testimonials and letters included in *Islamism in Australia* were his way of bringing home this point and demonstrating the importance of his place and work within the communities in which he lived. Allum was perhaps one of the most outspoken of the early Muslim settlers and what sources we have about his life provide researches with the active voice often missing from studies of this group of early Muslims settlers.

What set Allum apart from men like Musakhan was his insistence on being treated as an equal, as an Australian, not because he was a subject of the 'British Empire' or because he felt he needed to praise its representatives, as was the case with Musakhan, but rather because he deserved equality and Australians *needed him*. On those occasions when Allum threatened to leave Australia because of the intolerance and Islamophobic tendencies of its politicians, it was the needy, the poor and those who appreciated his work that influenced his decision to stay. Perhaps it was his ego and his blind conviction that gave him the incentive to continue defending his place within society to the point of sounding like Allum was doing Australia a favor by remaining within its shores. This idealism appears to have remained despite active resistance to his presence.

Like the range of correspondence included by Musakhan in *Islamism in Australia*, Allum's letters contain more than pure testimonials to a herbalist. It is no mere coincidence that all 48 letters included in the final section of this history were written by Anglo-Australians, both male and female, with not a single letter by a local Muslim included, despite evidence which clearly suggests that Allum's treatments were also highly popular among the local Muslim population.[54] Whilst Musakhan epitomized the loyal British subject, Allum was represented as the model 'citizen' who *through* his 'great faith in the Almighty's power' and as a 'friend of the people', was able to foster the ideal sense of belonging to what was presented as a largely egalitarian society. From the Royal visitors to the symbolic returned soldier who sought Allum's services, all were used to affirm the contribution of both Musakhan and Allum to Australian society and legitimize their place within it. Although both men are depicted as having a strong identification with 'Islam' as a faith, they focus on affirming a wider allegiance to the Australian 'nation' (and the wider British Empire to which it belonged).

A look at the experiences of Australia's early Muslim settlers through *Islamism in Australia* offers glimpses into the ideals and hopes that preoccupied this group of immigrants outside of the radicalized racial and Islamophobic discourses that presented them as a group of misunderstood, exotic, 'different' and 'alien' cameleers. With its unequivocally positivist approach, the book begins with an outline of these Muslim settlers' critical pioneering work both in the outback and as a group seeking to institutionalize their faith in their new homeland. It also reflects on, and highlights, their 'acceptance' by the Australian public who willingly embraced this group of immigrants due to the efforts and social engagement of men like Musakhan and Allum. This book reflects a diplomatic response to the racially-exclusive national narrative that often employed radicalized social and political discourses to alienate 'coloured foreigners'. Despite the racism, economic hardships, social exclusion and blatant Islamophobia, both these men like many of their Muslim contemporaries, chose to actively engage and appropriate both imperial ideologies as well as the emerging frameworks of the Australian national mythology to *be* Australian Muslims. In doing so, they left behind a bold, socially responsible and engaging version of *their* place within Australia's history.

NOTES

1. Poem cited in Madeleine Brunato, *Hanji Mahomet Allum: Afghan camel Driver, Herbalist, and Healer in Australia* (Adelaide: Investigator Press, 1972), 69.
2. ABC Radio Canberra, Web site, http://www.abc.net.au/news/2014-07-15/white-australia-game/5588280, accessed April 15, 2018.
3. ABC Canberra, Web site, http://www.abc.net.au/local/stories/2014/07/15/4046338.htm, accessed April 15, 2018.
4. Donald Horne, *Ideas for a Nation* (Sydney: Pan Books, 1989), 55.
5. Richard White, *Inventing Australia* (Sydney: Allen & Unwin, 1981), 63–83.
6. Ann Curthoys, 'Mythologies,' in *The Australian Legend and Its Discontents*, ed. Richard Nile (Queensland: University of Queensland Press, 2000), 21.
7. Linzi Murrie, 'Australian Legend and Australian Men,' in *The Australian Legend and Its Discontents*, ed. Richard Nile (Queensland: University of Queensland Press, 2000), 89.
8. Curthoys, 'Mythologies.' 33.
9. Pamela Rajkowski, *In the Tracks of the Camelmen: Outback Australia's Most Exotic Pioneers* (Sydney: Angus and Robertson, 1987); Christine Stevens, *Tin Mosques and Ghantowns: A History of Afghan Cameldrivers in Australia* (Melbourne: Oxford University Press, 1989).
10. For detailed explanations of the Australian 'type' see: David Day, eds., *Australian Identities* (Melbourne: Australian Scholarly Publishing, 1998); Horne, *Ideas for a Nation*, 51–66; Wayne Hudson and Geoffrey Bolton, eds., *Creating Australia: Changing Australian History* (Sydney: Allen & Unwin, 1997); John Thornhill, *Making Australia: Exploring our National Conversation* (Sydney: Millennium Books, 1992); and White, *Inventing Australia*, 63–84.
11. White, *Inventing Australia*, 83.
12. John Derek Mulvaney, 'The Australian Aborigines, 1606–1929: Opinions and Fieldwork,' *Historical Studies: Australia and New Zealand* 8, no. 30 (2008): 131–151.

13. See Raelene Frances, 'Green Demons: Irish-Catholics and Muslims in Australian History,' *Islam and Christian-Muslim Relations* 22, no. 4 (2011): 443–450.
14. Max Colwell, *The Journey of Burke and Wills* (Sydney: Lansdowne Press, 1985), 47.
15. Ibid., 11.
16. Ibid., 71.
17. Edward Said, *Culture and Imperialism* (London: Vintage, 1994), xvii, 73.
18. Ibid., 73–75.
19. Alfred Deakin, 'The New Commonwealth,' *Sources of Australian Immigration History: 1901–1945*, ed. John Lack and Jacqueline Templeton (Melbourne: Melbourne University Press, 1988), 11–13.
20. This number is based on estimates made by the Aboriginal Heritage Office, Web site, http://www.aboriginalheritage.org/history/history/.
21. Regina Ganter explores early Muslim interactions with indigenous peoples before European settlement in 'Remembering Muslim Histories of Australia,' *La Trobe Journal* 89 (2012): 48–62.
22. Stevens, *Tin Mosques*, viii.
23. Rajkowski, *In the Tracks*, 145.
24. David Gunn, *The Story of Lafsu Beg, the Camel Driver* (Sydney: Geo Robertson & Co, 1896), 96.
25. Mitchell Library, NSW, Newspaper Clippings, 'The Afghan Camel Invasion,' Q980.1/N, vol 67.
26. Andrew Markus, *Fear and Hatred: Purifying Australia and California, 1850–1901* (Sydney: Hale & Iremonger, 1979).
27. Cited in ibid., 196. See also *Coolgardie Miner*, October 30, 1894.
28. Mohamed Hasan Musakhan, *History of Islamism in Australia: 1863–1932* (Adelaide: Commercial Printing House, 1932).
29. George Farwell, *Land of Mirage* (Adelaide: Rigby, 1950), 8–9.
30. Mary Lucille Jones, 'The Years of Decline: Australian Muslims 1900–1940,' in *An Australian Pilgrimage: Muslims in Australia from the Seventh Century to the Present*, ed. Mary Lucille Jones (Melbourne: Victoria Press, 1993), 64. Herbert Barker, *Camels and the Outback* (Melbourne: Sir Isaac Pitman & Sons, 1964), 89.
31. Musakhan, *History of Islamism*, 2.
32. Cited in Nahid, Kabir, *Muslims in Australia* (Routledge, 2013), 71.
33. Ibid.
34. Ibid., 60.
35. Musakhan, *History of Islamism*, 3.
36. Ibid., 8–11.
37. Ibid., 14.
38. Ibid.

39. Ibid.
40. Horne, *Ideas*, 55.
41. Musakhan, *History of Islamism*, 14.
42. Helen Irving, *To Constitute a Nation: A Cultural History of Australia's Constitution* (Melbourne: Cambridge University Press, 1999), 101–104.
43. David Walker, "Race Building and the Disciplining of White Australia," in *Legacies of White Australia*, ed. Laksiri Jayasuriya, David Walker, and Jan Gothard (Crawley: University of Western Australia Press, 2003), 43.
44. Musakhan, *The History of Islamism*, 51.
45. Ibid.
46. Stevens, *Tin Mosques*, 267–275.
47. Ibid., 66.
48. Ibid., 66–96.
49. Ibid., 94–95.
50. Stephen Harold Riggins, 'The Rhetoric of Othering,' in *The Language and Politics of Exclusion: Others in Discourse*, ed. Stephen Harold Riggins (Thousand Oaks: Sage, 1997), 3–4.
51. Cited in Brunato, *Hanji Mahomet*, 23.
52. Ibid., 31.
53. Cited in Riggins, 'The Rhetoric,' 5.
54. Michael Cigler, *The Afghans in Australia* (Blackburn, VIC: Australasian Educa Press, 1986), 124–134.

CHAPTER 13

Islamophobia and Stigmatising Discourses: A Driving Force for Muslim Active Citizenship?

Mario Peucker

INTRODUCTION

The ongoing and seemingly every increasing securitisation of Muslims every-day life and, more broadly, stigmatising and exclusionary anti-Muslim discourses in Australia and other Western societies have multiple, often devastating, implications for intergroup relations and trust and for Muslim communities and individuals. Muslims are forced to position themselves in and respond, in one way or another, to these anti-Muslim discourses. This scope of potential, emotional and behavioural, responses is vast, and ranges from deliberate in-action and civic disengagement to

---

This contribution draws on an empirical study, published in Mario Peucker, *Muslim Citizenship in Liberal Democracies* (Basingstoke: Palgrave Macmillan, 2016). The pertinent chapters in the book have been revised and extended for this contribution.

M. Peucker (✉)
Victoria University, Melbourne, VIC, Australia
e-mail: Mario.Peucker@vu.edu.au

various forms of civic and political activism, including 'rebellious, critical, angry and disappointed'[1] performance of citizenship.

This chapter is concerned with the relationship between Islamophobia and citizenship, exploring Muslims' active response to personal and collective experiences of being subjected to Islamophobia in all its facets—structural and systemic, through the media, policymaking and public debates, verbal abuse and physical harassment in public and semi-public spaces, or discrimination in the labour market, to name but a few. While fully acknowledging the individually devastating and socially harmful effects, as discussed in other chapters of this volume, I focus on another dimension of Muslims' response to Islamophobia in Australia, which seeks to underscore Muslims' autonomy and agency in this societal context: their active citizenship and its relation to Islamophobia.

Citizenship is an inherently egalitarian concept,[2] but it also has, by definition, exclusionary dimensions drawing boundaries between those inside the citizenry and those who are not.[3] Historically, these boundaries have shifted towards more inclusiveness, primarily as a result of ongoing processes of contestation, protests and claim-making by previously excluded groups in society, who refuse to accept their status as second-class citizens. While these collective struggles continue around the world until today, liberal democracies in the twenty-first century have, in principle, all come to acknowledge that refusing equal rights on the basis of personal characteristics such as sex, ethnicity or religion is irreconcilable with the very values these democracies are built upon. Recognising this basic principle of equal legal status is, however, only one side of the citizenship coin; the other one is about substantive equality (or the lack thereof), 'equal standing in civil society'[4] and the persistence of *de facto* second-class citizenship.[5] This egalitarian promise of citizenship in modern democracies has not been fully achieved yet; it remains work in progress, driven by the 'claim to be accepted as full member of society' as the British sociologist Thomas Marshall put it in the 1950s.[6]

In Australia and many other western countries, Muslims' substantive equal citizenship has been inhibited in two interconnected ways, which resonate with what Nancy Fraser described as the two fundamental claims for social justice: redistribution and recognition.[7] Regarding the former, Australian Muslims' citizenship is hampered by their, on average, socioeconomic disadvantage as they disproportionally face unequal access to key resources, such as employment.[8] The second type of social justice and citizenship claims has been raised in response to the persistent lack of Muslims' collective recognition as full and equal members of society. This contested citizenship status manifests itself in a variety of ways, from discrimination, vilification, stigmatisation and experiences of exclusion in everyday life to political and public debates on Muslims as potential security threat (see part III of this volume) and their religion's alleged incompatibility with liberal democratic principles.[9]

There is no shortage in empirical evidence showing the prevalence of anti-Muslim sentiments among relatively large parts of Australia's society[10] and the dominant Islam-sceptical and, sometimes, overtly hostile media misrepresentation and public debates.[11] The exclusion and 'othering' of Muslims has manifested itself also in very tangible ways, beyond mere negative attitudes and skewed public discourses: Muslims face, more than other minority groups, interpersonal discrimination, for example in accessing the housing[12] and labour market,[13] anti-Muslim vilification, harassment and everyday racism.[14] This climate of public stigmatisation and interpersonal and institutional racism has been described by communities, human rights advocates and critical scholars with a reference to the term of Islamophobia.[15] The terminology is not unproblematic and has attracted some criticism—for different (sometimes polemic and political) reasons. Despite this criticism and conceptual weaknesses, Islamophobia has become, and seems to remain for the foreseeable future, a key notion to capture the empirically undeniable, complex social phenomena of Muslims' marginalisation, linked to the contestation of their recognition as equal members of pluralistic, liberal societies in the West, including Australia. In short, Islamophobia inhibits Muslims from enjoying citizenship in a truly egalitarian sense.

This chapter explores how Muslims in Australia claim, enact and negotiate their citizenship within such a sceptical, at times hostile societal environment. Some previous studies have emphasised the exclusionary effects of this Islamophobic discourse and its paralysing implications for Muslims' active citizenship. In Al-Momani et al.'s (2010) study on Australian Muslims' political participation, for example, many of the interviewed politically active Muslims described 'negative images of Islam as a barrier' for political engagement.[16] Another Australian study, conducted in New South Wales in 2009/2010 among Muslim families, found that some Muslim mothers of school-aged children refrained from becoming more engaged in school-related volunteer activities because of, among others, their lack of 'confidence due to stigmatisation of Muslims and negative media portrayal'.[17]

Drawing on research conducted between 2012 and 2015, this paper examines the indirectly 'positive' effects of Islamophobia on Muslims' active citizenship, without calling into doubt the devastating implications of these exclusionary discourses and experiences of racism.

THEORETICAL AND CONCEPTUAL FRAMEWORK: ACTIVE CITIZENSHIP

Citizenship is a much-discussed concept referring to someone's full membership of a society and political community. There is little disagreement that equal legal status is a key component of this membership and that citizenship by definition encompasses equal—civil, social and political—rights.[18] Such a rights-and-status based understanding used to prevail in the academic discourse on citizenship for many decades. This has ultimately changed, however, since the 1990s, leading the two leading citizenship scholars Engin Isin and Bryan Turner to assert in 2002 that 'there is now an agreement that citizenship must also be defined as a social process through which individuals and social groups engage in claiming ... rights'.[19]

Conceptualising citizenship as a combination of legal status, rights and responsibilities, on the one hand, and social processes of claim-making as performed citizenship, on the other, calls for greater attention to the complex ways in which people negotiate and enact their citizenship. Against this backdrop the notion of active citizenship has acquired not only new prominence, but also a more normative dimension especially in critical scholarship and the political debates. Advocating a radical and more inclusive form of democracy, Chantal Mouffe argues: 'A radical, democratic citizen must be an active citizen, somebody who *acts* as a citizen, who conceives of herself as a participant in a collective undertaking'[20] (emphasis in the original).

While there is broad consensus among most scholars, policymakers and practitioners that citizens' participation, or civic engagement, is at the core of active citizenship, the nature and scope of what constitutes participation as enacted citizenship has been less clear. One of the few explicit definitions of active citizenship, proposed by Hoskins and Mascherini, includes three locations of participation and specifies some basic framework conditions. Active citizenship is 'participation in civil society, community and/or political life, characterised by mutual respect and non-violence and in accordance with human rights and democracy'.[21] The two US researchers Richard Adler and Judy Goggin[22] use the broad concept of civic engagement to capture the manifold facets of active citizenship: '[C]ivic engagement describes how an active citizen participates in the life of a community in order to improve conditions for others or to help shape the community's future'. This definition is further specified with a two-axis model. The horizontal axis refers to the degree of institutionalisation of civic engagement, 'between individual or informal activities and more formal, collective actions that involve participation in organisations'. The vertical dimension focusses on the site of participation, locating engagement 'between involvement in community activities ... and involvement in political activities'.[23] The latter axis oscillates between civic and political participation, without making a clear-cut distinction between both.

Isin and Nielsen[24] propose an alternative paradigm of performed citizenship with their elaborations on 'acts of citizenship'. They advocate a more fluid understanding of citizenship, enacted by 'activist citizens' who constantly reinvent and create new 'scenes' and 'scripts' for the performance of their citizenship.[25] Isin and Nielsen underscore the performative nature of citizenship, calling for an open approach to the investigation of active citizenship, without pre-defined concepts of how citizenship might be enacted. This aligns well with other contemporary debates in citizenship scholarship, illustrating that the notion of active citizenship needs to flexibly include a range of existing—and newly emerging—performative expressions. This has changed the field and analytical lens of citizenship studies in the recent past, as more informal, temporary and highly personalised manifestations of enacted citizenship, especially of young people, has received increasing empirical attention (e.g. on young Muslims' citizenship in Australia[26]). There is no doubt that the previously narrow focus on conventional expressions of civic and political participation has ceased to dominate citizenship studies. Online social media,[27] the arts[28] or comedy performance[29] as sites of enacted citizenship, for example, may have been overlooked in the past, but have come to be regarded as vehicles of political participation and community engagement, especially for young people today.

Another related stream in contemporary citizenship discourse, which has its origin in empirical research on the civic performance of Muslims youth in the United States, explores 'dissenting citizenship'[30] as manifestation of informal political participation in the face of experienced stigmatisation. In their study on Muslim youth in the UK, Ben O'Loughlin and Marie Gillespie argue:

> With diminishing prospects for effective participation in formal political processes, except through the domineering framework of counter-terrorism, young British Muslims sought alternative arenas and modes of political debate and engagement. They expressed their dissent from the suffocating politics of security in informal ways that were deemed efficacious in their own terms… young British Muslims responded in politically creative ways that can be described as 'dissenting citizenship'.[31]

O'Loughlin and Gillespie's study sheds light on the often overlooked 'rebellious, critical, angry and disappointed'[32] performance of citizenship—and it addresses the theme of this chapter: the link between experiences of exclusion and Muslims' active citizenship.

While the exclusionary 'othering' and stigmatisation of Muslims is, by definition, irreconcilable with the egalitarian *principle* of citizenship, it is less clear how these anti-Muslim phenomena affect Muslims' negotiation and performance of their citizenship in everyday *practice*. Experiences of marginalisation and exclusion, including the skewed media misrepresentation of Muslims, have often been described as barriers for civic and political participation.[33] There is evidence, however, that suggests this exclusionary effects are only one part of the story. Historically, it has often been the very sense of injustice and exclusion that has motivated— not deterred—members of hitherto marginalised social groups (women, Blacks, gays etc.) to join forces in social movements, thrusting them into the arena of active citizenship, publicly expressing dissent whilst claiming recognition and equal rights. More specifically, as scholars like Tariq Modood have argued, experiences of racism and inequality may motivate ethnic minorities to perform their citizenship by 'mobilis[ing] around identities of cultural difference and demand equality of respect'.[34]

Research specifically on Muslims in the West confirms such arguments, highlighting that at least some Muslims have actively sought to challenge anti-Muslim racism and Islamophobic discourse and misrepresentation by engaging in a range of civic and political activities. Almost two decades ago, the Pnina Werbner already described British Muslims' mobilisation against what they considered unfair treatment of their faith group (for example, during the Rushdie affair) as 'key moments in the development of a Muslim British civic consciousness and capacity for active citizenship'.[35] In the Australian context, scholars have argued that in the aftermaths of 9/11 Muslims felt the urge to engage in outreach and dialogue initiatives to counter the backlash against their communities.[36] Hence, the rising tide of Islamophobia has had a civically encouraging impact on many Muslim community members. Examining Muslim community organisations' responses to the changed social climate after the 9/11 terror attacks, Nora Amath came to similar conclusions, identifying 'three main forms of interaction with the wider society: interfaith dialogue, media engagement and consultation with government'.[37]

These research findings show that Islamophobia-driven exclusion and injustice experienced by Muslims is not necessarily a deterrent for active citizenship. For some within Muslim communities, the opposite seems to be the case. This argument has been confirmed by a recently concluded empirical study, which has generated innovative insights into these mechanisms and Muslims' personal rationales.

Effect of Islamophobia on Muslims' Active Citizenship

This paper draws on empirical fieldwork carried out as part of a cross-national comparative study between 2012 and 2015 in Australia and Germany. In-depth, partially biographic, interviews were conducted with 30 self-declared Muslims in both countries. The following sections focus on the Australian sub-sample, which comprises 14 Australian Muslims from Melbourne and Sydney.

Participants were selected on the basis of a sampling rationale aimed at ensuring a maximum diversity in terms of their demographics and covering various different forms of civic and political participation, including:

- Engagement within Muslim community and non-Muslim organisations;
- Engagement within an organisational context or enacted independently;
- Engagement pursuing Muslim-specific goals (e.g. advancing Muslim communities), goals related to a particular non-Muslim community or group (e.g. workers' rights), or republican 'greater good' focussed civic agendas.

The realised sample covers these diverse manifestations of active citizenship, and it was also diverse in terms of its demographic composition. It included seven Muslim men and seven Muslim women, aged between mid-20s to above 75 years, four of them born in Australia (the others migrated, six of them when they were still children), and with various ethnic-national backgrounds (mainly Lebanese but also Egyptian, Turkish, Iraqi, Fiji, Pakistani and Eritrean). The sample was characterised by participants' high educational attainments with 11 out of 14 holding a university degree. The majority of participants appear to be practicing Muslims, but their religious practices and religiosity (beyond their self-identification as Muslim) was not a selection criteria, and the interview did not seek to elicit any information on this (although it has been brought up by many participants themselves).

The analysis of the interview data yielded innovative insights into the complex manifestations and dynamic trajectories of Muslims' active citizenship. Among many other findings, the study offers evidence on how personal or collective experiences of anti-Muslim exclusion and the skewed public discourse on Islam and Muslims have affected Muslims' performance of citizenship. Elaborating on their own biographies as committed citizens, interview partners referred to these phenomena in two interconnected ways: first, in the context of the aims pursued through their active citizenship and, secondly, as a source of motivation and encouragement for their civic or political engagement.

Performing Citizenship Aimed at Countering Negative Misconceptions of Muslims

Most Australian Muslims interviewed for this study explained that their civic or political engagement has been driven, generally, by their desire to have a transformative impact on the world around them. The envisaged changes and pursued goals vary broadly and are often complexly intertwined. Some interview partners have sought to achieve different aims, either simultaneously or consecutively, through different forms of engagement. The data analysis identified four basic types of goals:

- serving humanity and bettering society (with a strong republican focus);
- helping disadvantaged population groups other than Muslims;

- advancing the Muslim community (with a strong communitarian focus);
- redressing the negative misconception of Muslims and Islam.

It is especially the latter of these four goals that highlights the link between Muslims' active citizenship and Islamophobia. Several interviewed Australian Muslims have become active in different forms of civic or political participation with the explicit agenda of presenting a more accurate image of Islam and tackling ignorance, stereotypes and prejudice towards Muslims. This activism was either framed as an attempt to improve intergroup relations and contribute to a greater level of social harmony and cohesion and Australia's diverse society; or participants pursued a more communitarian agenda seeking to primarily advance the wellbeing and recognition of Muslims. In some cases, both rationales were closely intertwined.

Ashtar,[38] for example, an Iraqi women in her mid-20s, emphasised that the purpose of her active citizenship is 'to dispel these myths and misconceptions' the Muslim community has been facing in Australia. She stated: 'I know it's a cliché, but even if [only] a couple of people changed their views, I would feel like I've achieved my aim. My goal at the end of the day is to help people view Muslim women on an equal playing field, to see them as active citizens of this country.' *Ashtar* described her civic goals as 'breaking barriers and misconceptions'. This has driven her civic engagement in various contexts, and it has been particularly vital for her media work as a blogger and community radio presenter. While her activism was primarily aimed at 'mak[ing] sure that I do something that will benefit my community', she considered it most effective to pursue this goal from 'outside the community' through mainstream media work as a journalist. This would enable her to reach a wider audience. Working as a community radio presenter was for her only a strategic first step to become a journalist for mainstream media, 'where I can do more for my community':

> I want to become a broadcast journalist, and I think by being a broadcast journalist, I can do more for the Muslim community... Just by the fact that I wear the hijab and appear on television I can send a very strong message to a lot of people ... And sometimes the best acts of advocacy and active citizenship is just being you... It's much more powerful and

resonates with more people when a Muslim woman talks about politics or sports or whatever.

Ashtar's personal accounts illustrate how she has tried to tackle misconceptions primarily indirectly by acting as a publicly visible Muslim role model, calling into doubt the essence of many of these anti-Muslim narratives.

A similar strategy was deployed by Sara (aged 25–30; born in Egypt). She has pursued a combination of goals through her multiple ways of enacting her citizenship, which include volunteering for a Muslim grassroots organisation, working for Amnesty International, and other unaffiliated forms of political participation. Parallel to her goal of 'helping the needy' and empowering young Muslims and non-Muslims in the local community, she has sought to tackle the widespread misconception that Muslim youth were isolating themselves and refrained from engaging with broader society and political issues.

These public allegations have motivated her to participate in the government's National Australian Youth Forum, which she applied for, got accepted and eventually was appointed chair. Besides her personal interest in political issues, she explained that through her participation in this youth forum she was eager to demonstrate to the government that young people—and especially young Muslims—are not necessarily disconnected from 'mainstream government infrastructure and institutions'. Contrary to such misconceptions, many of them are interested, she argued, but need more platforms and support to become involved. Sara explained: 'So I thought [participating in this forum] would be a really good way to make sure the government is listening and sees there is this Muslim community, young Muslims are doing some great things. They need to see that'. Sara is optimistic about the effectiveness of her engagement within the National Australian Youth Forum, stressing that after some time 'people started to recognise that this [Muslim] community exists and that they were doing great things'.

In contrast to this indirect 'role modelling' strategy, some interviewed Muslims have tried to counter stereotypes and misrepresentation of Muslims directly, by providing accurate information about Islam and engaging in cross-community or interreligious dialogue. Often both approaches—role modelling and information sharing and dialogue—coincided. Riad, an Egyptian-born Melbourne imam (aged over 75), who has been active in several interfaith initiatives for many years, described his personal motivation for his cross-community engagement in reference to fostering mutual understanding: 'It is important that neighbours talk to each other and understand one another. That is important to me personally, very important, that we try to remove any misunderstandings; that would lead to a better life—for everyone.'

For Saara, Lebanon-born co-founder of Young Muslims of Australia and, later on, of the Muslim community organisation Benevolence, the desire to engage in a dialogue with non-Muslim Australians on Islam has been driven by her broadly defined civic-spiritual goal of 'serving humanity'. She emphasised that 'it is a deep concern for humanity as a whole to be proactive and try to create change. And it is not service to Muslims [only]'. One key element of this transformative agenda is her commitment to cross-community dialogue with, among others, church or women's groups and students at schools, which is ultimately aimed at breaking down misconceptions of Islam. She elaborated in particular on one of her many projects:

> I wanted to work with the wider community ... There are many projects that I worked on. I worked on the *My Dress, My Image, My Choice* show, which is a fashion show that I created ... to bring communities together to discuss what is Islam really about ... to demystify the hijab and to engage and really discuss why women dress the way they do. That's one point, but it was really about: Let's talk! The hijab was just a means to engage. Because this show was so successful, it only finished in 2011. So ten years, it was an ongoing show, it travelled all around Australia.

All these Muslims pursue the aim of tackling public misconceptions and prejudices towards Muslims, but their specific rationales differ significantly. While some, like Sara or *Ashtar*, articulated a primarily community-oriented focus on advancing the recognition of Muslims, others, like Saara, framed their cross-community dialogue work (undertaken as representatives of the Muslim community) in republican terms ('common good') of improving cross-community relationship and promoting social cohesion more generally.

Active Citizenship Encouraged by Islamophobia?

Experiences of Islamophobia, from collective stigmatisation to incidents of personal vilification and harassment, have not only shaped the goals behind Muslims' civic and political commitment; they have also been described by many Australian Muslims in this study as a motivating factors for their active citizenship. Instead of having a deterring effect, these Muslims highlighted that such negative, collective and often also individual, experiences have urged them to invest more time and effort in their activism. Several interviewees, however, also stressed that these positive effects do not apply to all Muslims, as some—or many—would feel civically paralysed by Islamophobia related experiences.

Abdul (aged 25–30), who migrated from Lebanon to Australia as a university student and has since then worked with many young Muslims from a mosque community in Melbourne's west, elaborated that the prejudice-laden climate towards Muslims has further encouraged his activism: 'It actually challenged me more', he explained. But he also noted that this does not apply to all Muslims within the community. To the contrary, he assumes a rather hampering impact on the inclination of the majority of Muslims to become active.

This is echoed by Hass Dellal, director of the Australian Multicultural Foundation, who has worked intensely with young Muslims. He asserted that while 'some [Muslims] withdraw' in response to the negative public discourse, others—including himself—feel even more encouraged to become active: '[Some] withdraw and keep within their own circles and do whatever. Some participate even more! For me it was like *bring it on*! The more [negative labelling of Muslims], the better'.

Maha Abdo, head of the Sydney-based United Muslim Women Association (UMWA) , expressed similar views, but applied them more broadly across Muslim communities. Elaborating on the effect of the negative climate for the Muslims collectively, she asserted: 'I honestly think the more [public scapegoating of Muslims] is taking place, the more we are encouraged to participate'. Similarly, *Ashtar*, online media activist and project officer at a government-funded agency for the promotion of multiculturalism, maintained that, in her view, many young Muslims 'are very active and I don't think they would disengage because they face racism … This is obviously not applicable to everybody, and everybody deals with it in his own personal way. [But] yeah, it is a lot more of a motivator than it is a deterrent.'

While this empowering dimension of Muslims' collective and individual experiences of marginalisation has emerged as a common narrative, the way in which active Muslims have dealt with, and responded to, these experiences differ. According to a small number of interviewed

Muslims, the sceptical or hostile climate affects the context within which actively engaged Muslims seek to enact their citizenship. It was suggested that certain Muslims may turn their back to mainstream-oriented forms of participation and instead focus on intra-community volunteering, where they can avoid potentially anti-Muslim confrontations. Joumanah El Matrah, representative of the Melbourne-based Australian Muslim Women's Centre for Human Rights, for example, expressed the view that the prevalent exclusionary discourse can push Muslims into minority-centric forms of citizenship, which she views somewhat critically: 'I think [the negative public climate] encourages them to do more, but it means that they misunderstand what the challenge is about. I think it increases the ethno-centric or religious-centric view to activism, which in the long term is bad for them and bad for society.'

Ferroz (aged 25–30), born in Sydney, who volunteered as a youth worker and board member of a Muslim grassroots organisation in Sydney, recalled an incident that supports Joumanah's view. He maintained that experiences of anti-Muslim racism can be a 'barrier for citizenship in the wider community'—although he did not consider such a community focus of Muslims' citizenship as problematic:

> I remember when I participated in Clean Up Australia …about a year ago with a friend [a Muslim girl]. We headed out to Cronulla… And the comments we got were like 'Clean up your own country! This is Clean Up Australia Day, and you are not Australian'. So it is definitely a barrier. She is too hurt to get into wider community citizenship [again]. She does local community work now, where she feels safe.

Such implications of Islamophobia on the location of performed citizenship were mentioned only by a minority. More commonly, interviewed Muslims elaborated on their extended commitment to mainstream-oriented or cross-community participation. This was often driven by their personal perception that there was an urgent need—or even a civic obligation—for themselves as Muslims to become active in order to break down stereotypes and overcome ignorance among segments of the mainstream society. 'More things need to be done', as Abdul put it, and Ferroz also expressed this view that Muslims need to act as model Australian citizens: 'We feel like we have to be the role models and the example of what an Australian Muslim is: just a normal Australian who has a faith … But we also know we have to work ten times as hard as any other group in the country to show that we don't have an agenda ... We just want to help.'

Some interviewed Muslims argued explicitly along religious lines, emphasising that their desire to redress the public misconception of Islam and Muslims is a direct reflection of their faith or Islamic duties. *Serap*, a 35-year old Australian born women of Turkish background, who volunteered for a Muslim women's group in Melbourne, explained:

> To please God runs down deep to a lot of things ... Me writing a letter to the editor because I don't like what he wrote about Muslim women in *The Age* is purely to please God for me. It's like I'm being an active citizen, I'm being an active Muslim. I'm going to defend what's right, and he [the editor] had a wrong understanding of what Muslim women are. So I have to correct that, so that the thousands of Australian readers who read that get a correct understanding of Muslim women, so that we can coexist in harmony. It's all about that...

Similarly, the Melbourne-based community activist Saara Sabbagh, who has been active in cross-cultural dialogue programmes, referred to the 'prophetic model' and her endeavour to follow the example of the Prophet in everything she does. Her personal experiences of anti-Muslim racism and harassment have made her civic engagement, in her words, 'more compassionate', because the Prophet also 'responded to ignorance with compassion and mercy. And this is the only way we are going to move forward'.

Concluding Discussion

These accounts of civically and politically active Australian Muslims demonstrate that the Muslim-sceptical or hostile climate, sometimes coupled with personal experiences of racism, affects Muslims' citizenship in different ways. There is little doubt that this can severely impede Muslims' sense of civic belonging, reinforce their feelings of alienation and hamper their eagerness to actively participate in the public sphere. Others within the Muslim community do not seem to disengage in the face of Islamophobia, but rather re-directed their civic commitment to what they perceived as a personally safe environment—the community-internal space of Muslim organisations. Here they feel confident to enact their citizenship and make a positive contribution to the lives of fellow

Muslims without having to justify their faith or even being racially or religiously vilified.

Australian Muslims interviewed for this study have witnessed these two responses among fellow Muslims, but they also stressed that neither of them apply to them personally. Instead, they asserted that Islamophobic discourses have encouraged them to become even more active in their effort to counteract ignorance and prejudice. This active citizenship response can be performed in two (often interconnected) ways: directly through media work (e.g. blogging), interfaith dialogue and other forms of cross-community exchange, or indirectly through civic and political participation as Australian 'model citizens' in a range of mainstream contexts. These findings further specify what Al-Momani and his colleagues found in their study on political participation of Australian Muslims: 'To some, the negative publicity about Muslims after September 11 2001 was a motivating force. Media stereotypes inspired some to demonstrate a different face of Islam. Others were moved by the discrimination Muslims experienced to help other Muslims understand and act on their rights.'[39]

Islamophobia fundamentally denies equal citizenship to Muslims, and some Muslims feel disempowered by this anti-egalitarian discourse and experiences of exclusion and refrain from active participation. But why is it that others respond by engaging even more in civic and political participation and cross-community exchange? What sets both groups apart? This is a crucial question that requires more empirical attention in the future. The present study was not designed to systematically explore this issue, but the interview data point to several potentially influential factors.

First, the individual's general personality or character traits of outspokenness, optimism and, very broadly, personal strength seem to play an important role in Muslims' accounts on their active citizenship. Those who refuse to withdraw in response to the stigmatising discourses and experiences of racism presented themselves as optimistic by nature, strong-minded and resilient. Moreover, many of them seem to deliberately ignore systemic-structural dimensions of Islamophobia and instead highlight that Islamophobia reflects primarily ignorance and a lack of information—which can in principle be changed—rather than a deeply entrenched personal animosity against Muslims or marginalising power structures. Hence, in their logic, Islamophobia poses a challenge for them—and it is up to them to do something about it, to reach out, and to provide an accurate image of what it means to be Muslim in Australia. Related to that, the analysis suggests a link between personal strength, having a clear sense of religious and civic identity, and the capacity to respond actively to collective or individual experiences of Islamophobia. Almost all interviewed Muslim stressed their civic belonging to Australia *and* their strong Islamic identity, and for some this was a major source of empowerment, enabling them to enact their citizenship through civic engagement in the face of these negative experiences.

These personality and identity-based characteristics of active Muslims have been mentioned in previous research. Al-Momami and colleagues, for example, concluded that many of the politically active Muslims, interviewed for their study, 'found in their family backgrounds the resources to be personally strong, willing to go out on a limb, unafraid to risk criticism—necessary attributes for anyone taking a public stand'.[40]

The second part of the puzzle of why some Muslims refrain from civic engagment, while others become even more active applies to all citizens regardless of their faith: Individual resources, including civic skills and knowledge as well social connectedness, increases one's disposition to civic and political participation. This also applies to Muslims' active citizenship. The analysis of the interviews suggests, for example, that Muslims' cross-community social networks and relationships of trust have often been regarded as a facilitator for enhanced civic engagement. Becoming active in civic or political participation may not be impossible but seems much more difficult for those who lack these cross-community forms of social capital. The same holds true for education-related resources. There is a broad consensus that people with a higher level of education are more likely to volunteer and become politically active.[41] Being articulate, having organisational and language skills, and being familiar with different cultural codes have been mentioned as important enablers of civic participation in this study.

The third factor that may explain why some Muslims remain passive, while others feel further encouraged by Islamophobia related experiences is linked to the fundamental drivers behind active Muslims' commitment and eagerness to contribute to positive changes. For Muslims interviewed for this study, remaining passive and not participating was not an option. They all felt urged to become active either by strong civic values, like their commitment to social justice, or by their faith. While civic and Islamic convictions were often described as inherently intertwined or even synonymous, it was especially the Islamic principle—or duty—of 'serving humanity' or 'doing good' that has driven their activism. This confirms emerging research on how Islamic practices enhance active citizenship.[42]

The interplay between these three factors—general traits of optimism and resilience, resources and social capital, and strong civic values or religiously driven motivation—seems to be part of the answer as to why some Muslims disengage in the face of Islamophobia, while others become even more eager to actively participate in one way or another. More research is necessary to explore these issues in greater depth.

These findings offer a starting point for future research, but they also highlight the need for targeted actions by governments and communities to strengthen the resilience and sense of multiple belonging of Muslim and other ethno religious minority youth, tackle their disadvantaged access to socioeconomic and educational resources, and help build supportive social networks and relationships of trust. A promoting citizenship agenda of empowering young Muslims to raise their voice, express themselves and their dissent, and to 'do citizenship' needs to go hand in hand with concerted efforts to counter Islamophobia. Presenting accurate counter-narratives is not only a task for Muslims themselves, but for everyone in society—especially for politicians and other public opinion leaders. Such a multidimensional approach is needed to promote substantive citizenship of Muslims, based on recognition and equal opportunities, beyond a merely legal status of equal rights. Applied more broadly, this will also be key to building a more cohesive and resilient Australian society for the future.

Notes

1. Ben O'Loughlin and Marie Gillespie, "Dissenting Citizenship? Young People and Political Participation in the Media-security Nexus," *Parliamentary Affairs* 65 (2012): 117.
2. Pamela J. Conover, Donald D. Searing, and Ivor Crewe, "The Elusive Ideal of Equal Citizenship: Political Theory and Political Psychology in the United States and Great Britain," *The Journal of Politics* 66, no. 4 (2004): 1037.
3. Peter Kivisto and Thomas Faist, *Citizenship. Discourse, Theory, and Transnational Prospects* (Malden: Blackwell, 2007), 132.
4. Conover, Searing and Crewe, "The Elusive Ideal," 1037.
5. Egin F. Isin, "Theorising Acts of Citizenship," in *Acts of Citizenship*, ed. Egin F. Isin and Greg M. Nielsen (London: Zed Books, 2008), 17.

6. Thomas H. Marshall, *Citizenship and Social Class* (Cambridge: Cambridge University Press, 1950), 5.
7. Nancy Fraser, "Social Justice in the Age of Identity Politics. Redistribution, Recognition, and Participation," in *Culture and Economy After the Cultural Turn*, ed. Larry Ray and Andrew Sayer (London: Sage, 1999).
8. Mario Peucker, Joshua M. Roose, and Shahram Akbarzadeh, "Muslim Active Citizenship in Australia: Socioeconomic Challenges and the Emergence of a Muslim Elite," *Australian Journal of Political Science* 49, no. 2 (2014).
9. Mario Peucker, "On the (In)compatibility of Islam and Citizenship in Western Democracies: The Role of Religiosity for Muslims' Civic and Political Engagement," *Politics and Religion*, https://doi.org/10.1017/S1755048317000700, (2018).
10. Andrew Markus, *Mapping Social Cohesion. The Scanlon Foundation Survey 2016* (Caulfield East: Monash University, 2016); University of South Australia, *Islamophobia, Social Distance and Fear of Terrorism in Australia. A Preliminary Report* (Adelaide: International Centre for Muslim and Non-Muslim Understanding, 2015).
11. For an overview, see Mario Peucker and Shahram Akbarzadeh, *Muslim Active Citizenship in the West* (London: Routledge, 2014), 78–90.
12. Heather MacDonald, et al., "Rental Discrimination in the Multi-Ethnic Metropolis: Evidence from Sydney," *Urban Policy and Research* 34, no. 4 (2016).
13. Alison L. Booth, Andrew Leigh, and Elena Varganova, "Does Ethnic Discrimination Vary Across Minority Groups? Evidence from a Field Experiment," *Oxford Bulletin of Economics and Statistics* 74, no. 4 (2012).
14. Kevin Dunn, et al., *The Resilience and Ordinariness of Australian Muslims* (Sydney: ISRA/Charles Sturt University, 2015); Derya Iner, ed., *Islamophobia in Australia 2014–2016* (Sydney: Islamophobia Register Australia, 2017).
15. The Runnymede Trust, *Islamophobia—A Challenge for Us All* (London: The Runnymede Trust, 1997); Erik Bleich, "What Is Islamophobia and How Much Is There? Theorizing and Measuring an Emerging Comparative Concept," *American Behavioral Scientist* 55, no. 12 (2011).
16. Kais Al-Momani, et al., *Political Participation of Muslims in Australia* (Sydney: Macquarie University, 2010), 39.
17. Sandra Gendera, Rogelia Pe-Pua, and Ilan Katz, "Social Cohesion and Social Capital: The Experience of Australian Muslim Families in Two Communities," in *Muslims in the West and the Challenge of Belonging*, ed. Fethi Mansouri and Vince Marotta (Melbourne: Melbourne University Press, 2012), 106.

18. Marshall, *Citizenship and Social Class*.
19. Engin F. Isin and Bryan S. Turner, "Citizenship Studies: An Introduction," in *Handbook of Citizenship Studies*, ed. Bryan S. Turner and Engin F. Isin (London: Sage, 2002), 4.
20. Chantal Mouffe, "Preface. Democratic Politics Today," in *Dimensions of Radical Democracy: Pluralism, Citizenship, Community*, ed. Chantal Mouffe (London: Verso, 1992), 4.
21. Bryon L. Hoskins and Massimiliano Mascherini, "Measuring Active Citizenship Through the Development of a Composite Indicator," *Social Indicators Research* 90, no. 3 (2009), 462.
22. Richard P. Adler and Judy Goggin, "What Do We Mean By 'Civic Engagement'," *Journal of Transformative Education* 3, no. 3 (2005).
23. Adler and Goggin, "What Do We Mean," 240.
24. Engin F. Isin and Greg M. Nielsen, ed., *Acts of Citizenship* (London: Zed Books, 2008).
25. Isin, "Theorising Acts," 38.
26. Anita Harris and Joshua Roose, "DIY Citizenship Amongst Young Muslims: Experiences of the 'Ordinary'," *Journal of Youth Studies* 17, no. 6 (2014); Chloe Patton, "Multicultural Citizenship and Religiosity: Young Australian Muslims Forging a Sense of Belonging After 9/11," *Journal for Intercultural Studies* 35, no. 1 (2014).
27. Amelia Johns, "Muslim Young People Online: 'Acts of Citizenship' in Socially Networked Spaces," *Social Inclusion* 2, no. 2 (2014).
28. Thea Renda Abu El-Haj, "Imagining postnationalism: Arts, Citizenship Education, and Arab American Youth," *Anthropology & Education Quarterly* 40, no. 1 (2009).
29. Mucahit Bilici, *Finding Mecca in America: How Islam Is Becoming an American Religion* (Chicago: University of Chicago Press, 2012); Riem Spielhaus, "Clichés Are Funny as Long as They Happen on Stage: Comedy as Political Criticism," *Muslim Political Participation in Europe*, ed. Jørgen S. Nielsen (Edinburgh: Edinburgh University Press, 2013).
30. Sunaina Maira, "Citizenship and Dissent: South Asian Muslim Youth in the US After 9/11," *South Asian Popular Cultures* 8, no. 1 (2010).
31. O'Loughlin and Gillespie, "Dissenting Citizenship?", 115.
32. Op. cit., 117.
33. Cultural and Indigenous Research Centre Australia (CIRCA), *Civic and Social Participation of Australian Muslim Men* (Leichhardt: CIRCA, 2010); Al-Momani, et al., *Political Participation of Muslims*.
34. Tariq Modood, *Post-Immigration 'Difference;' and Integration. The Case of Muslims in Western Europe* (London: The British Academy, 2012), 46.
35. Pnina Werbner, "Divided Loyalties, Empowered Citizenship? Muslims in Britain," *Citizenship Studies* 4, no. 3 (2000), 309.

36. Peucker and Akbarzadeh, *Muslim Active Citizenship*, 162–165.
37. Nora Amath, "The Impact of 9/11 on Australian Muslim Civil Society Organisations," *Communication, Politics & Culture* 46 (2013), 116.
38. Interview partners whose name is written in *italics* chose to remain anonymous; the used name is a pseudonym.
39. Al-Momani, et al., *Political Participation*, 35.
40. Ibid.
41. Sidney Verba, Kay. L. Schlozman and Henry E. Brady, *Voice and Equality. Civic Voluntarims in American Politics* (Cambridge: Harvard University Press, 1995), 270–271; CIRCA, *Civic and Social Participation*; Australian Bureau of Statistics (ABS), *Voluntary Work Australia* (Canberra: Commonwealth of Australia, 2011).
42. Amelia Johns, Fethi Mansouri, and Michele Lobo, "Religiosity, Citizenship and Belonging: The Everyday Experiences of Young Australian Muslims," *Journal for Muslim Minority Affairs* 35, no. 2 (2015), 185; Harris and Roose, "DIY Citizenship"; Mario Peucker, "On the (In)compatibility of Islam and Citizenship in Western Democracies: The Role of Religiosity for Muslims' Civic and Political Engagement," *Politics and Religion*, https://doi.org/10.1017/S1755048317000700, (2018).

CHAPTER 14

Tackling the Twin Threats of Islamophobia and Puritanical Islamist Extremism: Case Study of the Hizmet Movement

Ozcan Keles, Ismail Mesut Sezgin and Ihsan Yilmaz

INTRODUCTION

In recent decades, Islam has been hijacked by some violently extremist global groups that have a pastiche ideology composed of terrorism, nihilism, fundamentalism, Islamist puritanism, conservatism and *takfirism*.[1] Khaled Abou El Fadl refers to these group of Muslims as "puritans" owing to their claims of "purism" which rejects competing points of view.[2] In this study we will call groups such as Al Qaida and ISIS as "Puritanical Islamist Extremists" and their ideology as "Puritanical Islamist Extremism."[3]

O. Keles (✉)
University of Sussex, Brighton, UK
e-mail: o.keles@sussex.ac.uk

I. M. Sezgin
Leeds Beckett University, Leeds, UK
e-mail: imsezgin@hizmetstudies.org

I. Yilmaz
Deakin University, Geelong, VIC, Australia
e-mail: ihsan.yilmaz@deakin.edu.au

© The Author(s) 2019
J. L. Esposito and D. Iner (Eds.), *Islamophobia and Radicalization*,
https://doi.org/10.1007/978-3-319-95237-6_14

Islamophobia, or anti-Muslimism on the one hand,[4] and Puritanical Islamist Extremism on the other, are closely related phenomena. Both extremes of the religio-political spectrum are concerned with the interpretation of Islam in the modern world and each feeds the other's existence. The tendency to conflate the religion of Islam and its socially ultraconservative manifestations with the Puritanical Islamist Extremism leads to Islamophobia. This in return can help fan the flames of anti-Muslim hate crime resulting in a self-perpetuating vicious cycle of violence and social animosity.

While these ostensibly opposite ideological camps consistently and symbiotically reinforce each, they are perpetuated in the absence of knowledge, practice and interaction that positively disrupts the confluence between and within both camps. It is at this juncture that the Hizmet Movement's work and example could be useful. Hizmet does not aim to defeat Islamophobia or Puritanical Islamist Extremism head on. Rather, it is our contention that the core Islamic teachings that underpin the movement's values and practice undermine the ideology and mindset of these two mutually reinforcing camps as a natural by-product and default outcome of its positive work. Accordingly, the goal of defeating extremism is made to *ensue* without being directly *pursued*. In addition, this process helps to complexify matters pertaining to religious interpretation and representation while also promoting critical thinking, self-reflexivity, proactivism, empathy, openness to the other and intercultural exchange. Together, that addresses some of the underlying dynamics at play in the production and internalization of extremist ideologies, such as identity crises, real or perceived grievances, a sense of helplessness, absolutism and charismatic recruiters.

THE TWIN THREATS OF ISLAMOPHOBIA AND PURITANICAL ISLAMIST EXTREMISM[5]

While Islam has been hijacked by Puritanical Islamist Extremists, Muslims all over the world face discrimination and attacks from the extremist, right-wing Islamophobia industry and its supporters (who also promote phobia of Jews, black people, and LGTBI people).[6]

Islamophobia is exacerbated by a number of contextual factors. One of these is the deeply skeptical, secular, and agnostic outlook on religion found in some parts of the media. This outlook is reflected implicitly, and sometimes explicitly, in the media, and perhaps particularly in the left-liberal media. Moreover, both the media coverage which tends to front extremism (*if it bleeds it leads*) and political commentators (media, politicians, far right groups) pave the way for Islamophobia. However, a group's ability to respond to malicious or ignorant media coverage is dependent on the context. For example, in the United Kingdom the Church of England has far more resources and opportunities to respond than does British Muslims. For Muslims, therefore, since they have less influence and less access to public platforms, such attacks are far more undermining.[7]

There is a widespread perception that the war on terror is, in fact, a war on Islam.[8] The cumulative effect of Islamophobia's various features, exacerbated by the contextual factors, is that Muslims are made to feel that they do not truly belong to the West—they feel that they are not truly accepted,[9] let alone welcomed, as full members of the wider society. On the contrary, they are seen as "an enemy within" or "a fifth column"[10] and they feel that they are under constant siege.[11] All these factors pave the way for resentment among some Western Muslims. The Puritanical Islamist Extremists have been taking advantage of this resentment.

Puritanical Islamist Extremists generally attract disillusioned and alienated young Muslims[12] who struggle to define their identity in a postmodern and post-truth world that they perceive to be producing only injustice and misery for Muslims. For the most part, the traditional, moderate Islamic scholars (*'ulama*) have been unable to develop Islamic social, cultural, and political discourses, frameworks, and paradigms that are in tune with this age and that address contemporary life challenges. This mediocre 'ulama class that, conditioned to mediocrity and protectionism as a result of its very training, and not sufficiently versed in the Zeitgeist, fails to re-read and re-interpret Islam and Islamic law in tune with the current time and space. This results in what Ihsan Yilmaz refers to as "theological deprivation".[13] Puritanical Islamist Extremists fill this gap with a rhetoric which is energetic, self-confident, challenging, masculinist and easily comprehensible.

Muslim societies are full of ethnic, sectarian, cultural, and ideological groups with strong bonding capital but with little to no bridging social capital, empathetic acceptance, or intercultural understanding. In such contexts, othering becomes the norm. This is where Puritanical Islamist Extremist ideology has the upper hand since it is based on binary oppositions and dichotomous othering.

Puritanical Islamist Extremists' and the Islamophobes' convergence extends to proclaiming that their absolutist, proscriptive, essentialized interpretation of Islam is the only authentic understanding of the richly diverse faith. While these ostensibly opposite ideological camps consistently and symbiotically reinforce each other, they are perpetuated in the absence of knowledge, practice and social interaction that positively disrupts the confluence between and within both camps. It is at this juncture that the Hizmet Movement's work and example are useful.

What Is the Hizmet Movement?

The Hizmet Movement (hereinafter, "Hizmet") is a transnational civil society movement inspired by the teachings, values, and principles espoused by Fethullah Gülen, an Islamic scholar and peace advocate.[14] It is a faith-inspired, grassroots, civic, independent movement connected through shared ideals and teachings on the one hand and a dense web of formal and informal networks on the other.[15] It is "faith-inspired in motivation, yet faith-neutral or inclusive in manifestation".[16] Until recently, the movement was estimated to have founded over two thousand schools and even more dialogue organizations, clinics and hospitals, media outlets, and humanitarian aid and other charitable NGOs in over 140 countries worldwide. The movement is funded predominantly by the voluntary contributions of movement participants and supportive businesspeople and staffed by voluntary participants who work as administrators or teachers for nominal wages.[17]

The movement has a successful history of activism which has fashioned a unique response to the questions and challenges posed by modernity. Although Hizmet has evolved organizationally, its point of departure and its central concern according to movement participants remains; that is to gain the pleasure of God through service to others. "So that others may live" is not just a motto among United States coast guards,[18] it also happens to reflect a vernacularized expression of Hizmet's basic ethos.[19] A more accurate understanding of Hizmet's concern is to exemplify what it means to be a Muslim in the twenty-first century, which is simultaneously faithful to the precepts of religion and spirituality while articulating a constructive position on issues such as democracy, pluralism, integration, globalization and violent extremism.

Hizmet's Direct Approach: Theological Refutation of Violent Extremism[20]

Hizmet's approach to countering extremism is two-fold, direct and indirect. Hizmet's theological refutations of especially Islamist Puritanical Extremism comprises its direct approach. Hizmet's core teachings and values, underpinned and popularized through practice, act as a positive counter-narrative and comprises Hizmet's indirect but more effective approach. Incidentally, these two methods also help undermine Islamophobic sentiment, representation and structural causes such as the lack of social interaction and cross-cultural fertilization.

In this era of rogue states and nebulous terrorist groupings such as ISIS, Al-Qaeda and its affiliates, Gülen undermines any legitimacy such entities may claim by warning Muslims that:

> [t]he rules of Islam are clear. Individuals cannot declare war. A group or an organization cannot declare war. War is declared by the state…Otherwise, it is an act of terror. In such a case war is entered into by gathering around oneself, forgive my language, a few bandits.[21]

While legitimate states may continue to have the right to arm for deterrence, Gülen says that they cannot and must not wage war in an attempt "to serve religion" by, for example, conquering lands as was done in the past by previous Muslim polities while claiming religious legitimacy.[22] Those wishing to serve religion, can only do so by appealing to the mind and reason of the civilized world.[23]

Gülen explains that the means and end must both be lawful in Islam, which incidentally and additionally requires that it is also in accordance with the law of the land. Therefore, "[e]ven during war you cannot touch or harass those that are innocent. No one can issue a religious decree (*fatwa*) that contradicts this position."[24]

When it concerns acts of violence without a legitimate declaration of war, Gülen says,

> Terror can never be used to achieve an Islamic goal… A Muslim cannot be a terrorist because Islam foresees the harshest penalty in this world for murder or for violating security, and in the afterlife, it foresees the harshest penalty for those that reject faith, those who associate partners with Him and against those who have committed murder. It warns that those who have deliberately [and unjustly] killed another will face an eternal life in Hell.[25]

Gülen puts that one cannot reach holy ends by unholy means. No form of pragmatic expediency or necessity permits this. Therefore, Gülen draws no distinction between suicide bombs in London, Tel Aviv or Istanbul.[26]

In Gülen's philosophy, the combination of religion and violence or indeed religion and force contradict and undermine the creation of human agency. It is free will that makes us human and humans that give meaning to creation according to Gülen. Therefore, the denial of free will, negates human nature undermining the purpose of creation.[27] For Gülen, diversity of race, religion, nation, and life style was intended by God and should be accepted and valued as a route to understanding.[28] Sympathy, love, and service therefore should not remain confined to the people of any particular religion, race or life style.[29]

Gülen's studies and teaching on war and terrorism in the modern era have led him to redefine the relations between Muslims and non-Muslims. He rejects the binary opposition of *dar al-Islam* (abode of peace/Islam, where Muslims rule and should live in peace) and *dar al-harb* (abode of war, where non-Muslims rule and Muslims are expected to live in a "state of war" or "preparedness for war"), political concepts coined by Muslim scholars in the medieval era to present a dichotomous worldview of "us" versus "them", reproduced in the contemporary era to perpetuate that division. Gülen opposes this worldview. Rather, he suggests that all human beings be valued for principles, merit, effort, attributes, and characteristics, and not for their religious or national identities. Working from the Qur'an, he proposed *dar al-hizmet* (the abode of service) as a single concept to replace the other two and to see the entire world as a place to serve God by helping others: "This path passes through the inescapable dimension of servanthood to God by means of serving, first of all, our families, relatives, and neighbors, then our country and nation, and finally humanity and creation."[30]

Thus, in Gülen's view "a true Muslim cannot be a terrorist and a terrorist cannot be a true Muslim," not just according to the letter of Islam but also according to the "heart, soul, and spirit of Islam."[31] Therefore, epistemically and hermeneutically, this interpretation of Islam contradicts puritanical extremist ideology that attempts to justify violent extremism in the name of religion.

The case of Gülen demonstrates that an authentically grounded religious interpretation can and is being put forward by not only "modernist scholars" speaking from the lectern but by ʿ*ulama*, (traditionally trained

Islamic scholars) preaching from the "pulpit", challenging the essentialized versions of Islam put forth by both Puritanical Islamist Extremists and absolutist Islamophobes alike.

Hizmet's Indirect Approach: Deradicalisation by Default[32]

Hizmet, at least for itself, does not advocate defeating violent extremism ideology or practice by meeting it head on. Instead, core teachings that negate violent extremist ideology are popularized to wider public through a series of activities, works and practice. Hizmet's core teachings and the values and activism they underpin are diametrically opposed to and mutually exclusive with those associated with puritanical extremism; therefore, the stronger one grows the weaker the other becomes. Accordingly, the goal of defeating extremism is made to *ensue* without being directly *pursued*, ensuring it avoids the pitfalls associated with being reactive. This process was dubbed *Deradicalisation by Default: The 'Dialogue' Approach to Rooting out Violent Extremism* in 2009[33] and is what we refer to in this paper as Hizmet's indirect approach.

Some of those core teachings, as discussed by Sleap and Sener,[34] Keles and Sezgin[35] and McMaster,[36] can be summarized here in their idealized forms as follows. Love and compassion; love and compassion must be the basis of all human interactions and of the pursuit of peace and justice. The middle path; every human faculty, emotion and potential must be used in the appropriate measure, manner, and context for which it was created; that is, it is essential to find the middle way in every instance (*sirat al-mustaqim*, the straight path). Positive social engagement; engagement is essential despite any actions or qualities in the "other" with which one might take issue. Unwillingness to engage can be overcome by an attribute-based social engagement model which differentiates between the composite parts of a person, community or civilization (i.e. actions, attributes or characteristics) and the whole. Self-reflexivity (or doubt) versus absolutism; while people can believe that their religion represents the Truth, their access to it is defined by their own limitations.

These teachings fundamentally contradict both a Puritanical Islamist Extremists' projection of Islam from within and an Islamophobes projection of Islam from outside, creating a cognitive dissonance between the two sets of propositions.

Gülen believes that the answer to the misrepresentation of Islam by violent extremists and Islamophobes is that Muslims must assume responsibility for its representation through practice and action.[37] From the very outset, Gülen has emphasized *temsil*, "the inadvertent overspill of genuine practice" rather than *tebliğ*, "the deliberate attempt to teach and proselytize through speech and/or action", as the way to achieving this.[38]

It is on the basis of *temsil*, that Hizmet has become one of most dynamic Muslim-led movements in the world primarily focused on non-denominational education, dialogue and relief work with an auxiliary yet substantial arm in broadcast and print media. Prior to the Turkish government's relentless clampdown and persecution, Hizmet was estimated to operate approximately two thousand educational institutions, including primary, secondary and tertiary education, in over 160 countries.[39] Today, and on the basis of indefinite proxies, the total number of schools that Hizmet continues to operate is closer to 1000 in approximately 140 countries worldwide.

Through this multi-directional and multi-layered practice, Hizmet is able to test, develop and diffuse its core teachings and values within and without through practice and action which is far more effective than mere promulgation. A Muslim or otherwise who believes that Islam necessitates dialogue and positive social relations with the other cannot simultaneously maintain that Islam necessitates war and hostility towards one's neighbor. This "roundabout way" of achieving the outcome of undermining extremist ideology without becoming reactionary is an approach that is being explored and adopted by the British Foreign and Commonwealth Office.[40]

In addition, and more specifically, the general characteristics of Hizmet's border transgressor practice, its sense of social responsibility and constructive change, its focus on dialogue and education, and its grass roots religious activism, tackle a number of dynamics that underpin the mindset and ideology of Islamophobia and puritanical Islam.

General Characteristics of Hizmet's Border Transgressor Practice

Faith-inspired in motivation yet capable of being faith-neutral, -inclusive and secular in the manifestation of its work demonstrates the movement's ability to synthesize on matters pertaining to religion, identity, pluralism, and modernity. In so doing, Hizmet acts as a border transgressor in its attempt to bridge build between religion and secularity, scripture and science and tradition and innovation. That a Muslim-led movement, grounded in traditional-Islamic Sunni Hanafi heritage, calls for the opening of secular schools (and later Alevi places worship), as opposed to mosques; rejects political Islam; encourages globalization; and adopts dialogue as its basis of social interaction are indicative of this type of border-transgressor call and practice.

Hizmet's synthesizing border transgressor approach forces Muslims and non-Muslims alike to reconsider their stereotypes and prejudices. By complexifying the issue, Hizmet offers an enriched understanding of Muslim identity and Islamic interpretation that demonstrates the possibility of a third-way and the existence of the *in-between* shades. This approach rejects the idea of an exclusionary mono-Muslim-identity. Instead, it urges its audience to recognize and celebrate its multiple identities by focusing on values, characteristics and attributes over labels, signs, and symbols. Hizmet's border transgressor example instils skill and confidence in its participants and beneficiaries to embrace and navigate the different parts and forms of their identity. The inability to reconcile competing identities (identity crises) precipitates the attraction of exclusionary purist racial or religious ideologies.

Social Responsibility and Constructive Change

Hizmet's teaching and practice on social responsibility is another over-arching feature that is relevant to the present discussion. It inculcates a positive and proactive view, disposition and mindset that focuses on personal responsibility to do what can be done here and now (i.e. the 'near'), rather than apportioning blame on others about what has happened elsewhere (often 'afar').[41] By channeling energy towards positive forms of activism on the 'near' that is not predicated on fear and animosity of the other and what is assumed to have happened or happening in the 'afar', Hizmet's teachings and practice undermines the mutually reinforcing cycle between and within both ideological camps.

What's more, by teaching that Muslims have a responsibility to do all they can to bring about positive development in the belief that their effort is a form of 'active prayer' (*fiili dua*) to God, Hizmet helps tackle a sense of helplessness which has been associated with acts of extreme, and at times, violent behavior. Furthermore, Hizmet attempts to address the structural causes of this problem by continually investing in upward social mobility projects and initiatives to help people develop the means and confidence to bring about improvements in their personal and communal lives. Hizmet's success in building a great number and range of modern institutions also inspires confidence in Muslims that they can act peacefully and successfully engage the world.

Dialogue and Education

Today, Hizmet's dialogue efforts are as widespread as it is its educational endeavors. Hizmet's dialogue organizations have expended significant energy in understanding what is meant by dialogue and how it can be conducted in a way in which it is most meaningful.[42] For Gülen, lasting dialogue is the dialogue achieved at the grass roots of society and is a generational project.[43] To achieve this, Hizmet is actively pursuing what the movement participants in Britain refer to as community engagement.[44]

Intergroup contact between individuals from different ethnic and religious groups can lead to both positive and negative outcomes depending on contextual, group and individual circumstances.[45] Hizmet's practice is therefore consciously to create a positive, friendly environment and context of intergroup contact where disparate groups can learn from, and about, each other. These dialogue activities also allowed Hizmet participants to practice (and thereby, *temsil*) their core teachings and values as discussed above.

As dialogue proceeds through various stages, those that partake in it may come to realize that the other is not in fact the other but a different version of the oneself. Dialogue involving Muslims allows for cross-cultural fertilization, reducing the scope for racism, xenophobia and Islamophobia which nourishes in the absence of genuine contact with the other.

Hizmet's schools and educational endeavors on the other hand support upward social mobility, providing the confidence and skill-sets for students to change their own circumstances; they expose students to different religions and cultures through mixed intake; and they support economically and socially-disadvantaged students through bursaries and supplementary education which in return facilitates further integration. That outcome in itself undermines the Islamophobic narrative of "ghettoized Muslims" projected as "living off the state."

The teaching and ancillary staff at these schools provide positive role models of harmonious interaction between people of diverse beliefs and backgrounds and exemplify positive activism, thus countering for non-Muslim staff and students the negative images promulgated by Islamophobes. Simultaneously, they provide Muslim students with an attractive and convincing alternative to the 'victimized' self-image of the Islamist and the false sense of idealism which is presented and preyed on by violent extremists.

Grass Roots Religious Activism

Another dimension of Hizmet's educational endeavors is its grass roots religious activism (*bölgecilik* or *halk hizmetleri*). While Hizmet's schools are nondenominational and target children, teenagers and young adults, Hizmet's grass roots activism is *religious* and targets adults of both genders and all forms of occupation. Hizmet participants in Britain have formalized this hitherto informal grass roots activism as the Sohbet Society (sohbetsociety.org); in this context, 'sohbet' means religious discussion circles.[46]

Another dimension of this grass roots religious activism is religious mentoring focused on teenagers. Hizmet participants in Britain have also formalized this hitherto informal activity under the auspices of Mentor Wise, a non-profit company (mentorwise.org.uk). Mentor Wise provides four types of mentoring (academic, skill, value, and religious) for young people. Parents and mentees are free to choose any combination of the mentoring types and programs on offer. The religious mentoring is "underpinned by an emphasis on love and compassion, empathetic acceptance of the other, ..positive action and positive thought, a rejection of a dichotomous worldview and an understanding that promotes free will and choice."[47]

Whether it is adult or adolescent-focused, Hizmet's grass roots religious activism is a conduit by which Hizmet disseminates its core teachings to wider society. Sohbet Society and Mentor Wise volunteers and mentors act as role models for both adults and adolescents exemplifying personal qualities such as altruism and selflessness. By exemplifying these *sincerity-affirming* characteristics, Hizmet participants contest the monopoly that extremist groups claim to have over commitment and self-sacrifice. With their positive and proactive modus operandi, these forms of grass roots religious activism demonstrate the worth and significance of *living*, not *dying*, for Islam. Overall, the example of Hizmet's mentors and participants challenge the charismatic demagogue's ability to recruit from among Muslim youth disillusioned by what they perceive to be the *folk Islam* of noncommittal mosque-going Muslims.

Overall, Hizmet's dialogic practice and its underlying teachings, delivered directly or indirectly, encourage a disposition and form of activism that is open, enquiring, reflexive, critical, consensus-seeking, collective-decision-making, socially outward while spiritually inward looking—all of which counter absolutist tendencies; a cornerstone of puritanical Islam and Islamophobia alike. Moreover, its indirect approach ensures that it reaches the much larger pool of 'non-radicalized' Muslims who are continuously targeted by violent extremists for new recruits, rather than those that have already been radicalized.

Hizmet's Limitations and Shortcomings

Hizmet has a number of shortcomings which limits the impact of its direct and indirect approach as discussed above. For example, while Hizmet's theology of activism and engagement genuinely necessitates faith-neutral and faith-inclusive activities which it has achieved, in part, by keeping its religious identity at bay, there are other aspects of its practice where greater transparency about its religious identity would be far more helpful. However, Hizmet's persecution at the hands of the aggressively secularist Kemalist regime in Turkey has caused it to push its religious identity into the background. This habit has inhibited Hizmet's ability to take a more public and proactive role in relation to tackling Puritanical Islamist Extremism and Islamophobia in Western Europe and North America. To counter this, Hizmet must become more vocal and more visible in the public debate about Islam without necessarily needing to change its basic praxis.

Another shortcoming is Hizmet's limited engagement with other Muslim groups in the West. Hizmet has been wary of engaging with Muslim groups and organizations in the West out of fear of upsetting authoritarian regimes elsewhere. An additional consideration has been upsetting the overly securitized Western governments who have been suspicious of Muslim groups. As a result, Hizmet sought to engage with non-Turkish Muslims in the West only on an individual as opposed to an organizational or communal level. In our view, these were misplaced sensitivities then and now, albeit with some room to argue for this approach at the very outset when branching out to the West for the first time but certainly not thereafter. Hizmet's persecution, this time at the hand of the 'Erdoganist regime'[48] in Turkey, is inadvertently helping it to diversify its support base and causing it to break into other than Turkish Muslim communities. Whilst that is a positive development, Hizmet's limited engagement to date has inhibited its ability to diffuse its teachings into the Muslim diaspora in the Western hemisphere and to learn and develop from that experience and interaction.

A further point is Hizmet's active effort to avoid controversy and confrontation. However, challenging Puritanical Islamist Extremism and hate-fueled Islamophobic ideology necessitates partaking in that which is inherently controversial and contested. This does not mean reversing Hizmet's praxis which places greater emphasis on practice and its indirect outcomes rather than those to accrue from its direct approach. It does however mean articulating those indirect outcomes more clearly and being prepared to engage in more of that direct refutation as and when needed. To achieve this, Hizmet needs vocal cultural interlocutors, home-grown local leaders and speakers who can formulate, articulate, contextualize and vernacularize Hizmet's values, aspirations and practices through a glocal cultural idiom that connects and resonates with non-Turkish communities and wider society. So far, it has had limited success in achieving this, despite its considerable investment in education.

Moreover, in recent years Hizmet's innovative practices such as opening non-denominational schools as opposed to more mosques appeared to take on a more dogmatic nature becoming solidified and often replicated in an unquestioned manner. Hizmet's inability to offer public self-criticism for its support of Turkey's Justice and Development Party and its uncritical support of the Ergenekon and Sledgehammer trials is indicative of a similar lack of dexterity where new thinking is in fact needed. Hizmet needs to apply the border transgressor qualities it so aptly demonstrated in the 1990s of Turkey when it took a synthesizing position on issues such as Islam and secularism and Islam and democracy. Today, it needs to demonstrate to itself and the wider world that it can admit mistake where mistakes were made while defending its good work in the many instances in which that work warrants respect and admiration. Its inability to adjust and innovate in light of new experiences and context, has limited Hizmet's capacity to engage with indigenous communities in the Western hemisphere on issues that are of concern to them such as Puritanical Islamist Extremism and the rise of the radical right.

Furthermore, considering the growth of radical right and racist movements all over the world in recent years, it is possible to argue that the movement has not placed sufficient emphasis on grassroots dialogue. Hizmet's dialogue organizations should place greater focus on grassroots activities, to empower those that are at greatest risk of the extremist ideology of puritanical Islamism and Islamophobia alike.

Concluding Remarks

The Hizmet Movement did not generate and grow to address the perils of Islamophobia or Puritanical Islamist Extremism. Rather, it grew out of the practice-focused teachings of Gülen which sought to articulate an authentic expression of faith and religion in light of contemporary challenges predicated on the notion of service to God and humanity. This is and was the stated motive of Gülen and the movement participants and supporters. However, as discussed above, the underlying teachings and practice of that self-declared aim have direct and indirect implications in terms of undermining the ground upon which Puritanical Islamist Extremist ideology and Islamophobia flourishes and connects with potential recruits. While it is challenging to prove negative results (the prevention of radicalization in the first instance), especially in the field of extremism, this can be surmised from Hizmet's visible success in inspiring millions, innovating new forms of practice and influencing public and religio-political debate in significant ways. Nonetheless, Hizmet's success in this respect is limited by a number of shortcomings, the most significant of which is its core identifier: its Turkishness. Can Hizmet transcend its cultural luggage with elements of its associated mindset which appears to be holding it back outside of Turkey? Can it genuinely achieve that Gülenian form of give-and-take cultural dialogue[49] within itself in order to retain what is meaningful while replacing what is not with local concerns, considerations and modes of practice? In addition to much more, the answer to such questions will determine Hizmet's ability to maximize its impact in tackling Puritanical Islamist Extremism and Islamophobia everywhere but Turkey.

NOTES

1. *Takfirism* is the ideology of easily excommunicating Muslims from Islam just because they do not share the ideas of these violent extremist groups. They produce fatwas to excommunicate their critics. These violent groups produce takfirist fatwas to mainstream political Islamists who denounce violence.
2. Khaled Abou El Fadl, *The Great Theft: Wrestling Islam from the Extremists* (New York: HarperOne, 2007), p. 18.
3. The authors appreciate that using the term 'Puritanical Islamist Extremism' is a rather long-winded way of referring to what is otherwise labelled as 'Islamic extremism'. However, cognitive linguistic research suggests that the use of derivative terms such as 'Islamic extremism' can convey and conflate concepts distinct from their intended meaning owing to their etymological roots. This is considered to be a contributing factor to the rise of Islamophobia. To mitigate this, this chapter will refer to this phenomenon of extremism that claims an Islamic justification as 'Puritanical Islamist Extremism'. See Emma Jane Harris, Victoria Bisset, and Paul Weller, *Violent Extremism: Naming, Framing and Challenging* (London: Dialogue Society, 2015) for more on cognitive linguistics in the context of the current debate.
4. Islamophobia is not an uncontested term. Some suggest that the hostility is principally towards the adherents of Islam, rather than Islam per se and that as a result, the term 'anti-Muslimism' or 'anti-Muslim' behavior and sentiment is better suited, see Fred Halliday, "Islamophobia' Reconsidered," *Ethnic and Racial Studies* 22, no. 5 (1999): 892–902. Others have suggested that it involves both racial and religious discrimination and discrimination and hostility and that it is therefore a form of 'cultural racism,' see Nasar Meer and Tariq Modood, "Refutations of Racism in the 'Muslim Question,'" *Patterns of Prejudice* 43, nos. 3–4 (2009): 335–354.
5. This sub-section is based on a shortened and revised version of Ihsan Yilmaz, "Two Major Challenges to Muslims and the World in the Age of Post-Truth: Islamist Extremism and Islamophobia," Deakin University Chair in Islamic Studies and Intercultural Dialogue Launch Speech, November 22, 2016, Deakin Downtown Corporate Centre, Melbourne, Australia.
6. Ihsan Yilmaz, "The Nature of Islamophobia: Some Key Features," in *Fear of Muslims? International Perspectives on Islamophobia. Boundaries of Religious Freedom: Regulating Religion in Diverse Societies*, ed. Douglas Pratt and Rachel Woodlock (Cham: Springer, 2016), pp. 19–30.

7. CBMI, *Islamophobia Issues, Challenges, and Action: A Report by the Commission on British Muslims and Islamophobia* (Stoke on Trent, UK: Trentham Books, 2004), p. 8.
8. Ibid.
9. Ihsan Yilmaz, *Dynamic Legal Pluralism and the Reconstruction of Unofficial Muslim Laws in England, Turkey and Pakistan* (London: SOAS, University of London, 1999), pp. 132–138.
10. Sayeeda Warsi, "Islamophobia" in *The Enemy Within: A Tale of Muslim Britain* (Milton Keynes: Allen Lane, 2017), pp. 134–158.
11. Ibid.
12. Ihsan Yilmaz, "An Analysis of the Factors That Pave the Way for the Radicalization of the British Youth," in *Muslim Youth: Challenges, Opportunities and Expectations*, ed. Mohammed Siddique Seddon, Fauzia Ahmad, and Shiraz Khan (London: Continuum, 2012), pp. 32–53.
13. Ihsan Yilmaz, "The Varied Performance of Hizb Ut-Tahrir: Success in Britain and Uzbekistan and Stalemate in Egypt and Turkey," *Journal of Muslim Minority Affairs* 30, no. 4 (2010): 501–517; Ihsan Yilmaz, "Socio-Economic, Political and Theological Deprivations' Role in the Radicalization of the British Muslim Youth: The Case of Hizb ut-Tahrir," *European Journal of Economic and Political Sciences* 2, no. 1 (2009): 89–101.
14. For the Hizmet (Gülen) Movement, see in detail, Paul G. Weller and Ihsan Yilmaz, *European Muslims, Civility and Public Life: Perspectives on and from the Gülen Movement* (London: Continuum Publishers, 2012); Greg J. Barton, Paul Weller, and Ihsan Yilmaz, *The Muslim World and Politics in Transition: Creative Contributions of the Gülen Movement* (London and New York: Bloomsbury Publishers, 2013); and Ihsan Yilmaz et al., *Peaceful Coexistence: Fethullah Gülen's Initiatives for Peace in the Contemporary World* (London: Leeds Metropolitan University Press, 2007). For the Movement's stance on pluralism, secularism and democracy, see Ihsan Yilmaz, "Changing Institutional Turkish-Muslim Discourses on Modernity, West and Dialogue," Congress of the International Association of Middle East Studies (IAMES), Freie Universitat Berlin, Germany, October 2000 and Ihsan Yilmaz, "Influence of Pluralism and Electoral Participation on the Transformation of Turkish Islamism," *Journal of Economic and Social Research* 10, no. 2 (2008): 43–65.
15. Ozcan Keles, *Written Evidence to the Foreign Affairs Committee on UK's Relations with Turkey* (London: Alliance for Shared Values and Dialogue Platform), para 7, p. 5. October 20, 2016.
16. Ibid., para 6, p. 5.

17. Helen Rose Ebaugh, *The Gülen Movement: A Sociological Analysis of a Civic Movement Rooted in Moderate Islam* (New York: Springer, 2010), pp. 83–108.
18. There are multiple references to the phrase among U.S. coast guard literature. See, for example, Martha J. Laguardia-Kotite and Tom Ridge, *So Others May Live: Coast Guard's Rescue Swimmers: Saving Lives, Defying Death* (Guilford, CT: The Lyons Press, 2008).
19. Fethullah Gülen, *A Fethullah Gülen Reader: So That Others May Live*, ed. Erkan M. Kurt (New York: Blue Dome, 2013).
20. This sub-section is based on a shortened and revised version of Ozcan Keles and Ismail Mesut Sezgin, *A Hizmet Approach to Rooting out Violent Extremism* (London: Centre for Hizmet Studies, 2015).
21. Fethullah Gülen, *Essays, Perspectives, Opinions* (Clifton, NJ: Light, 2006), p. 129.
22. Ali Ünal and Alphonse Williams, *Advocate of Dialogue: Fethullah Gülen* (Fairfax, VA: The Fountain, 2000), pp. 63–66.
23. "Hizmet Studies Responds to Gülen's 23rd December 2014 Video Blog, 23.12.2014," Centre for Hizmet Studies Website, https://www.hizmet-studies.org/news/response/hizmet-studies-responds-gulens-23rd-december-2014-video-blog/, accessed April 21, 2018.
24. "Nuriye Akman, Zaman gazetesi roportaji, 2004." Fethullah Gülen Website, fgulen.com/tr/turk-basininda-fethullah-gulen/fethullah-gulen-le-gazete-roportajlari/zamanda-nuriye-akmanla/12070-zaman-bugun-islam-dunyasi-diye-bir-dunya-yok, accessed April 21, 2018.
25. "Nevval Sevindi, Fethullah Gülen İle New York Sohbeti, 2002." Fethullah Gülen Website, www.fethullahgulen.com/tr/turk-basininda-fethullah-gulen/dizi-yazilar-dosyalar/fethullah-Gülen-ile-new-york-sohbeti/3438-nevval-sevindi-11-eylulsonrasi-islam-ve-teror-arasindaki-iliski-butun-dunyada-cok-tartisildi-bu-konuda-nediyorsunuz.html, accessed April 21, 2018.
26. Fethullah Gülen, "Filistin ve İntihar Saldırıları. Kirik Testi, 13.5.2002," Herkul Website, www.herkul.org/kirik-testi/filistin-ve-intihar-saldirilari/, accessed April 21, 2018.
27. Ozcan Keles, "The Gülen Movement and Promoting Human Rights Values" in *The Muslim World and Politics in Transition: Creative Contributions of the Gülen Movement*, ed. G. Barton, P. Weller, and I. Yilmaz (London: Bloomsbury, 2013), pp. 200–201.
28. Frances Sleap and Omer Sener, *Dialogue Theories*, ed. Paul Weller (London: Dialogue Society, 2013), p. 89.
29. Fethullah Gülen, *Essays, Perspectives, Opinions* (Clifton, NJ: Light, 2006), p. 18.

30. Gülen, *Essays, Perspectives*, op. cit., p. 90.
31. Ozcan Keles, "The Gülen Movement and Promoting Human Rights Values" in *The Muslim World and Politics in Transition: Creative Contributions of the Gülen Movement*, ed. G. Barton, P. Weller, and I. Yilmaz (London: Bloomsbury, 2013), pp. 193–194.
32. This sub-section is based on a shortened and revised version of Ozcan Keles and Ismail Mesut Sezgin, *A Hizmet Approach to Rooting out Violent Extremism* (London: Centre for Hizmet Studies, 2015).
33. Ozcan Keles, *Deradicalisation by Default: The 'Dialogue' Approach to Rooting out Violent Extremism* (London: Dialogue Society, 2009).
34. Sleap and Sener, *Dialogue Theories*, pp. 89–92.
35. Keles and Sezgin, *A Hizmet Approach to Rooting out Violent Extremism*, pp. 29–31.
36. Johnston McMaster, *A Word Between Us: Ethics in Interfaith Dialogue* (London: Centre for Hizmet Studies, 2015), pp. 88–90.
37. Fethullah Gülen, "Kanlı Arenada İslam İmajı (Londra'da Terör). Bamteli. 9.7.2005," Herkul Website, accessed November 11, 2017, www.herkul.org/bamteli/kanli-arenada-islam-imaji-londrada-teror/, accessed April 21, 2018.
38. Ozcan Keles, "Tamsil: The Inadvertent Overspill of Internalisation. 13.6.2014," Ozcan Keles Website, accessed December 1, 2017, http://www.ozcankeles.org/tamsil-the-inadvertent-overspill-of-internalisation-21/.
39. Ozcan Keles, "The Gülen Movement and Promoting," pp. 192–208.
40. "FCO Leads Global Action on Freedom of Religion. 19.10.2016," HM Government Services Website, accessed February 2, 2017, https://www.gov.uk/government/news/fco-leads-global-action-on-freedom-of-religion. "Preventing Violent Extremism," Freedom of Religion or Belief & Foreign Policy Website, accessed January 1, 2018, http://forbforeignpolicy.net/preventing-violent-extremism/.
41. Yahya Birt and Sadek Hamid, "Jihadi Movements in the United Kingdom" in *Islamic Movements of Europe: Public Religion and Islamophobia in the Modern World*, ed. F. Peter and R. Ortega (London: I.B. Tauris), p. 172.
42. Dialogue Society, *Making Dialogue Effective* (London: Dialogue Society, 2013).
43. Sleap and Sener, *Dialogue Theories*, p. 86.
44. "Community," Dialogue Society Website, accessed December 1, 2017, http://www.dialoguesociety.org/publications/community.html.
45. Pettigrew, T. F. "Intergroup Contact Theory," *Annual Review of Psychology* 49, no. 1 (1998), pp. 65–85.

46. "About Us," Sohbet Society Website, accessed January 1, 2018, http://www.sohbetsociety.org/about-us/.
47. "Religious Belief Focused Spirituality and Teaching," Mentor Wise Website, accessed January 2, 2018, http://www.mentorwise.org.uk/religious-belief-focused-spirituality-and-teaching/.
48. Ihsan Yilmaz and Galip Bashirov, "The AKP After 15 Years: Emergence of Erdoganism in Turkey," *Third World Quarterly*, March 2018.
49. Sleap and Sener, *Dialogue Theories*, p. 91.

INDEX

A
Abbott, Tony, 75, 80, 81, 101
Abu Gharib, 26
Al-Awalaki, Anwar, 142, 180, 181, 192
Al-Qaeda (alternate spellings al-Qaeda, Al Qaida), 28, 30, 39, 148, 181, 209, 269
America, 15–17, 19, 22, 27, 29–31, 47, 189, 194, 239, 276
Australia, 4, 8, 9, 36, 47, 48, 63, 73–76, 79, 85, 87, 88, 100–102, 106–108, 110, 113, 180, 185–187, 189, 190, 203, 204, 209, 210, 219, 225–233, 238–242, 245–247, 249, 253, 255, 260
Austria, 21, 117, 119, 125–127, 130
Ayatollah Khomeini, 16, 195

B
Bernardi, Cory, 74, 88, 101
Blair, Tony, 193
Boko Haram, 35, 39, 81, 110

Breivik, Anders Behring, 3, 4, 37, 38, 44–47, 49, 68, 82
Britain, 6, 7, 17, 19, 161, 164, 166, 171, 173, 174, 229, 274, 275
Britain's PREVENT Program, 7, 162
Building communities of Trust (BCOT), 208
Burqa/Burka, 100, 102
Bush, George W., 3, 193

C
Cameron, David, 176
Centrum Democraten, 61
Charlie Hebdo, 59, 102, 105, 110, 111
Charlie Hebdo incident, 104, 105, 109, 111
Christian Conservative People's Part (ÖVP), 127
Christian/Muslim dichotomy, 109
Co-radicalisation, 3, 37, 43, 47, 49, 50, 68

Council on American-Islamic Relations (CAIR), 23, 32, 122
Counterterrorism strategies, 142

E
Egypt, 16, 28–30, 123, 228, 254
el-Sisi, Abdel Fatteh, 20
European Foundation for Democracy (EFD), 5, 117, 119–121, 123–126
Extreme right, 58, 67, 82, 190, 195
Extremist ideology, 10, 39, 190, 267, 270–272, 278

F
Far-right extremists, 40, 83, 84, 86
Fethullah, Gülen, 268, 269, 272, 274, 278, 280–282
Foreign policy, 23, 120
Foundation for Defence of Democracy (FDD), 119, 120
France, 18, 21, 57, 60, 61, 67, 121
Fundamentalism, 16, 41, 42, 46, 48, 49, 265

G
Geller, Pamela, 19
Germany, 21, 36, 55, 57, 63, 67, 121, 251
"Ground Zero Mosque", 19
Guantanamo, 26, 194
Gulf War, 16, 165

H
Haider, Numan, 101, 107
Hirsi Ali, Ajan, 63
Hizmet Movement, 10, 266, 268, 278
Huntington, Samuel, 16, 22, 31
Hussein, Saddam, 16

I
Iatrogenic Radicalization, 7, 179–185, 190, 191, 193, 194, 196
Indonesia, 29, 39, 62
Iran
   Islamic Revolution, 15, 16
ISIS (Islamic State, IS, Daesh), 2, 27
Islamic extremism, 35, 36, 39, 42, 47, 50, 86
Islamism, 35, 39, 41, 47, 170, 232, 235, 238–241, 278
Islamist ideology, 2, 10, 86
Islamists, 87, 104, 107–109, 179, 187, 195
Islamophobia (Islamaphobes, Anti-Muslimism), 266

J
Jihad, 16, 17, 61, 63, 78, 100, 102, 129, 143, 151, 188, 189

K
Khalifah (Caliphate), 188, 192, 194
Kouachi, Chérif, 102
Kouachi, Saïd, 102

L
Lee Rigby, 171
Lindt Café Attach (Sydney Siege), 194
7/7 London Bombings, 109, 161

M
Malaysia, 29, 39
Media
   Islamophobia in the, 99
   Sensationalism, 98, 103, 106, 112, 113
   Stereotypes, 99, 259

Monis, Man Haron, 101, 102, 104–106, 180, 194, 195, 201
Mujahidin, 189, 192, 194
Muslim
  alienation, 55, 99, 187
  assimilation, 18
  discrimination, 6, 17, 18, 28, 99, 140, 152–154, 259
  ghettos, 164
  immigration, 22, 20
  integration, 107
  moderate, 107, 126
  "Othering" (alternative "Other", "Fear of the other"), 36, 48, 247, 250
  stereotypes, 17, 114, 253, 254
  youth, 3, 5, 6, 8, 26, 56, 99, 113, 126, 127, 167, 189, 250
Muslim Brotherhood, 5, 78, 117, 122–131

N
Netherlands, 3, 17, 21, 55–58, 61–68

O
Organized Islamophobic Network (OIN), 23, 117

P
Party for Freedom (PVV), 57, 58, 60–65, 67, 68
Pipes, Daniel, 17, 31, 92, 129

Q
Quilliam Foundation, 167
Qur'an (Koran), 17, 21, 100, 102, 109–111, 153, 270

R
Racism, 2, 8, 9, 15, 18
Radicalisation, 3, 77, 120, 121, 126, 161, 163, 170–174
Refugees, 21, 22, 25, 55, 76, 80, 82, 84, 123

S
Said, Edward, 243
Salafists, 123
Saudi Arabia, 16, 27–30, 39, 109
Sharrouf, Khaled, 106
Social media, 20, 22, 23, 28, 73, 74, 80, 84, 88, 249
Spencer, Robert, 19, 92
Sudan, 16
Sweden, 117, 119, 121, 125, 128–130
Syria, 22, 27, 28, 39, 56, 57, 61, 67, 68, 101, 143, 148, 149, 151, 152, 162, 164, 170, 172, 174, 188, 209, 215

T
Takfirism, 265
Terrorism, 2, 4, 5, 10, 15–19, 21, 23–26, 28, 42, 43, 48, 74–86, 88, 89, 101, 112, 121, 131, 141, 142, 151, 161, 162, 166, 170, 172, 206, 208, 210, 219, 270
Terrorism prevention programs
  Australian Anti-Terror Legislation, 88
  Terror raids, 104, 108
Terrorist actors, 204
Trump, Donald, 3, 11, 20–22, 47, 57, 75
Turkey, 29, 39, 56, 60, 105, 228, 276–278
9/11 Twin Tower Attack, 97

U

United Arab Emirates, 28
United Muslim Women's Association (UMWA), 256

V

Van Gogh, Theo, 59, 66, 68
Violent Extremism, 2, 7, 10, 20, 23, 76–78, 80, 81, 84, 86, 89, 121, 122, 140–142, 163, 171, 179, 180, 190, 191, 196, 204, 205, 216, 270, 271

W

"War on Terror", 3, 10, 21, 121, 267

Wilders, Geert, 3, 17, 21, 31, 56–58, 60, 61, 63–67

X

Xenophobia, 2, 15, 18, 23, 30, 48, 226, 274

Y

Youth, 38, 57, 58, 60, 66, 68, 84, 126–128, 130, 131, 163, 165, 167, 168, 254, 257, 276

Printed by Printforce, United Kingdom